THE Gaggle

How the Guys You Know
Will Help You Find the Love You Want

JESSICA MASSA

SIMON & SCHUSTER

NEW YORK   LONDON   TORONTO   SYDNEY   NEW DELHI

Simon & Schuster
1230 Avenue of the Americas
New York, NY 10020

First Simon & Schuster hardcover edition June 2012.

SIMON & SCHUSTER and colophon are registered trademarks of Simon &
Schuster, Inc.

For information about special discounts for bulk purchases, please contact Simon
& Schuster Special Sales at 1-866-506-1949 or business@simonandschuster.com.

The Simon & Schuster Speakers Bureau can bring authors to your live event. For
more information or to book an event contact the Simon & Schuster Speakers
Bureau at 1-866-248-3049 or visit our website at www.simonspeakers.com.

Designed by Akasha Archer

Manufactured in the United States of America

10 9 8 7 6 5 4 3 2 1

Library of Congress Cataloging-in-Publication Data is available.

ISBN 978–1–4516–5752–4
ISBN 978–1–4516–5754–8 (ebook)

To the women of my Millennial Generation:
may the world—and the guys in our gaggle—be worthy of us.

CONTENTS

PART FOUR: THE GUY'S GAGGLE

PART FIVE: LOVE IN THE TIME OF TWITTER

INTRODUCTION: THE PROBLEM
THAT HAS BEEN MISNAMED

There is a big, looming, inescapable problem with your love life. But—surprise—it's *not* that you are single.

The problem begins with the fact that you are a young woman, living in the modern world. Statistics show that you and the rest of the women of your generation are mere minutes away from taking over the planet (no need to be humble here!). At this very moment, countless articles, books, news stories, and TV shows are singing your praises.

True to form, you are in the process of getting this whole L.I.F.E. thing under control. Acing your education? Check. Building strong, lasting relationships with your family and friends? Check. Scoring the winning run for your kickball team? Check. Becoming a star employee at work? Check. Mastering that risotto—and taking care of the pots, pans, and dishes that same night? Check and double check.

Of course, you are not Little Miss Perfect. No one is suggesting that you have it *all* together, *all* the time. You still have your moments of insecurity, mornings where you go heavy on the snooze button, and days where you disappoint your boss and forget to call your mom. But truth be told, Martha Stewart–style perfection creeps you out a little anyway, and besides, you're doing the best you can. In fact, by and large, you are thriving, in your unique way, as part of one of the most empowered and successful generations of women ever to live.

No big deal or anything. **brush your shoulders off**

But back to that problem.

While your professional life, social life, and home life might generally feel like they are all on the right track, there tends to be one other "life" that anxiously tugs at the worries and uncertainties that lie just beneath your confident surface. This would be your love life.

By day, you are the very picture of the infallible modern woman.

But by night (and maybe during your lunch hour), you find yourself biting your nails and obsessing over some guy's Facebook status. You rewrite four versions of the same "casual" email to your cute new co-worker. You strive for physical perfection, silently comparing yourself to your super-skinny friend who always seems to have men falling all over her. You feel nauseous when your mother (and grandmother and mentor and older sister and smug married friend . . .) asks who you're dating. And while you are mulling over your new Match.com photo, your phone buzzes with a vague check-in from a guy you've maybe-sort-of been hanging out with, leading you to end the evening sitting around a table of empty cocktails with your girlfriends, wild-eyed, phone in hand, crazily begging each and every one of them to explain, "What does this text message meeeean???"

Obviously, you don't want to be this neurotic girl. And so, ever the proactive and logical modern woman, you want a solution. You want to "fix" your love life.

And lucky you—it turns out that in this day and age, *everyone* is eager to help fix the single girl's love life. Whether you embrace the world of online dating or hit up the beauty counter at your mall or tune into the never-ending parade of "dating experts" who have flooded bookstores, magazine racks, blog rolls, and TV shows, you can rest assured that you will never lack for resources and experts who insist that they know the best way to help you master your whole dating problem.

Because clearly you have a problem, right? You're single! *Something* must be wrong with you . . .

You are constantly inundated with advice about how to fix your love life. But even so, you can't help but notice that it doesn't seem to be *working*. Why haven't you found love yet? Why aren't you having more fun? Should you be lowering your standards? Are you going for the wrong guys? And when you meet the *right* guys, are you messing it all up somehow?

Lest you feel alone in all this, allow me to get personal for a moment. I was finally struck by the scope of this "problem" over the course of one random night at my apartment in Brooklyn.

The epiphany came courtesy of my childhood best friend, roommate, and now business partner, Rebecca Wiegand (but always Becky to me). We have known each other since we were twelve years old, and ever since then she has been one of the most empowered, can-do young women in my life.

Becky has always been a definition go-getter, especially when it comes to men. But on that fateful night, she came home from a cocktail party and suddenly began unloading an overwhelming host of romantic doubts and insecurities to me. Despite our years of close friendship, I was shocked. If anyone had seemed immune to romantic anxiety, it had been "If He's Not Into Me, Then He's an Idiot" Becky.

Her first question—*"Why aren't guys asking me out?!"*—quickly turned into a spiraling cascade of neuroses. Why wasn't she in a relationship? Why hadn't that dude texted her back? Why hadn't she been on a date in forever? In her exact words, *what the fuck was up with her love life?!*

Determined to pinpoint her problem, Becky began trying to analyze her flaws. Was she too strong? Too needy? Too assertive? Too passive? Too ambitious? Too attracted to the wrong guys? Was she painfully unappealing in some glaring, deal-breaking way, and simply no one had the heart to break the news to her?

As I listened, I was not only taken aback that my uber-confident friend was having these troubling thoughts, but I was also dismayed to find that, as a then-twenty-six-year-old woman whose love life had been all over the map, some part of me, deep down inside, could relate. I typically err on the side of positivity, and I generally like myself—quite a bit, actually. But watching Becky unleash her fears, I felt every one of my own insecurities rise to the surface and threaten my self-worth.

But I forced myself to pull it together. My best friend was upset, and I was supposed to make her feel better. I was going to have to talk her through this.

As I thought about Becky's love life and looked for some silver linings, a realization hit me. My own love life might have looked dire to me, with its lack of dates, formal suitors, and legitimate tales to tell my mother so that she could sleep at night. But I was sure that *Becky's* love life was full of ambiguous-but-promising connections. I had been hearing about them in bits and pieces from her every day. A Gchat conversation with a soccer teammate here, an ex-boyfriend who still came around there, not to mention that coworker who was always sending her funny texts, and then there was that random make-out session with some guy at a Halloween party . . .

In reality, Becky's life couldn't have been further from the cliché of the lonely single girl sitting on her couch, waiting for the phone to ring. And by analyzing *her* love life instead of my own, I had given myself an opportunity to lift the veil of my own personal pressures and standards and insecurities, and see the truth: for a girl who wasn't "dating" anyone, Becky certainly had a busy calendar and a complex network of people—and guys—in her life. And amazingly enough, Becky pointed out that she could say the same for me.

We paused our pity party just long enough to ask ourselves: was it possible that we were simply thinking about our love lives the wrong way?

Yes! It turned out that our perspective was outdated. *This* was our problem. And in fact, it was our *only* problem.

As we talked throughout that night, Becky and I saw that we were limiting ourselves—and our understanding of our actual romantic options—by clinging to archaic expectations, labels, and fantasies that had nothing to do with the current state of modern romance. How could we get ahead in this brave new romantic world? We weren't sure yet. But *this* sounded like a quandary that we could actually figure out.

In an effort to understand the new romantic norms of our generation, I decided to spend a year traveling the country, interviewing hundreds of young people about their love lives. As a longtime world traveler and amateur psychologist by nature (and undergraduate degree), no one had to ask me twice—this nationwide trip was a dream come true.

I hit major cities like Chicago, Houston, Atlanta, and Salt Lake City, and I spent time in smaller areas like Green Bay, Baton Rouge, Boulder, and Provo. My interviewees, both female and male, were in the age range of 22 to 35. They ran the spectrum of life experience, from both a personal perspective (everyone from lawyers to kite surfers to "Sultry Shakedown" party planners) and a romantic one (from club-hopping single ladies to blissfully happy couples to divorced single parents). Over countless hours, I recorded their romantic recollections, gathered their perspectives, and made it my business to connect as many bigger-picture dots as I could. Their stories, thoughts, and advice infuse this book.

(Disclaimer: Though I interviewed people who fell on every inch of the spectrum of sexual preference, this book focuses primarily on the modern heterosexual romantic landscape. While many of my findings seem to apply as well in the gay, bisexual, and transgendered spheres, the nuanced similarities and differences there could—and should!—fill another book entirely.)

While I was letting my trusty GPS lead me around the country, Becky and I—along with our newly formed team—launched a website, aptly named WTF Is Up With My Love Life?! (WTFLoveLife. com). As word spread, stories from WTF?!'s nationwide readers began pouring in, and we met more young women and men who were eager to get involved and share their experiences. Becky and I soon learned that young people *everywhere* were also wondering WTF was up with their love lives. Our initial night of private desperation had tapped into a generation-wide sense of romantic confusion. Suddenly, via our project, Becky and I were shedding light on startling truths and deciphering the newfound romantic wisdom all around us.

And here is what we learned. We learned that nothing was wrong with us. And that nothing is wrong with *you*. We all just need to update our romantic perspective a bit.

As a generation, it is time to start seeing our love lives for what they actually are, and not what we've been taught that they *should* be. You already have everything you could ever need to find love, and you have all the power to use it. You just have to tune out the external noise, discard the advice and expectations of yesteryear, and start thinking about courtship, romance, and love a little differently. And that is exactly what this book is here to help you do.

First, we will discuss the reality of living in a *post-dating world* and pinpoint the *non-dates* that, whether you realize it yet or not, are comprising the bulk of your love life and offering you an ideal atmosphere to learn about your romantic needs, desires, and tendencies in a relatively stress-free environment. Next, we will look at the ten types of guys with whom you're going on all these non-dates—aka the guys in your *gaggle*—and discuss how to best cultivate your connections with them.

Of course, those guys have their own gaggle (of which you are definitely a part), so we'll go through the roles that girls play in the *guy's gaggle* as well. Then, we'll figure out how to make the most important tool in all of this—*techno-romance*—work for, instead of against, us. And finally, we'll take a peek into the *relationship of the future* and allow ourselves to get excited about the amazing partnerships that are awaiting us at the end of this journey.

You now have a choice—the same choice that Becky and I faced that night on our couch. You can hold on to those traditional dating expectations and stick to the old-fashioned rules. You can obsess over your "problems," trying to figure out what is wrong with you and testing out all the experts' plans to fix it.

Or, you can recognize that the *real* problem is your outdated perspective. You can make the choice to embrace the new romantic landscape. You can throw away that pernicious "single girl" label and learn to understand your love life. You can get better at navigating it and explore all of the amazing romantic possibilities that are popping up right under your nose.

Really not much of a choice, is it?

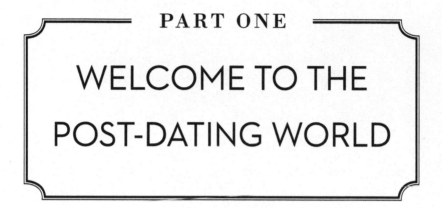

PART ONE

WELCOME TO THE POST-DATING WORLD

SO HERE'S MY FIRST QUESTION . . .

How would you define your romantic status right now?

- *"Single. Incredibly, unbelievably single."*
- *"Ha! Well, it's sort of up in the air."*
- *"Gray . . . ?"*
- *"In a relationship for—well, two months later we asked each other, 'So when would you say that we started dating?' And we were like, 'Oh, New Year's Eve, when we got wasted and made out.'"*
- *"It's really complicated. How much time do you have?"*
- *"I'm on Match.com. I was a little tipsy when I decided to do it. I wasn't going on any dates, really—so I figured, why not."*
- *"I am in a very boring relationship with a man who is exactly like my mother."*
- *"I'm single. As of—well, I thought it was as of a couple of weeks ago. But apparently we weren't even in a relationship! So I guess I've been single since November."*
- *"My romantic status . . . I would define it as, hmm, dating? Ish? Dating-ish?"*
- *"Dating. Although we don't actually go on dates, per se."*
- *"I don't have a love life—I date gay men!"*
- *"Completely single! Completely. But I mean, in the sense that, I guess I have been seeing people, but it's not necessarily, you know . . ."*
- *"I wouldn't say that I'm dating around. I'm just trying to see what I like."*
- *"It's a fucking mess, I'll tell you that."*

When I hit the road and sat down with young women and men all around the United States during the course of a year, I started each conversation by asking one seemingly simple question: how would you define your romantic status right now? Initially I thought, no big deal. The question was simply meant to be a jumping-off point—a way to ease these strangers into opening up to me, and a clue that would help me categorize them into clear boxes (single, in a relationship, married, etc.) that would further direct our conversation. I was expecting one-word answers. Maybe five words, max.

As you can see, that's not exactly what happened.

These varied, fraught, and uniquely personal answers made one thing clear to me—the times, they have a-changed. Gone are the days when one stock word or phrase could be used to sum up a person's entire romantic reality. Ambiguity in our interactions and connections is now the norm, and thus, the traditional labels that we all supposedly know and understand now require caveats, qualifiers, embarrassed laughter, and crazy hand gestures to ring even slightly true. As it turns out, modern romance has gotten a little . . . complicated.

Blame the ubiquity of technology and all the miscommunications and mixed signals that it breeds. Blame the rise of the powerful modern woman and the insecurity of our male counterparts. Blame our Millennial Generation's penchant for innovation and tradition breaking. Blame the disastrous divorce rates of our parents. Blame our childhoods, which revolved around participation trophies, parent-organized playdates, and consistent efforts to shield us from rejection. Blame reality television. (Why? Who knows—but it's fun to blame it for stuff, isn't it?)

Blame whatever and whomever you want. It doesn't change the fact that the romantic landscape has changed—and we're all standing in the center of it, trying to calm the storm just long enough to find love. Earth-shattering love, mind you. Because we're Millennials. We don't settle!

Luckily, this mystifying new romantic landscape is now ours for the taking. *Yours*, for the taking. So now I ask you, dear reader, just to start things off: how would you define your romantic status right now? In this very moment.

. . . Right. That's what I thought. And no, "single" doesn't count if you have to take ten minutes to explain what that even means to you.

There is a much more exciting romantic status out there waiting for you. An empowering one at that. So whatever your answer, ditch it!

Don't worry too much about all the ambiguity for now. Once you figure out how to embrace it (instead of letting it drive you crazy), you will remember that finding love can feel like a fun and exciting adventure—not like an annoying chore to check off your to-do list or a frustrating goal to steadfastly work toward. Your love life will feel natural and comfortable and positive and enriching, and not like you are skirting a dangerous minefield where the smallest missteps threaten to blow you up at every turn.

So now, the moment we've all been waiting for . . .

Let's start figuring out your love life.

DATING 101: A CRASH COURSE

I broke up with my last boyfriend to embark on this single journey, and I had absolutely no clue what I was getting myself into. I was like, "I'm going to find myself and become an independent woman and focus on me," and it's just turned into this big clusterfuck.

I thought it was going to be so much better! I thought it was going to be so much fun and I was going to be getting asked out on dates like every night, and eventually I would find a guy who I could date for a while— like on Sex and the City, *all Carrie Bradshaw. And it's just NOT. It's not what you think it's going to be, once you get yourself into it.*

—Clarissa, 21, PR account executive, New Orleans

There is no shortage of advice out there on how to date.

Want to ace a date? Easy! Just spend as much time as possible up until the big night reading how-to articles, brushing up on self-help bibles, and frantically trying on dozens of cute-but-not-too-revealing outfits in front of your mirror. Dating is now presented to us as a scientifically provable formula. Do X, and he will respond with Y. Say Q, and you will ignite an evolutionary hormone in his brain that will make him think of R and react with S. Get a little adventurous by trying out Z, and he'll go running and leave you alone and loveless for the rest of your life. DON'T DO Z!!!!

Need a refresher on some of these classic tips? Please, allow me the honor:

- Only say yes if he asks you out a few days in advance.
- When in doubt, wear red—it will make him think of sex (and how much he wants to have it, with you!).

- No getting drunk.
- Don't talk politics, religion, or past relationships. Mostly just ask questions.
- Eat more than a salad, but avoid red sauce and garlic.
- Pretend to reach for your wallet when the check comes—but if he actually makes you chip in, what a douchebag! End this doozy of a relationship before it even begins.
- You can contact him afterward to say that you had a good time, but DO NOT suggest another date (that's his job, obviously).
- Hold off on sleeping with him for . . . a very long time.
- Rinse and repeat until he declares his undying love for you. And then maybe you'll even be engaged before your next birthday!

Like I said, easy.

You've got all this tangible dating advice right at your fingertips. You've memorized all the rules and adhered to all the tips, so . . . why does your love life still feel like such a confusing mess?

Oh, right. Because there's one little secret that no one has told you yet.

All the dating advice out there is useless—because no one is really dating anymore. Traditional dating is all but dead. You are now living in a post-dating world.

POST-DATING WORLD (n.)

A new romantic landscape developed in reaction to the strict rules, terrifying divorce rates, and now-irrelevant benchmarks of traditional dating culture; characterized by a generational embrace of ambiguous interpersonal connections and the rise of non-dates, techno-romance, and the gaggle.

Does that sound really serious? It should. A romantic revolution is taking place. Pick your weapon of choice, and let's soldier on!

DING, DONG, DATING IS DEAD!

I think that the times are changing where you MUST "go out." I used to ask girls on dates. I would be like, let's get alone, let's talk. Not to get in your pants, ultimately, but to get to know each other.

But now I think that's inappropriate. There are a bunch of girls who I would just love to cut to the chase with and go on a date, but I just don't think it's done anymore.

What's done instead? Fucked if I know!

—Bryan, 30, carpenter, New Orleans

Remember all the conventional wisdom that we just went over? Great. Now forget it! It was written for women who lived in a romantic universe that no longer exists. All that "advice" doesn't apply to you—or the guys who you're supposed to be "dating"—anymore.

Of course, you may find yourself on a date every now and then. But what you need to understand is that dating, in the standard, explicit, traditional sense, is no longer the primary path to love. Flowers, chocolate, dinner and a movie, classy Italian restaurants, expectations, labels, timelines . . . these well-worn symbols of romance no longer signify our main opportunities to find love. Dates are now the exception, instead of the rule. They have become one *very small* piece of the huge, mystifying puzzle that we call "modern romance."

Look at your calendar. Do you have a date scheduled anywhere on there? Has a guy recently said to you, "It was great to meet you. Can I please take you out for dinner on Saturday night?" If yes, then, great! Make the most of it. Enjoy the free meal, and while you're at it, have fun exploring the connection that you and this guy might have.

But just remember, please, don't look at him too intensely, order the spaghetti, or talk a lot. That's just unladylike.

But any upcoming dates that you may have on your calendar are likely to be outnumbered by other types of plans. Happy hours at work, parties, soccer games, networking coffees, reunions with old friends, ladies' nights out, business trips, concerts, dinner gatherings, conferences, sporting events . . . you get the point. And you probably think of these plans as part of your social life, or professional life, or personal life—as opposed to "dates," which are supposed to be the most important part of your *love life*.

And here we have a problem.

Let me make a comparison. These days, expecting to find love by going on dates is like expecting to get in shape by going to a really hardcore spin class . . . once every few weeks. Sure, spin class is a step in the right direction. Of course, it can only further your cause. But one spin class every other Thursday is *not* going to lead you to your fitness goal all by itself. You need to get the rest of your life together and adopt a healthier day-to-day perspective as well.

Also, let's be honest: spin class kind of sucks. Even though it's good for you, some part of you is going to be dreading it, even as you get on that stationary bike and pretend to crank up the dial to whatever difficulty level the instructor is yelling about.

Nowadays, it's the same with dates. In this post-dating world, dates don't happen very often. And even when they do, they're not guaranteed to be all that fun—or lead you to love.

There *has* to be a better method than dating for women to cultivate amazing connections with guys and find love. People are falling in love every day all around us. Often with nary an old-fashioned date in sight. So how are they doing it? What has replaced the culture of traditional dating?

The mainstream media has recognized that some kind of transition is taking place, with everyone from *The New York Times* to *The Wall Street Journal* to *Glamour* calling out the chaotic shift in the romantic landscape and shaking their heads at those crazy young'uns and their crazy cell phones. Those kids and their booty calls! And delayed marriages! And cross-sex platonic friendships! And refusal to be realistic and accept that relationships are mostly work and sacrifice and, let's face it, drudgery! Haven't they seen the reruns of *Everybody Loves Raymond?*

The complaints, judgments, and unhelpful warnings about modern-day romance are unending. But what about clear insights from within our generation? Where is the tangible advice for how to make the absolute most out of it? All that has been nowhere to be found.

Until now. Because luckily, you picked up this book.

We need, and we deserve, a coherent explanation of this new post-dating landscape. And we require a useful set of tools, language, and tips to clarify the confusion and help us navigate the post-dating world.

Let's start with non-dates.

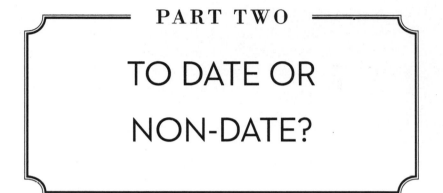

PART TWO

TO DATE OR
NON-DATE?

INTRODUCING THE NON-DATE

"Everyone asks us what our first date was. We don't have one."
"We, like, ate in the dining hall together."
"Yeah—there was no clear beginning to our relationship, which I think has some advantages to it."
—Shawn and Elaina, 27, psychologist and freelance fundraiser,
Minneapolis, married

Here's the bad news: unless you're online dating, getting involved with older men who abide by traditional rules, or letting your mother set you up with her friend's son (the dentist!), dating is probably playing a very small role in your love life.

Not to fear! Here's the good news: whether you realize it or not, you still *have* a love life. An active one, at that. Because in the post-dating world, everything and nothing is a date.

Let me say that again: *in the post-dating world, everything and nothing is a date.*

Romantic possibility is all around you. Once upon a time, you needed to wait for a date to find out if there might be a spark between you and a new romantic prospect. But now, you have the green light to explore meaningful connections *everywhere*, all the time, in any setting, as you go about your daily life—without needing to schedule (and stress about) a date in advance.

Everything and nothing is a date these days. Because what *is* a date, really, except an opportunity for two people to see if they connect? And who exactly determined that connecting on a romantic level *has* to include candlelight and white linen tablecloths and Saturday night plans that are made days, even weeks, beforehand?

If you open your eyes, you'll realize that these days, it's like you're on a date *all the time*. Or more accurately, you're on a non-date.

NON-DATE (n.)

An ambiguous interaction, sometimes face-to-face and sometimes involving technology, that is not explicitly romantic but does not feel entirely platonic either.

What are your plans over the next few weeks? A friend's birthday party? Lunch with an old college pal? A night of dancing with the girls? A conference? A volleyball game?

And now, think back over the past few weeks. What social opportunities came up at the last minute? Happy hour after a stressful presentation? A lazy day in the park with neighbors? Coffee with a professional contact who was in from out of town? Random nighttime meet-ups with an assortment of people who had tentatively promised to text you and "see what you're up to"? And how many emails, texts, Facebook messages, BlackBerry Messenger conversations, and Gchat sessions with guys happened in the midst of all that?

These are all potential non-dates. Which is why, starting right now, you should see these interactions as opportunities to meet guys and further explore your connections with them—be they romantic, platonic, or somewhere in between (be prepared, there will be *a lot* of "in between"). Not only is it *okay* to read into these ambiguous interactions, but in order to cultivate a fulfilling love life in this post-dating world, you *must*.

I've done the research and heard the stories, and these non-dates are often the start of amazing relationships. They are also the start of connections that aren't the be-all and end-all—but are still a truly fun, intriguing, instructive, and pleasant way to pass the time and enjoy your love life until that epic love comes along.

When you look at your calendar, instead of seeing a *lack* of dates, you should see an *abundance* of potential non-dates instead. From now on, the goal is to realize that you're on a non-date *while it's still happening.* That way, you can open your mind to spontaneous moments of romantic possibility as they arise and begin to embrace the craziness of the post-dating world.

Now for the non-dates. Leave no potentially romantic stone unturned!

THE GROUP-NON-DATE

A group outing where you and another member of the group connect, flirt, and talk mostly to each other—but never actually separate from everyone else. This is where birthday parties, sports leagues, and nights out with the crew come into play. If you both have a wide range of other people with whom you could be speaking, and you choose to speak to each other for most of the outing . . . that means something, right?

We were playing flip-cup after kickball, just joking around a lot, and, you know, kind of had a really funny dynamic going.

Then I got this Facebook message from him! But he was writing the message in MY voice, as if I was talking to one of my friends. It said:

"Oh my god, so I met this guy at a bar, and when I got home, he had already Facebooked me. Is that creepy?"

"I don't know, was he at least cute?"

"He was sunburned and dressed for kickball, but yeah, he was cute. Even though he had cut off his sleeves and put them around his thigh."

"Tell me more, tell me more. Like did he have a car . . ."

"No, he rode his bike home."

"Oh, well, do you think he'll call?"

"Yeah, I think so. I made a stupendous first impression, and told him I was horny, so he would be dumb not to."

—Abby, 26, special ed teacher's assistant, Chicago

FINDING YOURSELF ON A GROUP-NON-DATE

You've recently joined a local soccer team that plays (and then drinks) on Sunday afternoons. On this particular Sunday, your team heads over to the closest dive bar to celebrate the first big win of the season.

You partner up with Josh, a cute junior architect on your team, for a rousing game of beer pong (two overtimes!). After losing to a couple of members of the green team, you and Josh continue to talk and drink and sing along to the Journey songs blasting from the jukebox. And when your teammates continue on to the burrito joint around the block, you and Josh consult with each other and decide to tag along. You then stick together throughout the meal, sitting at the same end of the table and bonding over your love of spicy salsa and the Dallas Cowboys.

The team then parts ways, and you and Josh head off in different directions as he casually drops, "See you next Sunday!" You're intrigued by your flirty chemistry but also confused about your next move. He had definitely seemed interested in you, but he also made it sound like you wouldn't be seeing each other until the following Sunday. What did the entire afternoon mean? Was he into you or not? And even if he was, where could a bunch of slightly drunken group outings lead?

HOW TO FOLLOW UP AFTER A GREAT GROUP-NON-DATE

You've noticed that you and a certain guy seem drawn to each other in crowded rooms, like moths to a flame. But is that flame real? Or is it like those fake battery-operated candles you buy at Target, all artificial light but no heat? How can you make some sort of move to find out?

NON-DATE TIP

You've got to get him alone. *Alone* alone. Not "alone" in a dark corner of the party. Get alone in a setting, in person and/or online, where you can start getting to know each other with no social distractions.

You don't need to ask him on a one-on-one date or make a grand gesture. Simply find a way to walk in the same direction as him after next weekend's game. Establish an e-conversation by sending him an email (not the whole group—just him!) with a further thought about something you were discussing over burritos. Say that you're meeting your friends after the game and you have an hour to kill in the meantime, and see if he offers to stick around for a bit. Send him a quick Facebook message about his latest funny status update.

Yes, it would be easier to use the fun, casual group dynamic to push your connection along. But connect as you may, there are certain places that flirting in a group might never take you. And one of those places is a committed relationship, living together on a thirty-five-acre horse ranch, talking about wedding rings and baby names—just ask Brittany and Marshall, a happily engaged couple in their late twenties from Denmark, Wisconsin.

Brittany and Marshall first met as teammates on a bar league's volleyball team. When they hit the courts, their attraction was instant. But even though there was a spark—"a little chemistry," Marshall called it—neither of them was sure how mutual the feeling was.

As Marshall described, "I'm very shy with relationships, and I'm not used to girls necessarily coming up and flirting with me, because I'm not out at bars all the time. So that's why, right away, I thought she was flirting with somebody else." Not to mention that Marshall found Brittany's habits of drinking, swearing, and smoking a bit "too wild" for his tastes, while Brittany, in turn, thought that Marshall was "too nice" and assumed that she would "just tear him apart."

But over the weeks, Brittany developed a palpable crush on Marshall. Then she made a move that she *thought* was smart. She invited him on another group-non-date. Oops.

As Brittany recalls, "It was St. Patrick's Day, and our mutual friend was gathering a group at another bar. And I totally tried to take him home that night—I tried to bait him in with 'just a snuggle'—and he was not having any of it! I definitely remember going home and asking my roommate, 'Do I have a horn growing out of my face? Did I do something wrong?'"

In fact, Marshall was just an old-fashioned guy with a very religious Lutheran upbringing, and he simply wanted to get to know Brittany better and "be friends first" before taking any sort of intimate plunge. He also wanted to "see if she could form a sentence without a swear word." Their big drunken group-non-date was *not* showing him any of those desirable qualities.

Luckily, Marshall rejected Brittany's overtures by saying that they should grab dinner instead. Brittany was *pretty* sure that he was asking her out on a date—although despite being in her mid-twenties, she had never *been* on an actual date, so who knew! Either way, the invitation was formal enough to make her nervous. But once they got alone in a more intimate setting, their connection exploded to a whole other level.

"Right away, the biggest thing is that we talked the whole night, and just talked about anything, and it just worked," explained Marshall. "The conversation flowed, and that's what I was really looking for."

Brittany agreed. "That was the turning point for me. I was like, holy shit, we can connect and talk and not have to go get wasted in order to have a relationship and have fun!"

NON-DATE TIP

If the opportunity for a one-on-one hangout arises, *take it.* Expect it to feel a little different from the group-non-date. That might ultimately be a good thing.

When I met Brittany and Marshall, more than a year after that night, their ability to communicate and have fun (with and without a party happening around them) was still a huge part of their life together. And even though they first connected on a series of group-non-dates, they first discovered their deeper bond once they left the group at home—or, fine, at the bar—and focused solely on each other.

THE E-NON-DATE

A series of online interactions, during which you and your correspondent share the personal stories, thoughts, and feelings that would have traditionally been discussed on dates. Long email chains, Gchat conversations, and text exchanges can cover personal ground that might feel out of proportion to how much time you've actually spent together. But hey, sometimes it's easier to open up in front of a screen.

I met him at the gym, and he was my roommate's type—long hair, kind of hipster-looking kid. I went to my roommate, and I was like, oh my god, you've got to check out this guy, he's so cute.

She was very shy, so instead I started talking to him. His mom makes designer bags, so then he was like, check out my mom's website. He had a link to his email through the website, so I emailed him and said, loved the bags, blah, blah, blah. I think I sort of threw it out there—like, you're hot—by emailing him.

So then he had my email. And he emailed me back, and we sort of emailed back and forth. I really, really liked him. Actually, he broke my heart a bit.

—Kara, 34, teacher, Madison

FINDING YOURSELF ON AN E-NON-DATE

While flipping burgers at your friend's birthday BBQ, you meet Chris, a cute, laid-back art director who works at an advertising firm. Although you lose track of him at some point during the party, he finds you before heading out and asks if you're on Facebook (who has business cards anymore?). This prompts you to make a mental note to remove those unflattering photos of you from the previous night, and you say that yes, you're on Facebook. The next morning, the friend request comes. Success!

A few days later, Chris messages you a link to the YouTube video that he had been telling you about at the BBQ, which moves over into emails, and then turns into two weeks' worth of almost daily correspondence. The emails cover everything from gossip about your mutual friends to descriptions of your respective jobs to stories from your college years. And more links, of course. As the days go on, your back-and-forth becomes increasingly personal and familiar, and you become fairly certain that he is not a weirdo, and in fact, seems to be getting cooler with every email.

Eventually, you can't help but forward an email or two to your best friend, looking for some clarification on what's going on. You've both casually dropped hints about hanging out, but neither one of you seems to be in much of a rush to transition from your e-convos to something more serious. You're intrigued by him and a little worried that he'll soon grow tired of your online witticisms, but you also don't want to be the one to push a face-to-face outing for fear of coming across as aggressive or desperate. You beg your friend to explain: what are the rules in this situation??

HOW TO FOLLOW UP ON A GREAT E-NON-DATE

NON-DATE TIP

This one is obvious—hang out in person!

No one is saying that you have to go from emailing this guy funny cat photos to asking him out on an official date. But presumably, you've both been sharing bits and pieces about yourselves in these e-non-dates, and opportunities to transfer some of those online interests to in-person outings should start subtly presenting themselves. Are you e-bonding over a band you both like? Well, they're coming to town soon! Did you both happen to have Mexican food for lunch and are now Gchatting about whose guacamole was better? Maybe you should gather a group of friends and hit up both spots for a guacamole taste-off. Does he like to throw out random facts via BBM? Say that you need him on your bar trivia team. At the very least, you've probably become Facebook friends by now, so make sure to shoot your birthday party Facebook invitation his way.

Just bite the bullet and suggest a casual way to hang out. Like Kara, the thirty-four-year-old teacher who emailed the cute guy about his mom's bags.

Before moving back to her home state of Wisconsin, Kara had been in a relationship with a "gorgeous celebrity personal trainer" in New York City, where she spent most of her twenties. They met when Kara's friend, who was working for a fitness magazine, asked her to be a guinea pig for an article that she was writing.

"So they sent me to his gym, and he did this whole physical analysis on me, and he was *hot*," Kara remembered. "He said, 'Well, I need to check your legs for your body mass index,' and I thought, oh my god, I didn't shave my legs! This guy is going to totally laugh at me. I was just gross. But he didn't, and then he had to email my results from all the fitness stuff, and we started a flirty email back-and-forth."

Could that email chain have gone on and on until it eventually fizzled out? Absolutely—but Kara wasn't going to let that happen. Kara made a move to get their connection out of email inboxes and into real life. A *casual* move.

NON-DATE TIP

Don't kid yourself—if he's e-communicating with you, then odds are *great* that he'll also be interested in continuing that communication in person. Any guy who is spending significant time writing to you would most likely rather be hanging out in person so that he can actually, you know, look at your pretty face instead of at his computer screen. Let that knowledge give you the confidence to throw an option or two out there.

"We had friended each other on Facebook, and I had looked at his pictures and thought, okay, he's cool," Kara explained. "So I said, 'Hey, if you ever want to come to the bar where I work sometime for a drink, I'll get you one.' And then he started coming to the bar with his brother to watch football. I would just have a great time with them. And we would flirt, and that went on for months and months and months. There were mixed messages from him, in the sense that he would come every single week and definitely was flirting with me, but he never pursued anything."

Have no fear—Kara and her hot trainer eventually got together after a few months of mixed signals and non-date miscommunications. His offer to play nursemaid while she recovered from surgery ended up sealing the relationship deal. But it all started with a few flirty emails.

THE FRIEND-NON-DATE

One of many hangouts with a close guy friend whom you know well, feel comfortable around, and maybe sporadically cuddle with (despite being "just friends").

I became the girl that would hang out with all the boys, always had guy friends. But I would never date any of them. I've always had that very easy sort of camaraderie with them, and it was less awkward getting to know them in a non-threatening way.

They were my boys, but I would never have thought that they would've found me attractive. I was not their type. Their girlfriends were always delightfully tiny little blond-haired, blue-eyed creatures.

What's really funny is that it wasn't until years later that we got together for reunions and people got hammered. And my guy friends were like, "God, I had a thing for you so badly! I was so in love with you!" And I'm like, "What? What are you talking about? Are you out of your mind?!"

—Larissa, 37, college admissions officer, Houston

FINDING YOURSELF ON A FRIEND-NON-DATE

Meet Jared, your good friend. You guys touch base most days—not in a getting-to-know-you, are-we-or-aren't-we way, but in the same continuous and conversational way that you keep up with your girlfriends. You know his boss's name, you know what he's doing over the weekend, and you know that he thinks your cousin is really hot. But you're just platonic friends, as you regularly explain with airtight ease and confidence to all the acquaintances, family members, and random partygoers who sometimes mistake your closeness for something more romantic.

On this particular night, a quick Gchat conversation about how you've both fallen behind in your quest to catch up on *How I Met Your Mother* brings him to your doorstep with season three in hand. He knows his way around your apartment, and he focuses on rounding up some popcorn and getting the DVDs ready as you wrap up a phone chat with your mother. You're finally settled in on the couch when, a few minutes into the first episode, he teases you about hogging the space. You respond by giving him a joking (but firm) kick in the side. One big, yawning stretch later, your feet end up on his lap and you both contentedly sink further into the couch to get comfortable. Nope, not cuddling. Just friends.

But as you giggle at the LEGEN . . . wait for it . . . DARY romantic mishaps of Barney Stinson and his gang of friends, your mind starts to wander toward *your* friend on the other end of the couch. There *are* some shades of gray in your friendship; you supportively share all your dating stories with each other, but you always end up thinking that his girlfriends are boring, while he argues that your boyfriends are dumb. You're physically comfortable with one another, curling up on the couch and resting your head on his shoulder after a few too many drinks at the bar, but you've never actually hooked up. You've also seen him talk about and interact with girls whom he *really* likes, and you're observant enough to see that he doesn't treat you like that.

You're *just friends*. Seriously! But as you lounge around on the couch together, you wonder how sustainable your "platonic" friendship really is. What does he want from you? And more importantly, what do *you* want from *him*?

HOW TO FOLLOW UP AFTER A GREAT FRIEND-NON-DATE

Maybe it's because of my own tendency to get involved in prolonged, semi-complicated friendships with guys (busted! although to any of my male friends reading this—no, *of course* I'm not talking about you). But whatever the reason, I find that friend-non-dates are often the trickiest connections to explore.

Tricky, but worthwhile—because they can also be the most rewarding.

Making the decision to push the romantic envelope with a friend can appear to have major, intimidating consequences. On one hand, you can't ignore the feeling that something in your friendship, no matter how subtle, might be shifting. Sure, hanging out with him might not give you the giddy-like-a-sixteen-year-old explosion of butterflies that some other guys do. But there's something stirring inside of you when you talk to him, some small inkling of questions like: Are we missing out on something great here? Are all those people who joke about us being a couple on to something? It's fine that it took Harry and Sally a million years to wake up and get it together, but really, who has that kind of time these days?

On the other hand, there are potentially serious risks involved. You're worried about ruining the friendship that you both so appreciate—and, let's be honest, you're worried about making a move, getting rejected, and feeling like an idiot.

Well, I say, life is short and love is grand. Hell, fun flirtation is grand! Why not go ahead and give your friend-non-date a little boost?

NON-DATE TIP

Don't worry about the fact that nothing has "happened" yet. Stop telling yourself that if he were *just that into you*, he would've made a move by now. This narrative is limiting, disempowering, and often untrue. He might just see you as a buddy for the time being ... but that's a very questionable "might."

For many of the guys I interviewed, friendship with girls was a complicated issue.

Yes, I met men who immediately and aggressively go after everything they want in life. If you're friends with a guy like that and he hasn't made a move, then maybe he does just want to be friends.

But more likely, the guy you are friend-non-dating is not exactly sure what he wants. And even once he becomes more sure, he might not really know how to get it, or he may not have the confidence to go for it.

When I asked a world-traveling Irishman in New Orleans what would make a girl "friend material," he admitted, "It's probably that I was too scared to approach her in a sexual way. I might know from the start that I'm interested in her, but oftentimes, it's the girl I am most attracted to that I will talk to last. Because (a) I'm scared and (b) I don't want to make it too obvious."

Is this guy a strange anomaly? Apparently not. A New York City man about town who seems to score more women than the Yankees lineup combined laid it out like this: "The more awesome a girl is, the less likely I am to hook up with her. Say I meet a girl and she's an 8 or 9 on the personality scale—then *boom*, she goes into the friend category, regardless of looks."

What the . . . ?!

Let's get this straight. Say you meet a guy who *doesn't* make a move on you, but *does* pursue your platonic friendship. Instead of assuming that he's just not romantically attracted to you, you're now supposed to assume that he's putting you in the friend zone because you're just *too freakin' awesome*? According to these guys, yes. At the very least, that is a definite possibility.

The good news here is that being a guy's friend is no longer a guarantee that, as far as he's concerned, you might as well be wearing a jock strap and farting every ten minutes. He might not be *intending* to make a move on you—or he might still be trying to figure out if and how he wants to, and whether that's a good idea, and whether you'd reject him—but the possibility of romance is almost always in the air.

With all this in mind, let's get back to your friend-non-date. How can you kick things up a notch and further explore this promising connection?

The answer to that question comes courtesy of Michelle, a twenty-five-year-old PhD student in Cincinnati who studies body language as part of her research in experimental psychology. She is also a self-described serial monogamist who has been in many serious long-term relationships—every single one with a guy who started out as a friend.

In her experience, "Maybe two of the guys that I dated actually liked me before I liked them. But the other ones, when I asked them later, they would say, 'Yes, we were just friends, and then all of a sudden one day I was, like, oh my god, she's great, why am I not pursuing her?'"

What are Michelle's secrets?

NON-DATE TIP

Don't significantly change your behavior once you decide to test the waters of your friendship. Remember that he's *already* your friend, so there's already a whole lot that he likes about you. Change yourself, and you risk getting, well, weird.

As Michelle theorized, "I think too many times when girls get 'that feeling,' they change themselves. I used to do that, too—when I had a crush on a friend, I used to get more girly. Like, stupid. Talk in a higher voice. Do the whole side-glance and eye-batting thing. Put more effort into how I looked. Wear more makeup. And it's a good thing I didn't do that with my current boyfriend, because he told me later that he hates when girls wear too much makeup!"

Now, I'm not saying that you should start stressing about how much eyeliner your guy friend prefers. In fact, I'm saying the opposite! Don't worry about all that. He knows you already. He's well aware of what you look and act like. And he's a fan. Don't mess with it.

NON-DATE TIP

On the flip side, you should also make an effort to play around with your *natural* sexuality a bit, as a reminder to your friend that, yes, you are a woman, and a pretty hot one at that. But that sexiness has to come from a comfortable place.

Wait, sexiness has a middle ground between unshowered in sweats and stuffed into a bandage dress and Louboutins? You don't say! Find that middle ground, and you'll evoke hints of your natural sexuality that might make your guy friend sneak a second glance at you across the couch.

"It has a lot to do with body language," Michelle confided. "You don't have to be *explicit* to be sexy. There's a difference between when a guy thinks of you as being just sexy, or as being an awesomely sexy amazing potential girlfriend. And it's when you act sexy in a way that makes him think, 'Wow, she's not even trying and she's really sexy,' like in a homey way. It has to come from a comfortable place."

So . . . no Spanx? Okay, got it. No Spanx.

"Guys aren't stupid—they're primal and basic, but not stupid," Michelle swore. "I remember one time I was trying to be 'sexy' with a guy, and he was like, 'Why did you just pull your shirt down and show me your cleavage?' I was like, oh crap, he caught me! But that's why it can't come from a calculated place.

"Instead, I just think, how would I act with my long-term boy-friend? How would I be sitting? What would I be doing or saying? You just have to put yourself in the mind-set that you want to be in. It's kind of backwards thinking."

Michelle's go-to move is to wear an oversized sweater that shows "one little part" of her body and thus makes her feel sexy, confident, *and* comfortable. Now think through your wardrobe. What's your equivalent? Next time you two hang out, wear it and then get settled in on that couch.

NON-DATE TIP

Don't overthink your interactions with your guy friend! Don't worry about who texted who last, or who initiated the previous friend-non-date. When in doubt, just act as you would with a close female friend.

The perk of already being friends is that you should be able to skip any annoying game playing. Instead, generally treat him like you would a close gal pal. If you want to see him again, make it happen. Set up another friend-non-date. And then simply break out whatever comfortable outfit makes you feel sexy, stay calm when your knee bumps into his on the couch, and look out for those butterfly feelings that may or may not come when you're together.

Michelle's advice certainly sounds better than the advice I got from an outspoken male interviewee. Want to know what he thinks you should do?

NON-DATE (NON-)TIP

"Get drunk together and make a move. If he's not into it, then you can always blame it on being drunk!"

I mean, yes. That's always an option, too. But for the modern woman who wants to explore a more-than-friendly connection in a *mature* and *sober* way—I'd go with Michelle's plan.

THE PLAY-NON-DATE

A non-date that revolves around a hookup but is not plagued by the shadiness and disrespect of a booty call. Just because you met him at a bar doesn't mean that he can't be cute, smart, and funny. You're pretty sure that he might be all three... but more importantly, you're pretty sure that you're both getting some action tonight.

It was the first time I'd seen him in five years, and he'd gone from this awkward, chubby-faced kid to this really tall and gorgeous, muscular, good-looking guy. I was like, oh my gosh, HELLO!

So we started talking on Facebook one night, and things just went from there. It went from Facebook to texting to phone, and talking every day, throughout the day, all day.

Our text messages led really quickly to sexting. Honestly, I was okay with that, because I wasn't sure that I wanted anything serious. But I was like, he's hot, I've liked him for a while, I'll go sleep with him and see how it goes. Then we decided to meet in Chattanooga and spend a weekend together.

So I headed back up here, and we just kept talking. And then Sunday we were talking, and he was like, "I want you to be my girlfriend." And I was like, "Okay."

—Liz, 26, nurse, Nashville

FINDING YOURSELF ON A PLAY-NON-DATE

Despite your plan to stay in and finally catch up on *True Blood* (speaking of hot hookups), your friend convinces you to meet her and some friends at a bar across town for "just one drink." You're reluctant to change out of your pajamas and refrigerate your order-in Thai food, but it's been a while since you've hung out with her, so off you go.

After settling into the bar booth with your vodka tonic, you say your hellos and start chatting up Sean, your friend's friend-of-a-friend who is sitting next to you. He's funny and cute, and four vodka tonics later, everyone is heading home and you're both deciding that you should share a cab because . . . you can't really remember why, but it sounded like a good plan! Next thing you know, you're making out in the cab and agreeing to, uh, check out his apartment.

You hook up that night (make of that what you will) and are surprised to find yourself having a fun conversation with him the next morning. You're prepared to consider this a one-night stand, but a flirty text exchange a few days later leads to another rendezvous, this time including a pre-hookup drink where you talk about your jobs, friends, and favorite *True Blood* episodes. This happens a few times— you have harmless but entertaining text convos during the week, which lead to weekend hookups that are preceded or followed by food and/or conversation. But the hookups are clearly the main event, as there is no preexisting friendly or romantic dynamic between the two of you.

You'd think of this as a booty call, since there are no promises of exclusivity or dating statuses and no one is talking about feelings or whispering sweet nothings. But you're also consistently texting in between hookups, and you kinda-sorta feel like you're actually getting to know him pretty well. Maybe you're both just taking it (emotionally) slow? Or are you simply a delusional multi-night stand?

HOW TO FOLLOW UP AFTER A GREAT PLAY-NON-DATE

There is one phrase in dating lore that I hate even more than "Sorry, but it sounds like he's just not that into you." This one concerns hook-ups. Here it goes:

"But why would he buy the cow when he can get the milk for free?"

So says your scandalized grandmother, your nosy boss, and your uber-traditional friend who never, ever *ever* sleeps with a guy before the three-month mark.

Why does this phrase offend me so much? Well, let's not even harp on the fact that anyone who says this is inherently comparing you to a cow. There's also a clear lack of logic here. Why would he buy the cow? Um, how about because the cow is *awesome*? And fun and smart and interesting and attractive? And because, hey, the milk is a pretty nice perk, too? And since when should your decision to hook up be based on whether it's going to make a guy want to *buy* you?

We will not be taking that approach here. You (and the guy on your play-non-date) can thank me later.

NON-DATE TIP

In order to turn a play-non-date into a connection that doesn't only revolve around the bar and the bedroom (or the park, taxi, kitchen floor ... wherever it is that you guys have been "playing"), you need to reset your brain. There will always be people out there telling you that you *ruined everything* by hooking up with a guy "too early." Tune them out. Forget everything that everyone has always told you about the timing of hooking up. Stop second-guessing your actions, and stop psyching yourself out. Instead, *trust in the connection.*

When I first decided to seek out perspectives on the new norms of non-dating, I made a beeline for Ruth, an old friend of mine who, despite now being a responsible lawyer, had always been the first to convince me that having a cocktail the night before my college thesis due date was a *marvelous plan* that could only make my work more brilliant.

Ruth has a rebellious romantic streak that she has embraced for years. Time and time again, she would defy every dating rule and warning that I'd ever heard and still find herself in one relationship after another, always with men who tended to fall hard and fast for her.

Ruth's love life always followed a simple formula: meet a guy, sleep with him ASAP, repeat often, discover feelings, and enter into a relationship. At the time of this writing, Ruth had been in a stable, fun, loving relationship for over a year.

This relationship began with one hazy night of work parties, screwdrivers, 1990s rap lyrics, and, ultimately, sex. The next day, the Facebook friend request came. It was not quite the standard fairy tale that our generation of Disney fans has come to expect, but given the love, dedication, and trust that imbued their relationship, it was a fairy tale nonetheless.

"I've never hesitated to hook up with someone I was into," Ruth told me over beers. "And it's always worked out surprisingly well, despite the fact that everything we've ever been told emphatically assures us that happy endings never follow from, well, happy endings."

NON-DATE TIP

First off, you need to make sure that you're hooking up for the right reasons.

"I'm not saying we should all run around and put out until we find love," Ruth warned. "I'm saying that if you are attracted to a guy, and you *want* to get intimate, then don't refrain solely because you think there will be dire consequences. Every woman needs to ask herself where her personal comfort line begins."

NON-DATE TIP

If you know that hookups tend to have a crazy or emotional effect on you, then that's cool, too—just avoid play-non-dates and hold off on jumping into bed until you feel comfortable.

But let's say you've determined that you actually, in your hormonal heart of hearts and for your own sake (and not because you think it will make him like you more), want to hook up with this guy. You've ignored all the naysayers who are already dooming your connection with Mr. Play-Non-Date, and you are down for a good time. What happens post-bliss?

NON-DATE TIP

It's simple: Be relaxed. Be yourself. Be a welcome break from the postcoital mess that he's (unfortunately) expecting you to be.

Sadly, because of the harmful social and cultural messages that your guy receives about women, he thinks that you are going to freak out, get emotional, and start making crazy demands on him post-hookup. Instead, continue to be what you *actually* are—a sane, rational, confident, undramatic human being who is pretty pleased with herself for embarking on a mutually satisfying sexual encounter.

Demonstrating that you are comfortable with yourself, and with your decision to hook up, is actually incredibly easy. When you wake up the next morning (or even right after you're done hooking up), just crack a joke. Start a conversation. Go back to sleep. Get some food. Hook up again. Whatever! And the next time you see him, planned or spontaneous, do that all again. Be normal. Be friendly. Show that you harbor no strange reactions to your play-non-date, and simply stay open to the possibility that you might both begin seeing opportunities to explore your connection in other types of settings.

A true connection is a true connection, whether it starts out at dinner over a white linen tablecloth or in bed under a set of sheets.

If hooking up ruins that, well, then it probably wasn't that fantastic a connection to begin with.

And as Ruth says, "If you're an individual who enjoys sex with someone you're physically and mentally attracted to, and are looking for someone who enjoys the same, then a good roll in the hay might actually be a great way to find what you're looking for. At the very least, it's a fun diversion as you conduct the hunt."

THE NETWORKING-NON-DATE

A non-date in which both parties meet up for supposedly professional purposes but end up discussing personal and/or flirtatious topics. Think revealing drinks with co-workers, surprisingly fun coffee conversations with career contacts, and intriguing sidelong glances around the group project table. At least you already have something in common, right? Your jobs!

We had known each other peripherally for years now, probably like three or four years. Through music stuff—she works with all the same people that I work with. So we had actually exchanged emails and messages over Facebook and MySpace a few times beforehand.

We work with the same people and we'd had minimal contact, but I had never met her in person. And then we worked together when she came down to Nashville, and it was instant. Literally, as soon as I saw her, I was like, oh my goodness!

—Caleb, 29, musician, Nashville

FINDING YOURSELF ON A NETWORKING-NON-DATE

You breathlessly run into Starbucks after work. Smoothing out your business-casual attire and breathing in the smell of espresso, you see Matt, an up-and-coming Web designer, playing with his iPhone on a comfy chair in the back corner. You guys know each other through your work circles and, after emailing back and forth for a few weeks about some marketing ideas that he had for your company, you had decided to meet up over coffee to discuss.

You're both "very busy people" and have made it clear that this will be a fairly short encounter. But as you begin talking, the conversation starts to take some surprising turns. He mentions his family; you show him a photo of your dog. He admits that his secret dream is to join the Peace Corps; you tell him about that time in seventh grade when you dyed your hair fire-engine red in an effort to emulate Angela Chase from *My So-Called Life*. Suddenly, you both look at your watches and realize that you've been sitting in the same spot for two hours. Where did the time go?

Worried that you've overstayed your welcome, you cut the conversation short and awkwardly hug Matt good-bye before running to your next engagement. But in retrospect, you feel a little confused. Do you usually talk about your crazy uncle at business meetings? Why are your palms sweaty? And why do you kind of feel like you were just on a date?

HOW TO FOLLOW UP AFTER A GREAT NETWORKING-NON-DATE

The Millennial Generation is serious about our professional aspirations. This means that we spend a lot of time engaging in career-related activities. You might even say that, for many of us, work and school have become our comfort zones.

No wonder it can feel so much easier to connect with someone in a professional setting than on a date!

NON-DATE TIP

Push yourself—and your networking-non-date—out of that comfortable work zone. Slowly but surely, *get away from work,* and all that it touches.

The fact that you and a guy can bond in some professional capacity already puts your odds for deeper connection at an advantage. By starting off with a networking-non-date, you and a guy have the potential to skip a lot of the awkward getting-to-know-you and are-we-attracted-to-each-other stuff that can kill a connection before it even begins. This was first explained to me by Bryan, a thirty-year-old carpenter in New Orleans who had recently reentered school to get a second degree in engineering.

Attractive, charming, and openly sensitive, Bryan had been around the romantic block once or twice ("My sisters would accuse me of always being in relationships!") and had succeeded and failed at connecting with women in a variety of settings. He hated picking up women in bars, fearing rejection and "all the complication of dating." As Bryan now knew, if he had his way, you would meet him in his element: at school. In his words:

"School is great for connecting because I like working with people. Put some Legos in our hand! Like, right now, I'm doing a project with this *knockout* girl. I don't know how to pick up girls in bars, but I'm really comfortable if she and I are going to be doing an AutoCAD drawing together. That's fine. That's cool. We can laugh. *I* can laugh."

Bryan and this knockout girl were getting together to advance their learning and careers. And laugh! This connection sounded promising. Except there was a problem.

As soon as Bryan brought up this girl, I realized that it was the first time he had mentioned her during our interview. And afterward, as we discussed the girls who occupied his mind and played a prominent role in his love life, she didn't come up again. He thought she was a knockout and was excited to feel so comfortable with her while they worked on a project—but it didn't sound like he thought of her much outside of class. He'd put her in a work-related box, and as long as they were only interacting over AutoCAD drawings, she seemed destined to remain in that box while he explored his other romantic connections more avidly.

I found myself wondering: what should this knockout be doing, if she did, in fact, want to get to know Bryan better?

NON-DATE TIP

Set up another non-date that will entice you both to leave most of the work talk at home. Try and become a bigger part of his non-work life.

Depending on your preferences, this could leave you with any number of non-date options.

Group-Non-Date: Invite Him to Happy Hour!

Whether your office crew is grabbing drinks on a Friday night or you are planning to attend an industry-specific gathering over cocktails, an outing with a group of people in your professional sphere is the perfect excuse to invite him along without feeling too forward or random. Once you are there, make sure to find things to talk about besides work (the bar, the people around you, and whatever you did that day are all good places to start).

E-Non-Date: Start Becoming Friends Online, Not Just Professional Contacts

Who says that your emails have to focus *entirely* on professional stuff? Infuse your online correspondence with a personal touch. Crack a joke here, ask a personal question there, and all of a sudden, you're e-friends.

Play-Non-Date: Use Your Professional Bond as a Segue to Bond in . . . Other Ways

Did I mention that work happy hours usually involve drinks? One more glass of wine, one extra touch on the arm while discussing market trends, and soon you might find yourself throwing away your professional cares in a dark corner somewhere. What do you think happens at all those company holiday parties?

NON-DATE TIP

Proceed with caution at all times!

While you're planning all these non-dates, just remember: you have a professional reputation to protect. You don't want to end up as the latest star in the take-no-prisoners work gossip mill. Try not to do anything—especially in public—that will make you want to hide under your desk the following day.

THE SURPRISE-NON-DATE

A non-date where you arrive expecting a casual, platonic vibe and are surprised by the traditionally date-like atmosphere. That old college pal? Oops, look like he thinks you are meeting him for a real, live DATE! Too bad you're still wearing your kickball jersey.

Having recently returned from a trip abroad, I ran into a doctor who I've worked with in the past, but haven't seen since I've been back. Although we were friendly, we weren't friends. He inquired about my trip and asked if I had plans for the weekend, because he wanted to hear more about it. We made plans and met up at a bar near my apartment.

We had a few drinks and shared an appetizer, and he asked if I would mind taking a walk so we could talk. We walked around laughing and having a great time. Three hours in, he asked if I would like to get dinner. So we wound up at this nice Italian spot. Wine, dinner, more amazing conversation.

After it was over, we headed back to our meeting spot and talked outside for another hour! We made tentative plans to get together again, but nothing is set in stone. When he got home, he texted me, thanking me for an "intellectually satisfying night."

What do you think? Date or Non-Date?

—Anonymous, *WTF?!* reader

FINDING YOURSELF ON A SURPRISE-NON-DATE

You make dinner plans with an old friend from college who just moved into town after getting his master's degree. He chooses a trendy restaurant, which you take as a sign of his fancy new graduate-level tastes, and when you arrive, straight from the office and with an unfortunate ink stain on your understated wool turtleneck, you're a little embarrassed to find that he's wearing a nicer outfit than you are.

He proceeds to order an expensive bottle of wine ("to celebrate my move here," he claims), and you keep thinking that your conversation feels more mature and intimate than the college talks that you remember. And when the check comes, he insists on paying, laughingly reminding you that graduate degrees are usually accompanied by a bump in salary (but wait, wasn't his degree in education? Whatever . . .). The evening ends when he walks you to your car and, after a quick hug, you both promise to hang out again soon.

The next morning, you're surprised to find yourself asking some unexpected questions. You'd just been thinking of him as a casual old friend, but you're having strange thoughts like, *Should I have worn my sexy heels? Was I funny enough?* And most tellingly, *Why am I overanalyzing this like it was a date? Wait, was it a date??*

HOW TO FOLLOW UP AFTER A GREAT SURPRISE-NON-DATE

Surprise! A surprise-non-date is often the easiest non-date to explore. That is, if you're actually feeling a spark worth exploring . . .

NON-DATE TIP

If you're not romantically interested in this guy (and are *sure* that you never, ever will be), then establish a clear friendship instead. Avoid one-on-one outings and hang out in groups. Maybe even introduce him to a cute friend of yours!

Welcome him to the friend zone! Don't play dumb—you know how to put a guy there, when you want to.

But what if you're interested in delving into this connection a little further?

NON-DATE TIP

Regardless of where your non-date fell on the platonic-to-romantic spectrum, a guy just tried to impress you and show you a particularly good time. Your only job now is *not* to over-think things.

The key here is to let your connection progress in a comfortable way—without worrying about whether you're going on "dates." Stop stressing about the exact nature of your time together, and you'll be much more likely to find yourself in the same situation as Chris, a twenty-four-year-old student in Portland, Oregon, who only realized that he was going on dates with his now-girlfriend once he was on them. As he tells it:

"We ended up walking around, getting frozen yogurt . . . but it was just like, yeah, I'll hang out with you. There were no expectations at that point. It just became so immediately comfortable and compatible that it morphed into something else. We call it a date now—but when we got there, we wouldn't have called it a date."

So just follow up on that surprise-non-date by . . . hanging out! There are a few potential scenarios here:

NON-DATE TIP

If he proposes another datelike activity, go—but don't automatically assume that he's in love with you, and that this is "serious," and that maybe you should start brainstorming baby names.

He picks another nice spot? Well, he might just be a guy who likes to travel in style. This is why you shouldn't automatically read into everything and get all worked up—at least until something unambiguously romantic comes of it (basically, until someone tries to kiss someone). Enjoy the burgeoning connection, and let it all play out as it will.

Of course, that doesn't mean you have to show up in your sweaty jersey again. Now would be a good time to heed some advice from one of my male interviewees and up the ante a bit; as he explained to me, "Even a non-date could turn into a date. So if you're a girl and you find a guy to be attractive, then just treat it like a date. Wear something cute, shave, and seem 13 percent less crazy than you really are."

(I know, I know—you're not crazy, and guys need to stop saying that. We'll get to this later, I promise.)

NON-DATE TIP

If his next offer to hang out involves watching a basketball game with ten of his rowdiest buddies, or something equally "unromantic," then same thing—don't read into it!

This is not a demotion. He's not taking a step back, or trying to un-date you. He's just exploring your connection in a variety of ways, whether he consciously means to or not. Just have a good time. End of story.

NON-DATE TIP

And if you don't hear from him? Let his surprise-non-date behavior give you the boost of confidence to reach out yourself.

Text him with an interesting thought you just had, or email him a funny article, or comment on his latest Facebook photo, or propose another non-date. Whatever you want! Especially if some part of him *did* see your time together as a date, and maybe even sensed that you hadn't been anticipating the same thing, then he might be waiting for *you* to show that you're interested in continuing to spend time together.

Bottom line: don't think too hard. Have fun exploring your connection via whatever follow-up non-date he suggests—or follow his lead and suggest one yourself. No more overanalyzing. Done!

So there are the six types of non-dates. See? Romantic potential can pop up in your post-dating life at any time!

Embrace the ambiguity and start living your love life immediately. Explore these connections in incremental ways, and watch as one non-date turns into more non-dates, which then turn into *more* non-dates, which might just turn into a relationship. . . .

"TO THINE OWN SELF BE TRUE . . ." AND THEN LET'S FIND SOME LOVE, SHALL WE?

The way I see it, relationships are icing on the cake—and YOU'RE the cake. If the cake hasn't been fully cooked yet, and it's not strong and sturdy and complete on its own, then there's no point in putting icing on it. It'll just fall apart!

—Amy, 27, marketing manager, Minneapolis

If the goal here were for you to find a guy—any guy—and make him fall in love with you, then we could be done right now. You could simply fill your calendar with non-dates, make a few casually strategic moves to push these budding connections along, and keep at it until some guy declares his devotion.

And that's usually the end goal of these sorts of books, right? To meet a guy, make him like you, and get him to commit? Wedding rings exchanged, babies birthed, case closed?

Not so fast. You are not a typical girl, this is not a typical dating book, and you are not looking for typical love.

We have to think *bigger*. Because if there is one refrain that I heard over and over again in my interviews, it was that we modern women DO NOT WANT TO SETTLE. And somehow, despite all the fear-inducing warnings that we are too picky or too successful or too old or too educated or too empowered or too crazy, we remain optimistic that we won't have to. We want to experience once-in-a-lifetime, soul-exploding love with someone who makes our lives better, richer, and fuller. And there's more to that than just making sure you've got some non-dates lined up.

You are about to enter an exciting new phase of your love life—and one simple question will be the starting point for your entire journey. This question is: "Who are these guys I'm going on non-dates with?" But the answer will not be as clear-cut as it might seem.

The answer to that question shouldn't be a laundry list of interchangeable men. We're not talking about John the hockey player who likes Greek food, or José the academic who makes funny jokes, or Alex the ad salesman who has a lot of money. You want a guy who is a perfect fit for *you*—and *you* are not just Rose the teacher who speaks three languages, or Bridget the office manager who ran two marathons, or Jane the nanny who knits gorgeous scarves in her free time. You are more complex than that, and your ideal love is going to jive with your unique combination of needs, desires, experiences, and preferences.

To find this great love, you need to know yourself. But of course, you're probably still in the process of figuring out who you really are and what you really want. Aren't we all?

The incredible thing about the post-dating world is that you do not have to separate your quest for love from your quest for identity, since they are both vital to your long-term fulfillment as a person. You don't have to take a hiatus from romance while you figure yourself out (as many women told me they had tried to do during certain phases of their lives—"I'm having Tina time!"). Your journey in the post-dating world can be a learning process on multiple levels. You can find love *and* find yourself all at the same time.

But in order to find yourself while you're finding love, you'll need to do things a little differently than you probably have in the past. You'll need to put *yourself* at the center of your love life.

Remember, you won't have to "date" at all.

Instead . . . you'll be cultivating your gaggle of guys.

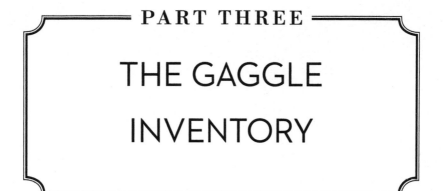

PART THREE

THE GAGGLE
INVENTORY

FACT: YOU HAVE A GAGGLE

I have surrounded myself my entire life since preschool with a group of guy friends. I am definitely a big believer that they all serve their different purposes as the men in my life, as the role models. Like, I would extract this from you, this from you, this from you . . . like all of this would make the perfect man. They all play their different roles.

I think that's crucial—crucial!—to women gaining confidence and strength in themselves. It's being smart. Keeping your options open, playing the field, figuring out what you want and keeping the people in your life who are giving it to you, who you're benefiting from, who are making you a better person, and who are helping you learn about yourself along the way.

To me, that's the best way to really develop as a person.

—Holly, 25, PhD student, Chicago

I've heard it called many things throughout my travels. Your As, Bs, Cs, and Ds. Your recycle bins. Your basket of eggs. Your balloons and your strings. Your "friends."

Starting now, we're going to call it your gaggle.

Gaggle, like a gaggle of geese? Sort of! Gaggle, like a bunch of catty, obnoxious women in clicky heels making a scene? Definitely not. I'm talking about a gaggle of guys. *Your* gaggle of guys. And as a modern-day woman, you have one.

Let's jump back to that fateful night when Becky and I sat on our couch and redefined our love lives.

In the midst of wallowing in the pit of despair (is it too late to blame hormones?), Becky and I realized that we were thinking about our loves lives only in terms of the guys we were dating. And thus, our love lives became boring, stressful, and disheartening (and, um, practically nonexistent). But instead, when we took into account *all* the guys in our lives, in all their various roles—ex-boyfriends who we still hung out with, supportive male colleagues from work, old college buddies who were willing to help us move apartments, that local bartender who was really hot (if not so smart), the random dude in Idaho who was always "liking" our Facebook status—then the lay of the land certainly got more interesting.

We discovered that we *did* have guys in our lives—a veritable gaggle of guys. Our relationships with these guys were less traditional than we'd been taught to expect. But we were learning bits and pieces about ourselves and our romantic desires through our interactions with them. We were exploring the many different sides of our personalities and experimenting with the different kinds of connection, attraction, and companionship that are out there. And *we were having fun.*

That very night, when we stopped obsessing over dating and started contemplating our gaggles, we felt the weight of the world lift off of our shoulders. So moving forward, instead of meeting a new guy and instantly wondering, "Could he be my soulmate?" we began thinking of him simply as a potential gaggle member with whom there might be a connection to explore. We shifted our focus to appreciating him for whatever little thing he was bringing to our lives, and we placed our vibe with him in the larger context of the various micro-dynamics that we were juggling.

Changing our perspective changed everything. And not only was the gaggle changing how we thought of men, but it was actually changing the very core of our bonds with them. We instantly saw our relationships with guys become more genuine and less fraught with expectation and insecurity, which allowed us to connect with them in a more fulfilling way. And as a result, we were getting closer than ever before to finding love.

Excited to place some helpful structure on our love lives, we immediately formalized the idea of the gaggle. When I began conducting my interviews, I also began talking to other women about the idea. Did they have these guys, too? What roles were they playing? What

were they learning? And under what circumstances had these ambiguous relationships turned into love?

It turned out that women had *a lot* to say about all the guys who
they *weren't* dating . . . the guys in their gaggles.

GAGGLE (n.)

The select group of guys in your life—many of whom you are *not*
explicitly romantically involved with—who play different roles, fulfill different needs, and help you to figure out who you are, what
you want, and what kind of relationship you ultimately desire.

Simply put, the gaggle has replaced dating as the primary path to
finding connection, love, and commitment.

Now, let's talk about *your* gaggle.

The guys in your gaggle are the guys who you are (or sometimes
want to be) going on all those non-dates with.

Here are the ten types of guys who may currently be in your
gaggle:

1. The Ex-Boyfriend Who's Still Around
2. The Super Horny Guy Who Happens to Be Around a Lot
3. The Accessory
4. The Hot Sex Prospect
5. The Unavailable Guy
6. The Ego Booster
7. The Guy Who Just Blew You Off
8. The Career Booster
9. The Boyfriend Prospect
10. The Prospect You're Not Sure Is a Prospect

You probably don't have all ten guys right now. Or you might have
a few Ego Boosters or Career Boosters, and none of the other guys. Or
a Hot Sex Prospect and an Unavailable Guy. No two gaggles are alike.

What differentiates a guy in your gaggle from all of the other guys in your life? If you put *any extra thought or effort* into an interaction with a guy, then he's in your gaggle. Do you re-read the text that you're sending him? Or consider wearing heels instead of flats when you see his name on the Evite list? Is there something that's just not 150 percent platonic about your relationship, a tiny spark of something that you might be exploring? Then he's in your gaggle.

And if you're not sure if a guy is in your gaggle . . . then, yes. He is in your gaggle.

The excitement comes from the fact that your relationships with the guys in your gaggle are evolving. If you are truly engaging in these relationships, then an intense conversation during a long car ride, an unexpected glimmer of sexual chemistry, or an extra shot at the bar can dramatically alter the role a guy plays in your life. The gaggle allows for that evolution. In fact, it counts on it.

Important note: having a gaggle is *not* about treating guys like disposable playthings, collecting them like baseball cards, or dating a bunch of them at once. We're not *dating* anyone—that's the whole point! The gaggle is also not about hooking up with every guy in sight. These connections are often distinctly mental, emotional, or intellectual in nature, and *not* always physical. But surprise—*it all still counts.* Exploring this complexity contributes to your current and future romantic happiness.

Most importantly, the gaggle is not an end in itself. It helps you find love. Here's how.

- **The gaggle allows you to figure out who you are, what you want, and what kind of guy you should end up with.**

You can't end up with the best guy for *you*, in the best relationship for *you*, if you don't know who *you* are. Do you need a guy who will boost your ego? Is it really important to you that your sexual connection is on fire? How warm and fuzzy do you feel whenever your plus-one is making the whole table laugh?

When you can compare the different types of connections you

have with the guys in your gaggle and figure out what you like and don't like, then you'll be ready for the right guy. *And* you'll be able to recognize him when he comes along (or pops out of your gaggle). As a bonus, you'll also know yourself well enough to actually make that relationship work.

- **The gaggle keeps you from feeling bad about yourself and thinking that everyone has this whole dating game worked out but you.**

Having great guys in your life, even ambiguously, is a fun, eye-opening confidence boost that will raise your whole demeanor and energy. This positive vibe will bring higher-quality guys into your sphere. *Guaranteed.*

- **The gaggle pushes you to engage in your love life all the time.**

No more compartmentalizing "dating" in your brain, and thinking that you don't have time for it or aren't good at it. With a gaggle, you're just living your life with some interesting guys in it, every day keeping yourself open to that moment when love will suddenly emerge out of it.

- **The gaggle increases your chances of ultimately meeting the right guy.**

Having an active gaggle encourages you to cultivate relationships with many different guys, most of which will not end up romantic or sexual. However, this will lead you to naturally expand your network and interact with people in circles that you enjoy, all making it much more likely that you'll put yourself "out there" and meet a guy who's right for you.

- **The gaggle forces you to be more open-minded about your tastes.**

When a guy asks you out on a traditional date, you're faced with a clear decision: say yes and give him a chance, or say no and reject him forever. The gaggle, with all its inexplicit connections and interactions, gives you more time and space to get to know guys and figure out if you are interested in them.

I've heard countless stories of women ending up with guys who they thought weren't their type and living happily ever after. The gaggle lets you try things out and surprise yourself—often debunking whatever you *thought* you were looking for.

- **The gaggle prevents you from putting all your eggs into one basket, at least until that basket is perfect and ready.**

By not investing every single ounce of hope and energy into one guy, at least until he has earned it, you avoid feeling desperate and obsessive. And since you're not feeling desperate, you won't settle for the wrong guy, and you'll be less likely to put premature pressure on a budding connection and scare that guy away.

Long story short, cultivating a gaggle is a way to get all the perks of dating without having to sit around in one little black dress after another, waiting and praying to be wined and dined. And because these guys tend to fall into one of ten categories (with overlap from time to time), you can cut down on the ambiguity by figuring out what specific role a guy plays in your life and engaging your brain, emotions, and actions accordingly.

No longer do you need to describe a certain guy in your life as, "I mean, he's my friend, but it's sort of confusing, because no, we haven't hooked up, but I feel like maybe there's . . . I don't know, you know what, forget it, we're just friends, I sound crazy and I'm sure it's all in my head, although let me read you this text because it's *so* weird!" Instead, he is now your Accessory. Or perhaps your Ego Booster. And tomorrow he might be your Boyfriend Prospect.

If you stop worrying about dating and start cultivating fulfilling relationships with the guys in your gaggle (and the new guys who could be entering it every day), then you can actually enjoy your love life. As I like to say—*right now, today, immediately.*

So let's get to it. Each type of guy in your gaggle is different, and you should approach the relationships differently as well. To get the most out of your love life, here's what you need to know.

THE EX-BOYFRIEND
WHO'S STILL AROUND

The guy who knows you best, eliciting a combination of fond memories and frustrating emotions. For better or worse, he's on a first-name basis with almost everyone in your life and understands what a pain your mother can be.

I have two very close friends—my best friend Michelle, and then the guy who my coworker likes to call my BFX (like BFF). He is my ex-boyfriend, who I broke up with a year ago exactly. He actually hated me, and we didn't speak for months, but he's my BFX now.

We talk every day. We text. And we go to dinner all the time—I buy him dinner, he buys me dinner, we buy our own dinners. But the romantic interest is totally gone.

I mean, he knows all about my love life. He thinks I'm insane. We even talk about our sex lives! You can't do that with someone you still have feelings for, you know what I mean?

—Clarissa, 21, PR account executive, New Orleans

MEET YOUR EX-BOYFRIEND
WHO'S STILL AROUND

Whether you broke up six days ago or six years ago, this guy has been around for a while and can identify and call you out on your patterns—when you're letting your boss steamroll you (again), when your sister is depending on you too much (again), and when you're finishing off an entire pint of ice cream by yourself because you don't like your new haircut (again). The Ex-Boyfriend has seen you through tough times and tough decisions, and there are moments when he's the only one you want to talk to because he knows you so well and has become a pro at guiding you through difficult situations.

You have many fond memories from your relationship—the magical night spent watching a snowstorm from the living room couch, the amazing sex you had on that hiking trip, the first time you said you loved each other. Some part of you might even think that maybe, just maybe, if the universe shifts in a certain direction and he finally matures in all the ways that you had once hoped, he might be the guy you end up with.

However, the Ex-Boyfriend is also a symbol of failure and all the pain and frustration that come with a breakup. Every time you hang out with him, you spend the first 90 percent of the time realizing you've forgotten how great he is and the last 10 percent remembering why you broke up in the first place. It turns out that the annoying things about him, and maybe about yourself when you're with him, haven't gone away. So you're content to stay in a holding pattern for now—hanging out with other people, flitting in and out of each other's lives, and secretly wondering if you should hook up one last time, just for old times' sake.

HOW TO HAVE AN EX-BOYFRIEND WHO'S STILL AROUND

When it comes to having an Ex-Boyfriend Who's Still Around in your gaggle, there's a trick to keeping the relationship healthy and fulfilling. It's something you won't hear me say a lot.

Minimize the ambiguity. In your *relationship*, and in your *feelings*.

I know, I know. The post-dating world thrives on ambiguity! The whole point of having a gaggle is to embrace that ambiguity in order to find love and learn about yourself!

Yes. True. But not when you're dealing with an Ex-Boyfriend Who's Still Around.

In all my travels, over the course of many interviews, I've heard countless tales about this gaggle guy. He's not just any Ex, but one who is still actively involved in our lives. When I sat down and thought about all the stories I'd heard, I realized that having an Ex-Boyfriend Who's Still Around can spell one of two things: friendship or disaster.

Friendship is obviously the preferred option.

"Friendship" might seem like a tricky word to describe your relationship with your Ex. It's always a little weird to be friends with someone who has seen you naked. There's an intimacy there that will always land this guy in your gaggle, and not on your list of best platonic male buddies. But done right, being friends with your Ex can be great. It can be a special kind of friendship that you have with no one else. And oddly enough, it can lead you closer to finding love—you know, with a guy who's not your Ex.

WHY BEING FRIENDS WITH YOUR EX-BOYFRIEND WHO'S STILL AROUND CAN BE AWESOME

There are major perks to having a guy in your gaggle who knows you as well as your Ex does!

He allows you to be yourself—and reminds you of who you really are.

Admit it: you put on an act in front of most guys. It's okay, we all do it. Whether you're acting just a bit too excited about a guy's favorite band, or laughing a little too hard at his cheesy joke, or pretending to be modest and swearing that your new promotion doesn't make you feel like the coolest, most successful chick *ever* . . . you're rarely 100 percent yourself in front of a new guy.

Enter your Ex! With him, there's no need for pretense. Try to put on a performance, and your Ex will laugh in your face. You've always preferred baseball to football, and oh wait, *now* you're a Patriots fan?

Yeah, right! He sees right through it. As annoying as that can be (and, god, it can be so annoying).

Hanging out with your Ex is like putting on that well-worn pair of slippers after a long day in heels. Sure, these aren't your coolest, sexiest shoes. And yeah, you're still pissed about that hole by your big toe that always lets in a little draft. These are not the shoes of your future—they're the shoes of your past, worn out and on the verge of falling apart. But sometimes, you'd rather sit back with your imperfect slippers than go through the trouble of breaking in a new pair. Just sometimes. When you don't feel like trying so hard.

The other guys in your gaggle help you grow: they introduce you to new things and push you to experiment with as yet unexplored parts of yourself. But your Ex brings you back to center. Hanging out with him—walls down, quirks known—gives you a chance to step back into your comfort zone, chill out, and reconnect with yourself.

He gives you the advice that you need to hear.

As a bonus, your Ex may know you and your past so well that you find yourself seeking advice from him. He's not like your best girlfriends, who often tell you exactly what you want to hear. Or your parents, who are always dying to tell you how problems were solved back in 1975. Or even the other guys in your gaggle, who may be willing to help but might so far be clueless as to what you *really* need, how you *really* act, and why you're *really* upset.

Your Ex can offer a much-needed male perspective, while also knowing how you need to hear it and how the situation fits into the larger story of your life. "The Ex as advice guru" is a concept I heard often in my interviews.

Alexandra, an attractive and ambitious thirty-four-year-old career woman, spelled it out to me this way while sitting outside a laid-back coffee shop in Austin, Texas. As a light wind blew through our hair, Alexandra went through her gaggle and stopped with a fond smile on one particular "guy friend" with whom she used to be romantically involved.

"I've known him for fifteen years," she explained while good-naturedly rolling her eyes at the reference to her age. "Now, he just offers me good advice. And sometimes, really fucking *bad* advice!"

(Yes, that's going to happen sometimes, too. No one gives good advice *all* the time.)

Alexandra loved having a guy in her life who had known her, warts and all, for a long time. She valued their relationship so much that she had refused to drop him from her life, even when later boyfriends had disapproved of their closeness and asked her to cut ties. But she also made it clear that they no longer "saw each other that way."

And this is where the lack of ambiguity comes in. If Alexandra and her Ex were still hazy in their intentions, then these advice sessions would go horribly awry. He would never want to rule her out as a romantic prospect by actually giving her *good* advice about another guy in her gaggle. And she would never be truly open and honest in her advice-seeking, afraid to come across as unappealing or instead using the opportunity to test the waters of his feelings.

Their genuine friendship, and the accompanying advice sessions, work because Alexandra and her Ex are committed to being just friends. They are both happy for him to be the Ex-Boyfriend in Alexandra's gaggle and nothing more.

Would they be as close if there wasn't a tiny spark of deeper connection there? Would he be so helpful if he weren't attracted to her? Ah! The mysteries of the gaggle. But for now, when it comes to Alexandra and her Ex, less ambiguity equals more friendship.

He gives you insight into what you want, need, and hate in a relationship.

When it comes to most of the guys in your gaggle, your assumptions about what it would be like to officially date them are hypothetical. Not the case with your Ex! You *know* what it's like to date him. You *know* what you loved about your relationship, and what drove you crazy. The fact that he's still around just makes it easier to recall how you felt during your relationship. All of these memories can provide opportunity for you to get some insight into what you should aim for in your next relationship.

Melissa, a twenty-nine-year-old nonprofit fundraiser, shared her unique version of this journey with me over several hangout sessions in The Big Easy. As one of many under-thirty divorcées I met in my travels, she was determined to avoid the cliché of the bitter, jilted ex-wife. With an inspired optimism, she told me how she had learned to appreciate her ex-husband as an integral guy in her gaggle.

"My Ex and I joke—not that you should joke about divorce—that our marriage died such a slow, painful death that we were kind of roommates and friends by the end of it," she said. "Which is great. Because my family loves him, he loves my family, I'm even friends with his girlfriend now. We have just maintained a really good friendship."

Melissa's friendship with her Ex is a constant reminder of what she is and is not looking for in her next relationship. He works in the military; therefore, they moved around a lot, which didn't allow Melissa the opportunity to pursue her own career and establish her own network of friends. When I met her, she was thrilled to be enjoying a busy social life in New Orleans alongside having a job that she cared about (she has since relocated to St. Louis for a "fantastic" career opportunity). Having already taken the path of following her Ex around the country, she had realized the importance of finding a guy who can work around *her* goals and passions as well.

Also, Melissa and her Ex got married when she was just twenty-one years old. They had dated for one and a half years and fallen head-over-heels in puppy love, but there was a catch: they had never actually lived in the same state. When they came together as husband and wife, they barely knew each other.

Melissa's Ex is a reminder to her that real, crazy, giddy love exists, and that she should hold out for nothing less. But he is also a wake-up call that infatuation needs to be followed up by a serious, careful getting-to-know-you process. This insight will help her create a new relationship that makes her happy—and, hopefully, doesn't end in divorce—when the next great guy comes along.

Her (unambiguous) friendship with her Ex has allowed both of them to move on and learn about themselves, while still caring deeply about each other.

What's the alternative to this awesome, supportive, drama-free relationship with your Ex-Boyfriend Who's Still Around?

Ugh. Disaster.

WHY BEING "FRIENDS" WITH YOUR EX-BOYFRIEND WHO'S STILL AROUND CAN SCREW UP YOUR LIFE

Done wrong, your Ex-Boyfriend Who's Still Around can hold you back from finding love with someone who's actually a better fit for you. And that tragic drama can go on for *ages*.

Your Ex can hold you back from exploring your immediate options.

Meet Vanessa. Vanessa is a confident, straight-talking guy's girl from Austin—and she's normally a pro at staying friends with her Exes. She even helped a few of them pick out engagement rings for their fiancées. As she put it, "With several of my Exes, clearly we were just better friends—or, that's what we should've been in the first place."

Clean, easy, and simple, right?

Not always. Even Vanessa gets sucked in to the dangers of communicating with an addictive Ex every once in a while. Here's how she described her relationship with her most recent Ex.

"There was a lot of post-drama, and in fact, there still *is* drama from that relationship. For a long time, I would go out and have fun, and then even though we'd been broken up and we 'hated each other' to our friends, we'd end up talking or texting at the end of the night. I think that kind of kept me from exploring other options."

Vanessa realized that keeping in touch with her Ex in a regular, consistent way was keeping her from cultivating her gaggle. Like any smart, reasonable, modern woman, she had a solution to this obviously unhealthy cycle.

"I've gotten much better at it! I've finally blocked his Facebook and taken his number out of my phone. All the measures."

Vanessa and I commiserated: being single can be tough. Putting yourself out there can be scary. Waiting around to meet someone for whom you actually have *real feelings* can be tedious. And this process can feel even less tempting when your Ex is just a text away.

This is where we come back to the issue of ambiguity. Remember: the key to having an Ex-Boyfriend Who's Still Around is to create as straightforward and platonic a friendship as possible. Because if, like Vanessa, you're still wondering, "Will we or won't we?" in an active, day-to-day way, then you are still romantically invested in him.

On one level, you're missing out on all the potential friendship, comfort, and constructive self-knowledge that can come with having an Ex-boyfriend in your gaggle. But on yet another, even more harmful level, you're taking the mental and emotional energy that you *should* be putting toward other guys in your gaggle, and instead putting it toward a secret plan to reunite with your Ex. You're holding yourself back.

You have two options when you realize that you're caught in a destructive pattern with an Ex. The first option: Give it a real go—date again! Be explicit in your desire to recommit to each other. Figure out what didn't work the first time around, and vow to change it. Promise that you'll move forward, not backward. Give it the ol' Elizabeth Taylor and Richard Burton try.

And what if you've already given it too many tries? What if you know that you're never going to stop loving your Ex . . . but it's never going to work out? This is where the second option comes into play.

Your Ex can hold you back from moving on.

Let's learn a thing or two from Rochelle, a San Francisco clinical psychologist in her thirties. She knows how to minimize ambiguity with an Ex.

Rochelle does not play around. She is one of those women who clearly knows what she wants and never doubts that she can get it. She's somewhat of a traditionalist, believing that women should never be too aggressive, too available, or too obvious in their desire to get married. She credits her dating do's and don'ts with landing her a great fiancé, and she is known for offering tough-love advice to her single friends.

So to hear that Rochelle has a weak spot was pretty shocking.

"I call him my Mr. Big. We're friends," Rochelle carefully articulated. "We still keep in touch through email, and every now and then a phone call. But I last saw him three years ago in person.

"We've both had so many opportunities. We've both broken up with each other a few times; we've both taken turns getting back in touch. It's a messy situation.

"So we have a mutual friend who ended up telling him that I'm now engaged. Apparently, he wasn't too happy. He was, like, 'What?! She's not even dating!' But honestly, I'd been too much of a chicken to call him up. He's like the first love of my life, and I always thought he had some kind of influence over me. It was dangerous, hanging out with him too much."

Here's something to remember when you're dealing with an Ex who is still pushing your buttons. Despite how romantic comedies make it seem, no relationship is inevitable. You are not destined to end up with someone who repeatedly makes you unhappy. Sometimes, when the connection is undeniable but you just can't make it work, the best way to move on is just to MOVE ON.

Do what Rochelle did after she realized that she was still mentally clinging to her Mr. Big: cut off your Ex. Don't feel pressured to deliver big news to him personally. Give yourself the time and space and mental clarity to invest wholeheartedly in another guy.

You may always feel a twinge of emotion when you think of your

Ex, and that's fine. But when you stop seeing him as the guy you are cosmically meant to end up with, you can build another, better relationship with someone else in your gaggle. Rochelle found a Boyfriend Prospect–turned-fiancé who fulfills her in ways that her Mr. Big didn't. Guess he'll have to rescue some other woman in Paris, because she'll be too busy marrying the man of her dreams in San Francisco.

═ KEY TIPS ═

For Cultivating an Ex-Boyfriend Who's Still Around

1. Minimize the ambiguity between you and your Ex. Also minimize the ambiguity in your *feelings* about your Ex. If you still have feelings for him, date him. And if you don't, then build a strong, unromantic friendship with him. No middle ground.

2. Be aware of the parts of yourself that he triggers. What sides come out when you're around him? Who are you when the façade drops? What personal flaws and positive qualities does he bring up in you? And are you sure that you're being true to yourself around the other guys in your life?

3. Ask him for advice. As long as your friendship is genuine, there is no one with a male perspective who will know you better and be more willing to tell you the cold, hard truth.

4. Think about your failed romantic relationship, and your now successful friendship, and determine: What did I like about our connection? What drove me crazy? What were the deal-breakers? And what does this all tell me about what I need in my next relationship?

5. Be honest with yourself about whether your Ex is holding you back from finding love with someone else (or even just from having fun with your gaggle). If you can't get over him, then stop kidding yourself and cut him out of your life. You owe it to yourself and your future happiness to be open and able to emotionally invest in other guys.

THE SUPER HORNY GUY
WHO HAPPENS TO BE AROUND A LOT

> A party boy who never stops thinking, talking, and joking about sex and has openly stated his desire to hook up with you (and almost everyone else). You don't take him seriously, but your inhibitions can't help but drop when you're around him. Livin' on a prayer, baby!

There's one guy I hooked up with from the bar—but no one knows about him, because afterward I realized that he's like a hobbit! He was always buying drinks for everybody. He was this short little white dude who liked big black girls. Any big black girl that was in the bar, he'd be on 'em.

So after I'd broken up with another guy, this guy started acting even more bold. And one night I was like, do you want to come to the café? We're going dancing . . . you know, I wasn't even really attracted to him. It was just that he kept trying so hard.

—Theresa, 29, financial auditor, San Francisco

MEET YOUR SUPER HORNY GUY
WHO HAPPENS TO BE AROUND A LOT

Although you intellectually disagree with everything that he stands for, this guy has the ability to turn you into a singing, dancing, binge-drinking, classic rock–loving party girl. He is a consummate party boy who clearly wants to sleep with you, if you ever got drunk enough to give him a chance. Luckily, you know that you shouldn't, especially considering the rumors you've heard about his short attention span and the naked photos of hookups that fill his iPhone.

But even as you turn down the Super Horny Guy with a laugh

and an exaggerated eye roll, you find yourself gravitating toward him and the fun, carefree, vivacious woman that you become when you're around him—one not bogged down by jobs, responsibilities, insecurities, the search for true love, or the fear of having unflattering photos of your Friday night posted on Facebook. You would never exert the effort of emailing or calling the Super Horny Guy directly, but you make a mental note when you hear that he'll be attending your mutual friend's party or stopping by the bar where you always seem to bump into him.

You share a sexual energy that is fun, light, and lacking in long-term potential, and you are easily convinced to have an extra drink (or three) while in his company. It's refreshing to have a guy be so open about his attraction to you, even when you know that his fearlessness stems from a belief that the whole world (or at least the whole bar) is his sexual playground.

HOW TO HAVE A SUPER HORNY GUY WHO HAPPENS TO BE AROUND A LOT

You have a lot to stress over. There's your job, your friendships, your finances, your family, your health, your looks, your future, and your apartment (which you're going to decorate any day now, promise!). Behind every free moment of time, there's the email you have to send, the dog you have to walk, the boss you have to please, and the grandmother you have to call. Not to mention the constantly nagging fear that you might be falling behind in your quest to fulfill every single one of those ambitious hopes and dreams that you first announced to the world in the pages of your high school yearbook.

You could use a break, couldn't you? A mindless, stress-free mini-vacation from your regular superwoman routine? A distraction from your never-ending to-do list?

Honestly, you could use a little freakin' fun. Enter your Super Horny Guy Who Happens to Be Around a Lot.

You may initially see this guy as a frivolous, tangential member of your gaggle. You're a kick-ass woman. What could that crazy party guy double-fisting beers have to teach you?

Believe it or not, let loose around the Super Horny Guys in your gaggle, and you just might end up learning quite a bit from them (and getting closer to finding love with more suitable guys in the process).

Just make sure that you're sober enough to remember it all the next day.

YOUR SUPER HORNY GUY REMINDS YOU THAT YOU *ARE*, IN FACT, A FUN CHICK

Feeling a bit boring lately? Wondering when you became an old lady who can't wait to collapse into her bed at 9:00 p.m.? Suspicious that the best days might already be behind you?

Let me tell you my story. It might make me sound like a frat boy, but I'm willing to take the risk. Because it was a key turning point in my personal gaggle journey, and one that I hope will inspire you to purchase your own beer tower, jump on the couch in the middle of a bar, and start singing "Party in the U.S.A." to a roaring crowd (true story, and yes, there are untagged photos somewhere . . .).

It was late 2008, and I had just transitioned from working in a mostly male environment to an entirely female company. I went from hanging out all day with my coworking Career Boosters (more on them soon) to never seeing a man who wasn't delivering my mail or my lunch. I was pushing myself really hard to make my name in a new field, and I was all business, all the time.

My professional life was barreling ahead. But my social life? It sucked. Which was unsurprising since, at the time, I was a walking ball of stress, focus, and determination. And fatigue. I was always *so* sleepy.

At twenty-five years old, I felt about as fun and likable as a root canal, sans the laughing gas.

I decided that I needed to kiss my supposed-to-be-fun-loving twenties good-bye—or force myself to have some fun. I also realized that it would do me some good to maybe even meet a boy or two in the process. I considered online dating, but actually, no, that didn't sound fun at all! So I tried to think of something that I would enjoy, whether there were boys there or not. And I came up with bowling. Because seriously, who doesn't love bowling?

Fast-forward a few weeks. I'd joined a bowling league, started my own team, recruited a few female friends to play, and demanded that they invite their guy pals to fill out the roster. To be clear, the point was not to meet the love of my life. I just wanted to expand my social circle and open myself up to a setting that wasn't my office or my couch. Four years later, as the captain of that same crew—what's up, Smells Like Team Spirit!—I'm so glad that I went through with it.

The team lineup has changed over the years, and at varying times, I've met Boyfriend Prospects, Hot Sex Prospects, Ego Boosters, and Unavailable Guys on my team and in the bowling league. But most importantly, I met a bunch of Super Horny Guys—and my love life is better for it.

Because you don't only bowl in these leagues. You party while you bowl, usually while wearing ridiculous team outfits. Then you go to a bar, "just for an hour," and spend the rest of your afternoon playing beer pong, competing in flip-cup tournaments, flirting with the guys you just played against, and eating french fries off some random dude's plate. It may all sound very immature and collegiate—and it is. But when you stop judging it, you end up having a ton of fun.

Long story short, I relearned how to party that winter. And along with the new awesome female friends that I was making, there was suddenly a cadre of guys who were buying me drinks, high-fiving me after a good beer-pong toss, dancing with me on the pool table, and yes, on one occasion, even catching me in a particularly carefree moment and inspiring me to make out in front of the entire league. Of course, these guys were doing this with all the girls there. But amidst the chaos, I still ended up learning something about myself.

I had been so stressed with work and the rest of my normal routine that I had completely forgotten how much fun there was to be had out there. At bowling, I remembered that I liked to laugh, dance, goof around, and come up with scandalous dares for the losing flip-cup team. It hit me that I didn't have to be all business, all the time—and that I wanted a guy who could understand and embrace that side of me, and himself, as well.

Did I fall in love with any of the Super Horny Guys who inspired me to have a little fun? No—at least, not yet! There's always next season. Are my Sundays still as wild? Nah, I've grown out of it a little and calmed down a bit.

But I absolutely bring that resurrected fun side of myself to my interactions with every other guy in my gaggle now—and I've found that most guys appreciate a girl who doesn't take herself uber-seriously 24/7. And if they don't get that, well, then they're probably not the right guy for me. I'll always know that there's a bar full of after-bowling guys who do get it.

Take my advice: let a Super Horny Guy into your sphere every once in a while. Enjoy his ridiculous advances without judging them. Be inspired by his life-isn't-that-serious-so-I-might-as-well-give-it-a-shot attitude. And don't be surprised if you walk away feeling a little less stressed about life and love. All in pursuit of one awesome good time.

YOUR SUPER HORNY GUY REMINDS YOU THAT YOU *ARE*, IN FACT, AN ATTRACTIVE WOMAN

Remember when you were in sixth grade, and you were all frizzy hair and big glasses and unibrows and baby fat and neon leggings? Okay, maybe that was just me. But there was probably a time in your life when you weren't quite as cute as you are now. And during that time, you probably appreciated *any* male attention. A car honk from a random guy on Main Street could make your day.

Now your reaction to male attention is probably a bit more complicated. You're annoyed by sketchy guys—and that's all well and good! No one wants to be harassed and treated like a sex object, and being grossly leered at by a slobbering loser doesn't *actually* translate to you feeling sexy.

We ladies should never have time for disrespectful guys who can only see us as collections of tits and ass. But there can also be a proper time and place for a more respectful middle ground of appreciation. Especially when the social pressure to be attractive can somehow still be overwhelming and disheartening these days.

Faced with public standards of beauty that feel unattainable to even the most confident woman, you might find yourself seeking a little reinforcement that you're hot every now and then. Because no matter how many hours you spend on the treadmill or in the makeup chair, you're still going to have moments when you fear that you're not pretty enough, or you need to lose weight, or your boobs are too small, or your style is outdated, or your legs are too short, or your hair is too brown. Especially when your Boyfriend Prospect doesn't text you back quickly enough, or your Hot Sex Prospect checks out another girl, or your trusty Ego Booster falls in love with his new next-door neighbor.

Confident as you may be, it can be all too easy in a weak moment to think, "If only I were more attractive!"

Well, guess what? That Super Horny Guy thinks you're *very* attractive. And he's going to be the first one in line to tell you so— whether you end up going home with him or not (let's be honest, probably not).

But don't just listen to me. Check out what Rachel in Chicago learned during her time in the city's famous bar scene.

Rachel, a twenty-five-year-old blond-haired, blue-eyed corporate regional assistant, is a cool, calm, even-keeled girl who has been weathering a roller-coaster social life in Chicago by sticking with a positive, optimistic attitude—part of which might be connected to her perspective on the Super Horny Guys in her gaggle.

Rachel broke it down.

"Sometimes a guy will come up to me in a bar and be like, um, my friend thinks you're really cute—he wants to talk to you. Or they'll be standing at the bar, and they'll look at me and wave. And sure, I get the feeling that they're just trying to hook up with me right now. I'm so not into that! That's just not what I want at all.

"But I think a lot of girls take that as, ugh, he's hitting on me, how annoying. Yet I think that it's always nice to get hit on. That's what

I'm trying to work on now—just trying to be positive and taking those compliments and seeing it as a huge ego boost when somebody hits on me. Now, I just say thank you. Even if I'm not interested, which, in that scene, I'm usually not."

A Super Horny Guy may not fulfill you mentally, emotionally, spiritually, or even physically. But that doesn't mean you have to hate on him! He is attracted to you. This is ultimately a *good* thing. So just take the compliment and tell him thanks but no thanks. Now you can bank on that confidence when you go to meet up with your Prospect You're Not Sure Is a Prospect. If that Super Horny Guy thinks you're hot, then why shouldn't he?

KEY TIPS

For Cultivating a Super Horny Guy Who Happens to Be Around a Lot

1. Let loose around him! Don't cling so hard to your "I'm smart and accomplished and you should take me seriously" persona. Or your "But what if someone sees me?!" paranoia. When you're around a Super Horny Guy, drop the judgment and have a little fun.

2. If your life is seeming too serious and stressful, find a setting where there will likely be some Super Horny Guys, like bars, parties, social sporting leagues, and beach vacation spots. Make yourself part of that crowd, and allow the fun, carefree side of you to emerge. And by the way, drinking is optional, not essential; trust me, the Super Horny Guys will be excited that you're there either way.

(cont.)

KEY TIPS

For Cultivating a Super Horny Guy
Who Happens to Be Around a Lot (cont.)

3. Even if you don't consider the Super Horny Guy to be an essential, long-term member of your gaggle, be aware of the lessons he might teach you and bring them to your interactions with the other guys in your gaggle. If he makes you feel fun, then be more fun with the rest of your gaggle. If he makes you feel attractive, then bring that confidence and sexiness to your interactions with other guys. You can learn a lot about the different sides of yourself when you're not trying so hard to make someone fall in love with you. The Super Horny Guy provides you with that freedom.

4. Take a compliment! The Super Horny Guy finds you attractive. Accept the flattery and don't try to qualify or brush it away. Carry it with you.

5. No matter how ridiculous a Super Horny Guy is being in his efforts to hit on you, reject him in a kind, respectful way. Treat him like that silly old friend who is always jokingly (or so you tell yourself) hitting on you. You'll end up transporting that positive energy around with you for the rest of the night. And who knows! Some of these guys can be pretty great when they're not trying to take you home. You might end up with a new friend who simply thinks you're a hot girl with a sense of humor who doesn't get offended by his over-the-top behavior.

THE ACCESSORY

> A standout guy who is a great plus-one. A perfect non-date for that wedding or work party, he makes a great impression on everyone around him. He is the first person you book for dinner when your out-of-town friends are visiting. You feel cooler just knowing this guy, but for some reason, the buck stops there.

I took one guy to my Christmas office party. He's an engineer grad from Tech, and he's crazy attractive as well, so I was like, this looks good!

One of the doctors where I used to work was so intimidating she would give me a stutter. She was the shit. But he could totally hold his own with her, and I was very impressed. I was like, thank you for taking the pressure off of me.

—Amanda, 24, physician's assistant, U.S. Navy, Atlanta

MEET YOUR ACCESSORY

This guy is fantastic—at least, on paper. He's so funny/smart/charismatic/talented/good-looking! People tend to really enjoy being around him, and his reliable likability makes him a great guy to have on your arm.

He is known for being exceptionally friendly and social—and always knowing just how to make your waiter (your parents, your cab driver, your boss) smile. You're proud to show off someone like him.

You know that the Accessory is awesome, but you also know that, for whatever reason, you're not really romantically into him. He makes everything more fun and interesting and is a great activity partner, but you're just not sure that there's a deeper connection there. So you do the responsible, fair thing and regularly encourage him to find a girl who appreciates him and all his wonderfulness to the fullest. Luckily, he usually returns the favor. Maybe, at times, half-heartedly.

He's just so awesome! So you keep the Accessory orbiting in your sphere and active in your social scene. You invite each other around a lot, and you know without a doubt that someday he'll find a girl who is as impressed with him as you are *and* who wants to rip off his clothes. But in the meantime, why not enjoy his company as much as possible?

HOW TO HAVE AN ACCESSORY

Today is your friend's wedding! You could go stag, and hope that one of the groomsmen is really hot . . . or, you could avoid the awkward singles table, bring your Accessory, and dance the night away.

You've been invited to your company's holiday party! You could show up by yourself, work the room, and rely on your knowledge of current events and fine wines to impress the higher-ups . . . or, you could use that plus-one for your Accessory and set him up to talk sports with the baseball-loving CEO.

Nice job scoring those tickets to an advance movie screening! You could give the extra stub to your roommate and deal with all her questions about how many calories are in a tub of movie theater popcorn . . . or, you could grab your Accessory and get those hands greasy while you watch the flick.

Sometimes, life is just more fun when your Accessory is there to join you for it.

You know that you can kick ass in pretty much any scenario, by yourself, relying on your own individual strengths and talents. You don't *need* a man. But every once in a while, it's kind of nice to have one there with you anyway.

Especially when you don't feel like dealing with the lame, pernicious social pressure that friends, family, and society at large might be putting on you to be in a relationship. You've become good at fighting off that pressure, feeling confident in your knowledge that you have a gaggle and are on your way to finding love, *on your own time, thank you very much.* But in the meantime, here and there, your Accessory can play the part of fill-in boyfriend nicely.

Your Accessory is not your *actual* Boyfriend Prospect because you're looking for real, passionate, true love—and, at least so far, you haven't found it with him. Your dynamic with him, well, it's great . . . but it's just not that deep. He feels like more of a friend than a serious romantic prospect. Yet while your quest for true love runs on whatever schedule it likes, your Accessory is there to fill in some boyfriend-like holes, at least until an actual boyfriend comes along.

YOUR ACCESSORY CAN *LOOK* LIKE YOUR BOYFRIEND

Do you sometimes get the sense that your relationship-ing friends see you as a poor single girl who can't find love? Have you caught extended family members looking at you quizzically across the table at your grandmother's eightieth birthday, wondering if you just might be a lesbian, because geez, *why doesn't she ever seem to bring boyfriends to our family events?* Well, worry no more. Nothing quiets the peanut gallery more than arriving somewhere with a charming guy on your arm.

To the nosy public, your Accessory can look like the perfect boyfriend. But he's not your boyfriend, you say? Doesn't matter. You don't even have to lie and say that he *is* your boyfriend. You can be honest and say that you're just friends! Everyone around you will still assume whatever they want. And that means they'll probably assume that you and your Accessory are one step away from falling in love and becoming the power couple of the year. This is what it looks like to make that ambiguity work *for* you.

The bonus? They'll stop badgering you with probing questions about your love life. Score!

Gia, a twenty-five-year-old office coordinator who was born and raised in the Chicago area, was all too aware of the social pressures and stresses that can come with being romantically unattached. She had a ton of guy friends, especially from her high school days, and her gaggle was active and lively. But still, she'd been feeling a bit disconnected from her friends in relationships lately. And honestly, their well-intentioned efforts to find her a boyfriend had been kind of ticking her off.

If Gia thought her coupled-up friends were nosy and annoying, then she was going to have to prep herself for the multiple weddings that she had coming up the following summer. She was on a kick to hit up as many as she could stand without a plus-one—she called it "coming to terms with the fact that I'm going to be single, and trying to think of it in a positive way, like, hey, I could meet somebody at these weddings!" But if and when the pressure got to be too much, Gia had a backup plan. Her Accessory.

"My friend from Tennessee is my Accessory," she declared with a laugh. "He is a really charismatic person, so I can take him anywhere and he makes friends with everybody there. He's super fun to be around, and I'm so comfortable with him. Even my parents know who he is, so if it's a family wedding or something, he would be an easy date!"

Herein lies the beauty of a great Accessory—not only does he make any event more fun simply by being there, but your friends and family will be impressed, and that will reflect back on you in a positive light. Instead of being seen as a single-girl charity case (who might even possess some crazy, secret quirk that scares men away), you'll be seen as that girl who was lucky enough to snag one of the coolest guys in the room.

And don't worry, he'll enjoy himself, too. What charming guy doesn't love showing off his goods *and* getting to spend the day hanging out with you? It's a win-win.

YOUR ACCESSORY CAN *ACT* LIKE YOUR BOYFRIEND

While it's nice to have your very own razzle-and-dazzle-'em charmer to bring out at parties, your Accessory can be much more than that.

You both might enjoy the faux-relationship dynamic so much that you keep it going, even when there's no one else there to see.

Your Accessory can end up being your go-to guy for pretty much any activity that would be more enjoyable with a partner. Basically, he can be your platonic boyfriend. No strings attached! And no hooking up involved. Remember: if you have loads of sexual chemistry, then maybe he's your Hot Sex Prospect. And if he's your plus-one to everything *and* you're making out with him, well, that sounds like a Boyfriend Prospect to me. The primarily platonic nature of your relationship is key to an Accessory dynamic.

I was lucky enough to meet both halves of an Accessory faux-couple in Minneapolis. As soon as I interviewed Jason, an unattached, high-living twenty-seven-year-old investment banker, he insisted that I also meet Maria, his close female friend.

"My friend Maria always jokes that she and I should be dating," Jason explained, after I asked him to go into depth about the most important girls in his life. "She's totally kidding, but it's because we do so much stuff that a couple would normally do. We go to the farmers market, or go out to dinner, or cook together. She kind of feels like a faux girlfriend, like a fill-in. Because you do need that activity partner, for lack of a better word. Someone to do those kinds of things with. So she always jokes, 'Okay, here we go! Jason and Maria, doing couples stuff.'"

When I explained the Accessory role to Jason, he immediately related. And it turns out that he was happy to fill that spot in her gaggle. He swore that, as much as he adored spending time with her, he didn't feel like a relationship was necessarily in the cards for them.

As he told me, "Maria is really good-looking. She's really fun. But for some reason, we've just never been into each other like that. And our relationship still works, because you don't need to sleep with someone in order to go to the farmers market."

While I don't always believe guys' claims that they can see an attractive female friend as just a friend, I believed Jason. As one of the most confident guys I interviewed, he didn't seem like the type to unwillingly fall into the friend zone with a girl who sparked romantic interest in him. Also, I happened to observe that he was getting plenty of action elsewhere.

Jason sounded like the perfect Accessory. But I had to wonder: did Maria see their relationship as truly platonic? Or was she secretly in love with him? Because we've all seen those romantic comedies! Two close friends, hanging out all the time, pretending that they're not going to end up together at the end . . .

Then I met Maria, and it all became clear. This girl had a gaggle. She wasn't in love with Jason. She just saw him as an important Accessory in her day-to-day life.

First, without my prompting, Maria confirmed everything that Jason had told me about their dynamic. "He's one of my best friends, and I can come to him with anything and he'll give me a straight-up, honest response. But he's not the physical type that I usually go for. We're so alike, but we're also extremely different. In so many ways, he reminds me of my brother."

And while Maria navigated the Match.com scene, which she was finding fairly frustrating, she was clearly appreciative of having such a stable, great guy in her life with whom she could spend time, *without* all the pressures and trappings of an official relationship.

Aside from just having a blast together, Jason and Maria's relationship was making it easier for both of them to be patient in their search for the right girlfriend or boyfriend. They weren't feeling starved for attention, or lonely, or desperate, because they had each other. They both realized that they shouldn't be together romantically. But that slight spark and feel-good vibe that they shared was allowing them to hold out more comfortably for the right person.

Your Accessory should provide you with that same patience. You'll still desire a deeper love, of course. But any desperation you may be feeling will dissipate with every home-cooked meal and trip to the gym that you and your Accessory embark on together.

That said, if your Accessory is so great, what could be keeping you guys from falling for each other?

THE ACCESSORY MIGHT ULTIMATELY BE BETTER ON PAPER (OR NOT)

As *my* Accessory once told me, "In life, as a guy, you end up with a bunch of almost-girlfriends. Great girls who are so close to what you're looking for, but just a little bit off. You could almost fall in love with them, but, when it comes down to it, you don't. There's just something missing there."

This basically sums up the questions you should be asking yourself about your Accessory. You love spending time with him, and you get a huge kick out of showing him off to people, right? So what, if anything, is keeping you from taking your relationship more seriously and pushing it to the next level? Why isn't he your Boyfriend Prospect?

If I had to pick one word to describe what most young people in the Millennial Generation seem to be looking for, it would be *connection*. Boyfriends, relationships, love—those concepts now come with a million expectations, pressures, and labels attached. They mean many different things to many different people. But connection tends to be something that you either feel or you don't. It's ambiguous, complex, personal, and hard to explain, but it's real. You know it—unmistakably and without doubt—when you feel it.

Ask yourself: do you have a profound connection with your Accessory?

Your Accessory might look fantastic on paper, and while he's twirling you around the dance floor at your cousin's wedding, you might think to yourself, "How great would life be with this guy on my arm?" But if you still feel like there's something else out there for you, some deeply felt connection that you just haven't found yet, then that's okay. Enjoy the dance, show your Accessory lots of love and appreciation, and keep your eyes open elsewhere for the connection that you're dreaming of.

However, while you're running around seeking that elusive magical connection, make sure that you're not overlooking the potential of a relationship that could be genuinely wonderful and positive—and right under your nose. If you and your Accessory have similar interests, wholeheartedly enjoy spending time together, and prefer to face the public as a team, well, that's half the battle to building a long-lasting relationship right there.

Intense connection absolutely matters, but happy couples also often tell me that they feel like best friends and partners in life, endeavoring to take on the world as an airtight duo. One San Francisco woman in a strong, happy, three-year relationship put it to me like this: "We're like co-pilots looking out the same window, watching the world go by and saying to each other, 'Hey, are you seeing this, too?'"

When considering your dynamic with your Accessory, be honest with yourself. If that connection isn't there, then play house with him and call it a (fun, happy) day. But don't be surprised if, while cooking dinner together one night or wowing the crowd at your company's holiday party, you get a glimpse of something more serious.

Don't be surprised if you start thinking that he might make a great co-pilot.

NOW, ABOUT YOUR GAY BEST FRIEND . . .

Weddings, dinners, farmers markets, movies, impromptu drinks—you may be thinking that these all sound like fabulous things to do with your favorite gay guy friends. And you're right! Having an Accessory can be just like having a gay best friend . . . except that unlike your gay best friend, your Accessory has probably thought at least once or twice about making out with you in a non-experimental way.

And that is essentially why the Accessory is in your gaggle—and the gay best friend is not.

Your relationship with any guy in your gaggle must have the potential, no matter how slight, to evolve in some sort of romantic fashion. It should involve at least the teeniest, tiniest bit of a spark that you're exploring. And as amazing as your gay best friend is, he is not in your gaggle because your connection is not based on that spark. You may love him, but you will never be *in* love with him (if you're smart). Just because you seductively dance up on him at parties sometimes, that doesn't mean that he's a potential life partner in your romantic sphere.

Go ahead and hang out with your gay best friend all day, every day! We have the opportunity to grow and learn about ourselves through every person who passes through our lives, whether they offer romantic potential or not. But don't trick yourself into thinking that you're cultivating your gaggle while you're with him. How about asking him to introduce you to some of his cute (heterosexual) coworkers and then adding *them* to your gaggle instead?

KEY TIPS

For Cultivating an Accessory

1. Don't let the idea of needing a plus-one stress you out anymore. If you have an Accessory, that spot will always be filled by the perfect faux boyfriend! Invite your Accessory to any gathering or event where you're worried about being "the single girl." After the crowd meets your Accessory, all doubts about your romantic appeal will be squashed. And you'll probably have a lot of fun with him, too.

2. Instead of feeling pressured to have a boyfriend in "couple" settings—and allowing that pressure to force you into moments of desperation—join up with your Accessory for some friend-non-dates. Go out to dinner, stroll through the park, or check out your latest Netflix movie. You'll have a good time, and as a bonus, having a buddy for those activities will give you more patience to wait for the right guy to eventually fill those roles as your true boyfriend.

3. Having an Accessory is fun, convenient, and safe—but you can't let that hold you back from meeting and exploring relationships with other new and existing guys in your gaggle. Especially Boyfriend Prospects! This may mean showing up to a wedding alone every once in a while or making the emotionally riskier choice of offering your second concert ticket to another guy. Don't get lazy and rest in a comfort zone with your Accessory.

(cont.)

KEY TIPS

For Cultivating an Accessory (cont.)

4. Don't try to force a deep connection with your Accessory just because you enjoy his company and he happens to be there. Despite what you might have grown up watching on *Friends* and *Dawson's Creek*, you and a guy can have a good time together and still not be destined to fall in love. Appreciate the level of your connection for whatever it is.

5. But also check in with your gut from time to time, making sure that you're not overlooking a great romantic opportunity with him. You just might have all the makings of a fantastic couple. Maybe you weren't simply fooling everyone at that wedding!

THE HOT SEX PROSPECT

A guy with whom you have physical and sexual chemistry, despite not being mentally, emotionally, or intellectually attracted to him. You don't really want to sit through a whole dinner conversation with this guy and hear about his hopes and his dreams and the way his parents met—although you'd be more than happy to grab a late-night drink...

I had a "rando" guy for months. We'd hang out four or five nights a week. I didn't want to be exclusive with him. Zero percent chance that I wanted to call him my boyfriend.

But he was super cute and we had phenomenal sex. I thought, well, this is probably going to end in about three months: I'm okay with that! And he's still kind of in the recycle bin, unless he gets a girlfriend.

—Trisha, 25, accountant, Atlanta

MEET YOUR HOT SEX PROSPECT

An in-depth heart-to-heart with this guy? Hmm, no thanks. You like to think that you're a good listener and that you really care about the people around you, but to be totally honest, the idea of spending time talking to this guy about his job, parents, life goals, and personal hobbies already starts your mind drifting. You probably don't have a lot in common with him, and he is likely missing at least one of the key characteristics that you expect from a relationship candidate: a baseline level of intelligence, a quirky sense of humor, a steady job, etc.

However, you and the Hot Sex Prospect share a physical chemistry and a sense of sexual possibility that defy your differences. You have a strong hunch that, given a few moments of privacy and a loss of inhibition, you two would have incredibly hot sex without any of the hangups or mishaps that can plague first-time hookups. Maybe it's the overt flirtatiousness in your exchanges or the electricity that leaves you feeling a little light-headed each time you touch, but there is a purely sexual energy between you and this guy that is begging to be explored.

The Hot Sex Prospect can remain a prospect even after you've finally hooked up with him. Although no promises were made at the time, a successful play-non-date may leave you wanting to test the waters of a repeat rendezvous (or five). Of course, the road from one-night stand to regular booty call is a tricky one cluttered with hurt feelings and broken hearts. But managed well, this is a friends-with-benefits situation that could actually work because, in truth, you don't really care about being friends.

HOW TO HAVE A HOT SEX PROSPECT

It's time to turn up the heat and talk about the most controversial of all the gaggle guys—the Hot Sex Prospect.

Gosh, why does sex *always* make things so confusing and complicated? Well, it does. Here's why.

We have come of age in a media culture saturated with images of overt sexuality. We grew up with the exhibitionist horrors of *Girls Gone Wild* and are now subjected to endless *Jersey Shore* reruns. Madonna showed us all how to push the sexual envelope when we were in elementary school, and Britney Spears carried that torch once we got to high school. Hit me baby one more time!

Errrrr . . . or don't. We are *not*, in fact, a generation of women who thrive on meaningless booty calls and spring-break-fueled hookups. We want more than that. We get offended when someone implies that we are a part of the so-called Hookup Generation. No matter that Kim Kardashian has built a legitimate media empire out of one golden-shower sex tape. She is clearly not a role model, in life or relationships, for what we are striving to become.

So many of us are stuck in the awkward middle here. We want to embrace our sexuality, but being forthright about it can seem like a tremendous liability. In our professional lives, we often get the impression that our sexuality—and even any hints of it—should stay under wraps. I met women in my interviews who felt like they had to delete their flattering photos from LinkedIn in order to be considered for prestigious jobs, or who got frustrated when potential clients didn't take them seriously because they had shiny blond hair and big blue eyes. And even outside of the office, sexuality doesn't always feel like a welcome card to throw out on the table. At the end of the day, many of us want to feel like (and be seen as) marriage material. Whatever the hell that means.

But then what does sexuality mean to *us*? How are we supposed to act? Despite all the mandatory sex ed classes we squeamishly sat through as youths, there is a lot that many women are still not comfortable with. When I interviewed Nina, an outgoing twenty-five-year-old health-care sales rep in Atlanta who runs "Sultry Shakedown" parties on the side, she could not make this point strongly enough. She gathers young women for sex-themed drinks (pink panty pulldowns) and desserts (éclairs shaped as penises) and sells sex equipment and toys directly to them. Yet even as she has aimed to empower women to take ownership over their sexuality, she has also witnessed firsthand the shortcomings of a culture that bombards women with in-your-face messages of sexuality but still lacks honest, genuine conversations around real women's sexual needs.

"I try to stay as calm and knowledgeable as I can, because these people really have problems," Nina told me. "Especially in the South, the topic of sex is so forbidden. So this is education I'm giving to girls. I feel like I'm helping, trying to sit there and explain. But girls are so afraid of it! And where are they supposed to go? Online? That's scary."

Nina has found that some women are terrified of embracing their sexuality at all. On the other hand, I also met women who have been taking a different path by trying to capitalize on it. I interviewed girls who were ambitious and career-driven businesswomen and academics by day—but cocktail waitresses and top-shelf brand models and shot girls by night. Not only were these women making some pretty decent supplemental income, but they were finding a certain enjoyment and confidence in putting on their tight referee outfits and tiny red dresses and acting out cartoonish notions of sexuality. Getting attention for being sexy—or at least for successfully portraying clichéd versions of sexy—was making these women feel, well, sexy.

But even owning these sexual stereotypes left each of these women yearning for more. Their time role-playing gave them a confident sexiness, but it also strengthened their desire to connect with men—and themselves—in a more authentic way and find something sexy in *that.*

For the rest of us, their lessons can be learned without having to carry around a blinking tray full of liquor or sign photo after photo of ourselves in a bikini. As Valerie, a poet and Bacardi shot girl, put it:

"For the Bacardi job . . . there's something really indulgent in that, really easy. It requires no mental energy—you basically become this MySpace girl, like TinyCutiePatootie444.

"But of course, I like myself better when I'm not all dressed up like a sex kitten. When I'm talking to a guy, usually I'm trying to be witty or cool, but I'm not trying to be the Cutest Little Thing You Ever Saw. And there's something awesome about connecting with someone in a natural, goofy way—as opposed to in this very choreographed way that feels like a *Dick Tracy* movie or something."

In many ways, our cultural notions of sexuality have fallen short of providing us with a clear, comfortable understanding of ourselves as sexual creatures. So hearing about the Hot Sex Prospect might evoke knee-jerk reactions: "But I'm not that kind of girl!" "What would my grandmother say?" "No way, I'm looking for love. I'm not a slut." (Are we still using that word? Really?)

But this is an important topic. We have to get past these stigmas to reach the most important question here: What does *your very own* authentic sexuality look like? How can you become empowered in a world that sends you such bizarre, offensive, and confusing signals about sex?

Let's welcome your Hot Sex Prospect. He's here to help you figure all that out.

WHY YOU PROBABLY NEED A HOT SEX PROSPECT—WHO IS ONLY A HOT SEX PROSPECT

The Hot Sex Prospect is a key gaggle guy.

Your gaggle is there to help you explore the many sides of yourself. This includes your emotional, intellectual, professional, public, private, and embarrassing karaoke-singing sides. It also includes your sexual side.

What turns you on? How do you like to be touched? Why do some settings make you feel more excited than others? Do you know the answers to all those questions?

Any episode of *Dr. Phil* will tell you that being comfortable with your sexuality and understanding yourself on a physical level is essential for eventually building a strong, long-lasting relationship with a life partner. And until that partner comes along, how great would it be to explore this side of yourself, on your own terms and within your comfort zone?

Umm, really great.

You can learn about your unique sexual needs and desires from your Hot Sex Prospect in a way that will make your life richer *now*, while also setting you up for a healthier long-term relationship down the line. But how can you create a healthy dynamic with your Hot Sex Prospect that works? What's the key?

The key is to explore what it feels like to be sexually attracted to this guy—*without trying to force him into boyfriend territory.*

All too often, when we meet a guy who starts our hormones flowing, we immediately ask ourselves, "Do I like him?" And the easiest answer to that question seems to be, "I want to kiss him! So, yes, I must like him! Maybe we're falling in love! I wonder if he'll be my boyfriend?"

And then we endeavor to fit a square peg into a round hole by trying to turn a sexual spark into a full-blown relationship, when maybe there was never more than that spark to begin with.

No more! I hereby grant you permission to see some guys solely as Hot Sex Prospects. You are allowed to meet a guy, feel an urge to rip his clothes off, and *not* try to make him your boyfriend—if you two just don't connect in that way. Rest assured, the connection that you have with a Hot Sex Prospect is still a connection. It's a pretty powerful, awesome connection, actually, and one that should allow you to engage in play-non-dates without guilt or regret. It's just a different kind of connection than the one you'll have with the potential love of your life.

However, it's not quite that easy. An essential aspect of enjoying your Hot Sex Prospect is actually knowing who he is and then trying to cut out the emotional ambiguity. As with anything having to do with physical intimacy, there is a sensitive, tricky line here. Between the flowing oxytocin and the dubious claims that we've all tricked ourselves into making in the past ("Yeah, it's cool, I'm not looking for a relationship either"), it can be tough to tell which guys you can handle just hooking up with, and which ones you can't. Not every guy you're attracted to should be a Hot Sex Prospect.

Oh, if only.

WHO IS YOUR HOT SEX PROSPECT?

Whenever I think of the ideal Hot Sex Prospect, I think of Valerie from Baton Rouge, Louisiana. She's the Bacardi girl we just met.

Valerie is twenty-four years old. When I met her, she was exploring her professional options not only by applying to graduate school and sidelining as a shot girl, but also by working part-time as a publishing receptionist, pet sitter, writer, and poet. Her colleagues saw her as an intellectual (I met up with her at a poetry reading), while men at bars saw her as the girl in the sexy referee outfit giving out free shots of rum. And she saw herself as a girl with wild, unkempt hair who hadn't worn matching socks in years.

At the time of our meeting, Valerie had been dealing for years with a painful, confusing ex-boyfriend. They had an undeniable connection, but, to put it bluntly, he didn't treat her very well. He disappeared for weeks at a time, he provided only sporadic support, and they'd had recurring sexual issues that involved him becoming emotionally overwhelmed and avoiding physical contact. Still, she was finding it hard not to obsess over him.

Luckily, a few weeks before we sat down for a night of drinks, a new guy had entered Valerie's gaggle. After showing me his photo on her phone—no shirt, towel around his waist, abs of steel blazing—she stopped suppressing her huge grin and told me about him.

"His name is Hot-Sex-Prospect-Kevin. He's a friend of my roommate. He's available, he's good in bed, and he's exciting to flirt with. Most of the time, I sort of back out at the last minute. But when I don't . . . he's got a really hot body, and he has a penis that works all the time!"

I already loved Valerie by this point and, after hearing about the emotional trauma with her Ex, was thrilled to see her sound so confident and secure about a guy. But how could she be sure that she wouldn't end up crying over this guy, just as she'd been crying over her Ex?

Valerie assured me that her feelings about Hot-Sex-Prospect-Kevin were completely different, and she was acting accordingly.

"We've never been out. We've never even been at the bar together. He comes over to my house, and we have sex. And afterward, we kind of lie around. And then he's like, 'Well, gotta go.' And I'm like, 'Yup.'"

What's so great about Valerie's Hot Sex Prospect? The fact that he's *only* a Hot Sex Prospect. He's not a Boyfriend Prospect in disguise. She's not in denial about what she really wants from him, and she's not waiting by the phone for him to call. He's also not an Ego Booster with a nice six-pack. She's not sleeping with him to feel better about herself or basing her self-worth on his attraction to her. She's having fun with him. She's getting something from him that she's not getting from anyone else. And she's being realistic about what he means to her—and not judging herself for enjoying it.

So who is the ideal Hot Sex Prospect? Simply put, he's the guy you don't necessarily like in a "Let's be friends and hang out all the time" way—but someone who really turns you on. We women are focused, driven, and analytical. We spend quite a bit of time in our heads. Don't we deserve a drama-free guy who reminds us that we should be spending time in our bodies as well?

Yes, we do.

WHO IS NOT YOUR HOT SEX PROSPECT?

If only hooking up were always that simple.

Think you have a Hot Sex Prospect? Here are two important questions to ask yourself first:

1. Is this all about my ego?
2. Do I want more from him?

If the answer to either of these questions is yes, then he's not your Hot Sex Prospect, and you're treading on very dangerous territory by getting sexually involved with him. Let's explore why the following guys are *not* your Hot Sex Prospect.

The Guy Who's Willing to Take You Home When You Feel Ugly

You know how I said that we're not part of the Hookup Generation? Well, let's remind ourselves why.

We all know what meaningless hookups look like. You spend hours getting ready. You head out to the house party. You notice that your friend looks really hot in her new dress, and you start to feel insecure. You get drunk. You flirt with lame guys. You start making out with one of these lame guys, because, well, he's there. You spend the next hour or so thinking, "Wow, this guy seems really into me, I *am* hot!" You ponder going home with him. And then you feel like crap the next day.

That guy is not your Hot Sex Prospect.

Having a Hot Sex Prospect is all about connection. Your interactions are built on attraction, magnetism, passion, and fire. The intense sexual tension is palpable. You can't keep your hands off each other. If and when you do hook up, it's a physical, sensual, exciting experience. Touching him makes you think, "Oh, hell yes! This is a necessary part of life."

Having a Hot Sex Prospect is not about the temporary validation of your ego. It's not about a guy making you feel hot. It's not about proving to your friends that you can get some action. It's not about hooking up because it's Saturday night and that's what people do on Saturday night, right? It's not about being some guy's Last Resort (see the guy's gaggle for more on that).

It's not about participating in some lame hookup culture. Because remember, the gaggle is supposed to help you learn about what you like and who you are. It's supposed to lead you closer to knowing yourself and finding the right guy and relationship for you. And is a random, passionless, drunken make-out session going to do all that for you?

Nope. Gross. Don't do it.

The Guy Who Doesn't Want to Be in a Relationship (Sigh . . .)

A guy is also not your Hot Sex Prospect if you are developing real feelings for him.

Be honest. Do you want more from him? If he's willing to give it, then consider him your Boyfriend Prospect. And if not . . . then it's time to follow the path of Marjorie, an Indianapolis expat living in New Orleans who works at the local library. When I met her, she was trying to scale things back with a former Hot Sex Prospect.

"It hasn't been strictly about the physical aspect of it, but a relationship just wouldn't have worked," she admitted to me. "Because he is the kind of guy who can just tune me out, and does his own thing whenever he wants, and doesn't tell other people about it. In some ways, he's pretty sketchy. And I liked him a lot, and could have just gone ahead and fallen in love with him. But I knew that was something that was going to end in tragedy and failure."

Marjorie was able to identify that this guy was *not* her Hot Sex Prospect—but only after she tried to treat him like one and started getting hurt. She liked him too much to think of him that way.

When we talked, I asked Marjorie if she was still drawn to him.

The answer was yes. But she was also realistic about their future together, which seemed like a healthy first step toward improving her situation. And since she couldn't just have fun with him, à la Valerie and Hot-Sex-Prospect-Kevin, how else could she fit him in her life? Let's just say that she was in the process of figuring that out.

"Are we still physically involved? Hmm . . . *ish*. Obviously I don't always stop myself, but I didn't let it turn into something where I threw myself into this relationship that I knew wasn't going to work. But that's probably going to stop. That's my dilemma. I had been periodically hooking up with him, prior to meeting my new Boyfriend Prospect. But it's happening less now. I haven't yet figured out a solution to that, but I'm working on it."

Perhaps more importantly, Marjorie was using her experience with this guy to inform her decisions with her new Boyfriend Prospect. It had been a learning experience about her own personal limits vis-à-vis sexuality and attachment.

Knowing that sex means a lot to her, Marjorie had made a decision to not sleep with her Boyfriend Prospect yet. Getting burned by her non–Hot Sex Prospect had shown her that she needed to take things slow, if she hoped to moderate her emotions and proceed carefully in her new potential relationship.

Learning about your sexual boundaries is an important part of dealing with potential Hot Sex Prospects. Like Marjorie, you may discover how fast or slow you can move and how you respond to physical intimacy.

HOW TO STICK TO YOUR VALUES AND STILL HAVE A HOT SEX PROSPECT

It can be done!

Whether your values are personal, religious, or up for grabs, having a Hot Sex Prospect should never be a departure from what you believe in. Yes, you should allow yourself to appreciate a purely physical connection for what it is: a purely physical connection. But aside from that, your relationship with your Hot Sex Prospect should run on your own terms and according to your own rules.

Take Liz, a young nursing student and blues singer in Nashville. Having grown up a devout Christian in the South, she was still in the process of integrating physicality and sex into her emotional and romantic life when I met her. But while sorting through her particular beliefs, she has made sure to keep careful tabs on her values and work them into her relationships with the guys in her gaggle.

Liz firmly believes that a strong relationship cannot start out with sex and partly blames premature sex for the demise of her last serious relationship. Throughout my interviews, I obviously met women who think differently. But Liz knows what works for her, and this knowledge is allowing her to build relationships without any guilt or fear that she has betrayed her core values.

That said, her traditional values haven't stopped her from having a Hot Sex Prospect. Because no one is saying that you have to have sex with your Hot Sex Prospect! Sexual attraction—and all the fun to be had with it—can take many forms.

"That's Mike. He's physically everything that I want," Liz described with a conspiratorial smile. "And he's such a good kisser. Luckily, I'm not attached to anything. Hooking up is all it's going to be, and that's fine with me. I don't know where I'm going to be living. I'm applying for nursing jobs in three different states. I can't work around a guy right now. So he may not be Mr. Right, but he's Mr. Right Now, and he's doing his job just fine."

Again, this goes back to knowing who you can handle a physical relationship with—and who you can't. Liz has realized that, according to her personal values, she cannot begin a serious relationship with sex. That's good for her to know. However, she's also learned that she can keep herself entertained with a casual fling in the meantime.

Can I get an amen to that?

KEY TIPS

For Cultivating a Hot Sex Prospect

1. Explore your sexuality through your relationship with your Hot Sex Prospect. On any given day, you are being hit with countless messages about what it means to be and feel sexy. Commit to figuring out your own unique definition.

2. Recognize your connection with your Hot Sex Prospect for what it is, a purely physical connection, and allow yourself to enjoy that. But also don't assume that every guy you're attracted to is your Hot Sex Prospect, and don't pretend that you can keep it casual when you can't. He's only your Hot Sex Prospect if you don't have emotional feelings for him. If you do, then he's your Boyfriend Prospect. Always be honest with yourself and be able to separate the two.

3. Don't hook up with lame guys in lame circumstances and then call them Hot Sex Prospects. Hold out for physical connection and passion and heat—not for just any guy who's willing to take you home from the bar.

4. Look at your time with your Hot Sex Prospect as a way to learn more about your unique sexual needs and desires. What turns you on? Who better than a Hot Sex Prospect to show you all that?

5. Know your own morals and values, and fit your Hot Sex Prospect into that structure accordingly. Your relationship with him should be on your own terms—whatever those terms may be.

THE UNAVAILABLE GUY

A guy who has a serious girlfriend but still engages in a light, outwardly nonthreatening flirtation with you. No one's wrecking any homes, but there's a mental and possibly emotional connection there. You may even wonder what could have happened between you two, if the timing were just a little different.

He has a girlfriend, but he texts and emails and calls me constantly. When we hang out, people always think he's my boyfriend. But that pesky girlfriend thing is in the way.

—Lindsey, 26, office manager, Atlanta

MEET YOUR UNAVAILABLE GUY

This guy has a girlfriend, and you probably know a lot about her. You've hung out with her at parties, friended her on Facebook, and helped pick out her birthday presents. You also counseled the Unavailable Guy during his latest relationship spat and basically wrote the lovely apology email that led them to better times. This girl has no reason to dislike you, as you would never steal another girl's boyfriend—in fact, she should thank you for advising her boyfriend on their relationship problems and convincing him to book the more expensive room for their surprise weekend getaway.

Others may have noted a flirtation between you and the Unavailable Guy, but you don't see the danger in giggling over a few private jokes and grabbing dinner together every once in a while. You both know that he is unavailable, which makes him less threatening than other guys and enables you to let your guard down more than you would with a viable romantic prospect. Because your relationship with him isn't going anywhere, you don't have to overanalyze your interactions and can continue to push the boundaries of your friendship into territory that never feels unsafe.

Good intentions aside, you're not oblivious to the fine lines of your relationship with him. You can imagine that his girlfriend wouldn't be thrilled to hear that he paid for dinner, or to know how many DVDs you lent him last month. You may even have set up unofficial, unspoken rules of communication just to be safe, like not texting him on weekends when you know that they're together.

You also can't help but be a little suspicious of her calculated friendliness—did anyone else catch her giving you the evil eye at your BBQ last weekend when she thought no one was looking? But whatever, she's not *your* girlfriend! So you allow yourself to get closer to the Unavailable Guy, rationalizing that *he* is the one in the relationship and thus responsible for pulling in the reins if your friendship crosses into dangerous territory.

HOW TO HAVE AN UNAVAILABLE GUY

Pop quiz: What's more distasteful than a homewrecker? Answer: Nothing! *Nothing* is more distasteful than a homewrecker. That is why you shouldn't be one.

Let's be clear about this, right off the bat. Gunning for a guy who is committed to someone else is desperate, disrespectful, and tacky. It couldn't be a less inspiring way to find love and happiness. How are you going to tell that story to your kids?

If a guy meets you, falls deeply in love, realizes he can't live without you, and then breaks up with his girlfriend to pursue you, then fine. You can't help being awesome. But playing any sort of active role in his change of heart is a lame move. It just is. Participating in the all too prevalent modern culture of infidelity and distrust makes you a less admirable woman.

Okay! Glad to have that out of the way, obvious as it may be. Now let's talk about the Unavailable Guy in your gaggle. You know, the guy who has a girlfriend.

When you're navigating a connection with an Unavailable Guy, you're bound to come across quite a few hazy lines and overly careful (but necessary) safeguards. Respect them: these safeguards are important ways to harness the ambiguity in your relationship before it gets out of control. You cannot think of your Unavailable Guy as just some guy in your gaggle, and you definitely can't treat him like one. He's committed to another girl, and she will—and should—always be a presence that dictates boundaries to your behavior.

Why is the Unavailable Guy worth keeping in your gaggle, even with all these unspoken lines and restrictive boundaries? The connection between the two of you is worth exploring because it is real. The time spent talking with this guy probably evokes something special in you, something that the other guys in your gaggle aren't reaching in quite the same way. This friendship really means something to you. You're learning and growing from it. It is in your best interests to figure out how to find a spot for this guy in your life. A spot that remains meaningful, while also staying ethical and respectful. (Have I mentioned that he has a girlfriend? Yeah, don't forget that.)

It is possible to cultivate a powerful connection with a guy and not have it result in unethical behavior or unrequited feelings. After all, you live in a post-dating world where women and men have reasons to interact in an endless variety of circumstances. Men and women can be just friends; in fact, between our jobs, our social networks, our hobbies, and our living situations, we're often forced to have opposite-gender friends these days. There can even be an attraction that remains unexplored. Despite what dirty baby-boomer politicians and feckless, philandering celebrities might be demonstrating, we *can* exercise self-discipline and exert control over our actions. We *can* keep it in our pants, at least when there is a really good reason to.

That said, relationships end all the time: further exploration of the connection between you and your Unavailable Guy may be a future possibility. But for now, friendship must be the big idea here.

So, how to cultivate this friendship while still reaping all the benefits of the Unavailable Guy's spot in your gaggle?

Weirdly enough, you should embrace and explore *his* relationship, in order to gain insight and wisdom about you and the rest of *your* relationships.

GETTING TO KNOW THE GIRLFRIEND

Want to explore your connection with an Unavailable Guy? If you ignore the existence of his girlfriend, then your friendship will be dead in the water before it even begins. No matter how irreproachable your intentions are, no girl is going to be super excited to hear that her boyfriend is talking to or spending time with another woman. If his girlfriend hears your name a few times and has no greater context in which to place it, she's going to get nervous. She's going to visualize you as an evil, man-stealing vixen who wants her guy. And you are going to quickly find out that you do not want to be in this power struggle.

There's a good chance that the girlfriend is not simply overreacting or being crazy. Good behavior or not, some part of your Unavailable Guy might be attracted to you. As one committed man in a *very* long-term relationship told me, "I do have female friends I spend time with. They're usually girls I would consider dating if I didn't have a girlfriend."

Yeesh. The knowledge that her boyfriend is hanging out with girls he could see himself dating (and therefore finds attractive) can be a little difficult for any girlfriend, no matter how cool, to wrap her mind around. But this is where trust factors into a relationship. The above guy swears, for example, that he would "never in a million years cheat! I think that a lot of guys cheat, but I would never do it. My girlfriend has *nothing* to worry about."

The only way to counteract a girlfriend's potentially valid nervousness is for you to get to know her. Your motivation should stem from a desire to show her that you really, truly just want to be friends with her boyfriend. And maybe even with her, too, if you end up getting along.

Let's take a cue from Trisha, a twenty-five-year-old take-no-bullshit accountant in Atlanta. She is confident and hot and has a huge gaggle—and not surprisingly, it includes an Unavailable Guy. However, she has had to be strategic in ensuring that their friendship can continue in an open, comfortable, and ethical way.

"I've got a work husband, a guy who I always talk to at work," she explained to me. "But he's in a relationship. It was kind of awkward until his girlfriend and I met. Before then, I'm sure she was like, 'Well, who's this girl?' And I'm a very flirty person, too, so sometimes it's not good."

As I sat there with Trisha, I tried to see her as a guy's girlfriend might. And although I consider myself to be a particularly confident and trusting partner, I had to be honest: if I had a boyfriend, I'd be nervous about his friendship with Trisha. She's fun and attractive and all too easy to hate. Except that once you meet her, you can just tell that she's a stand-up, straightforward person. You can tell that she's not the type of girl to purposefully break up a relationship. And this is what Trisha realized, and set out to fix.

"[My Unavailable Guy's girlfriend] works at our company, too, so I got to know her. And I like her! Now we know each other, and we're totally cool. So he and I can grab a drink, and she's 100 percent okay with it. It's great, and I think that's really rare—to find a girl who's really just fine with it. But she's completely okay with him and me hanging out, now that she knows me."

If your intentions are actually pure (which they should be), then a sane girlfriend will recognize that once she meets you. And if her relationship is worth its salt, she'll trust her boyfriend. This will allow you and your Unavailable Guy to explore your friendship without ever feeling guilty or evoking unnecessary drama. Being friends with her will also provide yet another incentive for you to not cross that platonic line, ever. If everyone is being open and honest, then everyone wins.

TALKING ABOUT THE GIRLFRIEND

Once you've gotten to know the girlfriend, and she's comfortable with you hanging out with her boyfriend, you need to talk about her with him. And probably even hang out with them as a couple.

You're not doing this to torture yourself. You're doing this so that you can personally learn and grow as a result of your friendship with him. Hanging out with only single guys can skew your perception of how men act and what they are capable of. This is why your Unavailable Guy's perspective and his status as a committed man can affect how you interact with guys in a larger capacity.

Look at it this way. You hear your female friends talk about their relationships *all the time*. But how often do you get a front-row seat to the guy's side of a relationship? How often can you ask those real questions, and pick a guy's brain about love and connection and commitment, without wondering if either one of you has ulterior motives? Your Unavailable Guy's perspective and advice can be priceless and incredibly useful for the rest of your love life.

As it was for Sonia, a twenty-seven-year-old entrepreneur in Denver who had once been reeling from her divorce from a guy who was, by all counts, bad news. Since the collapse of her marriage, she had totally rebuilt her life in an inspiring way. She'd refocused herself professionally, gotten more involved in her church and her Christian faith, and invested in a new, solid group of friends. She'd even started talking about dating again. But, she wasn't feeling inspired by the guys she knew or was meeting in the Denver singles scene.

However, she did know a few guys who were in relationships, and by getting closer to those guys, she was beginning to find hope for her own romantic future again.

"I now have some guy friends here, and most of them have girlfriends," Sonia told me. "In some cases, I'm friends with their girlfriends, too, so it's not like there's a weird overlap there. But through these guys, I'm starting to see how a guy could treat a girl nicely. They're just good examples of nice guys. They're not douches."

Seeing solid evidence of good, caring guys was providing Sonia with the optimism to put her painful past behind her and embark on a positive path to love. And, as it turns out, it was strengthening her resolve to further explore the religious faith—and relationships with others who followed it—that had also gotten her through a tough time.

If your Unavailable Guy is in a good relationship, then having him in your life can act as inspiration when the other guys in your gaggle are being annoying or falling short of their potential. And if your Unavailable Guy is in a bad relationship, you can also learn from his experiences and reflect on them when you're dealing with your own relationships.

All of that can only happen if you openly acknowledge his relationship and assert yourself as someone in his life who is willing to talk with him about it. You should aim to become a genuine part of the life that he has built with his girlfriend.

ADJUSTING YOUR DYNAMIC WHEN YOUR UNAVAILABLE GUY'S RELATIONSHIP WITH HIS GIRLFRIEND GETS MORE SERIOUS

Your connection with your Unavailable Guy can take several different paths. Here are some of the most common:

1. It will fade out with time (or with you focusing more of your energy on other guys in your gaggle).
2. He and his girlfriend will break up one day, potentially allowing your friendship to blossom into something more romantic.
3. He and his girlfriend will break up one day, leading you both to realize that, even when you're both available, you don't actually want to be together.
4. His relationship will become more serious, and you will find yourself doing the Electric Slide at his wedding.

Path 4 is what happened to Jenn, a twenty-eight-year-old consultant in Pittsburgh. And as Jenn can testify, any girl with an Unavailable Guy should be ready to cope with that phone call (or more likely, that email or Gchat or Facebook relationship status update).

Jenn and her Unavailable Guy had been close ever since their university placed them in the same freshman dorm. They spent their four years at college staying up late, stretching out on futons, and sharing all their hopes, dreams, and thoughts on life. In the years since undergrad, they'd partied together, bonded over professional successes and frustrations, and been present whenever the other needed them. They each considered the other a close friend.

There was only one hitch: Jenn's Unavailable Guy had been dating the same girl since high school. Then, three years out of college and seven years into their friendship, he called Jenn one evening and told her some big news: he and his girlfriend had gotten engaged!

Jenn congratulated him. Jenn hung up the phone. Jenn cried her eyes out.

"I was so confused!" Jenn told me while still shaking her head in disbelief. "I had never, ever considered trying to break up his relationship. I never *actively* wanted to be with him. But still, when he told me that he was getting married, even though I was happy that he was happy, I cried."

What was Jenn crying over? It was not a sudden revelation that she'd been in love with him all these years. But she realized she'd been harboring a tiny thought that maybe, one day, in the unforeseeable future, they would end up together. And that possibility ended with his engagement. It was the death of that slight chance, that unexplored potential, that unrealized connection, that she was mourning.

Remembers Jenn, "I think some part of me thought that maybe, just maybe, we'd give it a go someday. I didn't even necessarily want that, and I definitely wasn't pining after him during all those years of friendship. But he really *got* me, and our connection was really meaningful to me, and I suddenly got scared that I was going to lose all that."

Jenn was right to prepare herself for a shift. After his engagement was announced, Jenn's Unavailable Guy became less available to her. She still hung out with him, but his fiancée now usually came along as well.

In good gaggle fashion, Jenn sat back and thought about what exactly drew her to this guy, even as a friend. She thought about his dependability, his incessantly fun teasing, and his willingness to call her out on her crap. She also thought about what it felt like to spend time with a guy who really seemed to understand and appreciate her, with all her neuroses and eccentricities. And she made a mental note to recognize when other guys in her gaggle displayed those likable traits—ideally, guys who she also wanted to be with romantically, more so than she ever had with her Unavailable Guy.

When your Unavailable Guy drops the news that his relationship has become more serious, you should accept your reaction, whatever it may be (although if tears or thrown objects are involved, try to save it for when you're alone). Support his big step forward. If you haven't already, build a real friendship with his partner. Prepare for your relationship to operate under clearer, stricter rules. And then realize what you appreciate about him and make a mental note to seek that out, or at least be aware of it in other, more available guys.

Most importantly, mourn the death of that potential romantic opportunity—and then get over it. There are many more possibilities where that came from. The beauty of the gaggle is that you will always be open to them.

KEY TIPS

For Cultivating an Unavailable Guy

1. Never try to break up someone's relationship. Period. Come on, that should be a given, right? Right.

2. Become friendly with your Unavailable Guy's girlfriend. Showing her that you are not trying to steal her boyfriend and are working to gain her approval will enable you to spend time with your Unavailable Guy with minimal drama attached. Putting a face to her name will also make it much harder to forget that he's not, in fact, a free agent.

3. Engage in open, honest conversation with him about his relationship and be aware of his behavior when he and his girlfriend are together. This is a chance to observe a guy in a relationship firsthand. Learn from it, and let your perceptions inform your own relationships!

4. Determine what it is that you like so much about your connection, and then keep an eye out for those traits in other (more available) guys.

5. When his relationship takes a big step forward, support him and get ready for your relationship to become more clear-cut. If you find yourself upset about that shift, then remember that if you weren't in love with him yesterday, you're not in love with him today. You're just mourning the death of potential. You will feel sad, and then you will get over it, and eventually you will meet someone who is a better (and again, more available) fit for you.

THE EGO BOOSTER

A "great guy" whose attention and stability always make you feel good about yourself—despite the fact that he never quite makes it to the top of your romantic list. He's the guy who will help you fix your broken cabinet and carry your boxes when you move. And the one who you know will text you back after that other guy blows you off. Let's be honest: no one wants to be the Ego Booster! But too bad. He's in your gaggle anyway.

John Richardson. I know that he would do anything for me. If I said, "I want to date you," he would be like, "Oh god!" and do cartwheels down the street. I know I can call him and be like, "Hey, let's go grab dinner," and he'll drop everything to do it. He's my Ego Booster. I love John Richardson to death. If he was a little bit taller, I could maybe date him.
—Carolina, 29, medical sales representative, Atlanta

MEET YOUR EGO BOOSTER

This guy is *such* a great guy, an undeniable fact that your friends and mother love to remind you of. He is very sweet—and very willing to pay for all the drinks when you're broke. You know that if you contact him and don't hear back within the hour, then he has a good reason and will get back to you as soon as he sees your message, usually with an unasked-for explanation of why it's taken him so long to respond. He's the first guy you text when that other guy doesn't get back to you, and it's amazing how quickly his response boosts your confidence, especially when you're feeling unlikable and unattractive.

You're guaranteed to feel good about yourself when you're with the Ego Booster.

Unfortunately, you're also somehow not attracted to him. Those closest to you think that he's a great catch and keep urging you to just "give him a try." They love to repeat the tale of their third cousin, who turned down her husband several times and swore that she could never see him as anything more than a friend before finally agreeing to a date with him and subsequently getting hitched.

Yet, what they don't understand is that they don't need to remind you of all this. You've already realized that if you could finally appreciate what is right in front of you and allow yourself to really fall in love with the Ego Booster, then you would be treated like an absolute queen. You would never again have to wonder, "Is he going to text me back?" or "Should I be nervous about that cute girl he works with?" You even notice that slight twinge of jealousy you feel whenever he starts telling you about a new girl and the great conversation they just had (although you can't help feeling that he'd happily cancel his plans with her if you asked him to come over and fix your broken bookcase).

Thinking that you have finally grown up and begun to see him in a new light, you decide to meet up with him and his friends on a Saturday night and give it a real try, once and for all. You've seen other girls fall for him; maybe it's your turn!

But then you get to the bar and notice that his friend is really hot, and the Ego Booster falls to the back burner once again.

HOW TO HAVE AN EGO BOOSTER

Ladies, I know it's tempting. But I *implore* you: do not abuse your Ego Booster.

As with all of the gaggle guys, the key here is to cultivate a mutually beneficial relationship that will teach you about what you want and need and what type of guy you're ultimately looking for. The point of the gaggle is never to milk some poor, doting sucker for all he's worth. And nowhere is that more true than with your Ego Booster.

Why? Because, duh, if your instincts are on point, he actually likes you! His interest in you makes him vulnerable. And if you knowingly manipulate him and break his heart, then he'll turn into a jaded jerk and you'll be ruining some other girl's Boyfriend Prospect. Don't forget that romantic karma's a bitch.

So be nice, and try not to take (too much) advantage of his eagerness to be around you. The Ego Booster is one of the most common guys in the gaggle, but his existence is still a very sensitive subject for all the guys out there who *don't want to be one*. Believe me, I wish you could see men's reactions when I tell them about the Ego Booster. They think of that one girl who they really like, something clicks, and then I am forced to watch as their faces melt into a flaming pile of horror, embarrassment, and hurt.

Kind of heartbreaking, right?

But, as long as we women are keeping an open mind about our Ego Boosters—which we should because, come on, they're *such* great guys—it turns out that the power of this fear can actually be used for good.

Let me share a story that proves how the threat of the Ego Booster can actually have a positive effect on everyone's love life, including that of a (former) Ego Booster.

ONE GUY'S TALE OF AVOIDING EGO BOOSTERDOM

One of my proudest moments of the interview tour occurred while I was having a second beer with Michael, a senior at Louisiana State University in Baton Rouge (Geaux Tigers!). Cute, smart, charming, and thoughtful, Michael didn't initially strike me as insecure or likely to always end up in the friend zone. He was a catch! But the friend zone is exactly where he'd ended up with a girl he'd liked five months prior to our interview.

In his own words:

"We started hanging out, and honestly, I felt like I was obvious in showing that I liked her. But then one day she said, 'It's so awesome how we can just hang out, and not be weird, or whatever.' And I thought, 'Oh. Not good. This is going to be frustrating.' Because the day that we're 'friends,' and she tells me, 'Oh, I met this guy,' that is going to be the day I realize that I ruined this whole thing, and I wasted so many months."

And yet, his next step was unclear to him. Was he supposed to make a move? Not make a move? Settle for friendship? Put his feelings on the line?

Hallelujah! He ended up making a move. He kissed her. Twice! And the second time, it worked.

What could've possibly inspired Michael to swallow his fear, face rejection, and go for the girl of his dreams? He told me that the deciding factor was a phone chat with a guy friend who happened to read the WTF?! site religiously. Familiar with the gaggle, his friend listened to his quandary and then spelled out the situation for him in clear terms. "Dude. You're turning into her Ego Booster!" the friend exclaimed. "Don't. Be. The. Ego. Booster."

Michael was horrified by the idea of being the Ego Booster, and felt compelled to make a move and break out of that box—and the rest is a post-dating love story.

Michael's tale is proof that the gaggle is in fact evolving, and that no guy has to necessarily be stuck in a role that he doesn't like. Michael transitioned from Ego Booster to Boyfriend Prospect with one—okay, two—assertive kisses.

WHAT YOU CAN LEARN FROM A GUY WHO ACTUALLY *IS* YOUR EGO BOOSTER

Now we know that guys are so terrified of being your Ego Booster that the possibility may compel them to make a move and leap into another gaggle category. It can happen! But in the meantime—how should you cultivate a relationship with your Ego Booster?

If the gaggle is meant to teach you about yourself, then your Ego

Booster is there to show you how much emotional support and adulation you, as a unique woman, need from your ideal guy in a relationship.

I've met some women who don't care to have Ego Boosters or aren't willing to put in a lot of work to keep them around. The takeaway message there is that these women don't ultimately need to be with a guy who is going to be constantly attentive to their emotional needs. A minimum of emotional bolstering is not going to be a deal breaker for them. Because when it comes down to it, these women don't really need that from their partners.

I've met other women—to be honest, many, many more women—who can identify their Ego Boosters all too easily. The Ego Booster is a huge part of their lives and their gaggles. Some women, and I don't necessarily recommend this, practically seem to collect them. And that tendency should alert them to a clear message as well.

If you always have a few Ego Boosters, or find yourself relying heavily on one, then you need a guy who is good at making you feel good about yourself. You'll struggle to be happy in a relationship that doesn't involve lots of open appreciation and love. So keep your eyes open for a guy who is willing to provide that consistent support.

Ego Boosters can remind you that if and when you are ready, there are solid, dependable guys out there. That you are worthy of being treated well. That you deserve a guy who can bring it emotionally. That there *are* men out there who will help you fix that damn cabinet.

Ladies, your Ego Booster is holding out for you, and he thinks you're worth it. Absorb that lesson.

HOW *NOT* TO TREAT YOUR EGO BOOSTER

Most of us don't mean to hurt anybody, which is why, if you're anything like me, you have moments when you hope and pray that your Ego Booster isn't going to make a move, lest he ruin the friendship that you two have created. You avoid getting into any romantic or sexual situations with him, fearing an inappropriate thigh touch or a sudden declaration of love. And that's fine. If he's not being clear in his intentions, then you don't need to be presumptuously clear in your rejection.

But once he puts his heart on the line, don't toy with him! Either give it a fair try or let him down gently but firmly. You owe him honesty, after all the ego boosting that he has bestowed on you.

Ultimately, both you and your Ego Booster will benefit from your ability to depend on him only in reasonable doses. He'll leave himself open to a girl who is attracted to all his wonderfulness, and you won't fall into the trap of settling for a guy who is simply nice to you when it feels like no one else is.

That's what Cynthia, a stunningly gorgeous, sweet, and divorced twenty-nine-year-old ex-Mormon in Salt Lake City, Utah, realized after years of relying on her Ego Boosters to pick her back up after a heartbreak. Quite the jet-setter, she reminisced a bit guiltily, "My out-of-town guys were always my Ego Boosters. When I got my heart broken, I would call them and say, 'I wanna leave!' And then I would fly out and hang with them for the weekend. I wouldn't sleep with them, but I'd just let them take me out. They'd treat me really well—which was a huge confidence booster—and then I'd come back into town on Monday."

Did it work? I asked her.

"No," Cynthia sighed, shaking her head. "At the end of the day, I was still alone. Because I didn't really like any of these guys. I just wanted someone to make me feel better, when the guy that I *really* wanted wasn't there."

The Ego Booster will not solve all of your problems and fix all of your insecurities. The more you expect him to, the more he'll disappoint you *and* read into your neediness in a dangerous way. Ironically, sometimes when you're at your lowest point, you should keep a safe distance from him, letting yourself work through the effects of your latest blowoff on your own terms instead of taking that easy path down Ego Booster Lane.

KEY TIPS

For Cultivating an Ego Booster

1. Remain open to the possibility that one day you'll wake up (or he'll finally make a real move), and suddenly this great guy will seem like perfect boyfriend material.

2. Pay close attention to your relationship and ask yourself how much attention and affection you'll need in your ideal relationship.

3. If your Ego Booster makes a romantic play for you and you're still not into him, then you *must* turn him down unambiguously—even though it means taking the chance that he won't want to remain in your life as "just a friend" anymore. For the sake of all women everywhere, don't string him along when he's at the end of his rope.

4. Don't expect your Ego Booster to fill the hole that the Guy Who Just Blew You Off left. You're setting the poor guy up for disappointment and shortchanging your own growth in the process.

5. That said, enjoy having an Ego Booster! He thinks you're worth jumping through flaming hoops for. And guess what? You are. Remember it.

THE GUY WHO JUST BLEW YOU OFF

> An undeserving guy who is not treating you well but is still on your mind. You're likely tempted to contact him in an effort to get closure or "fix things."

So this guy was kind of blowing me off, and after a while you realize you're the one always making contact and sending the first text. We went from hanging out two or three times a week to nothing. I was kind of blaming it on his business, and finally, on Facebook chat, of all things, I was like, "Hey, what's going on?" And he started laying it out: it was because it freaked him out that I called him sweetie.

And I was like, don't flatter yourself, I'm a "sweetie" whore! But for whatever reason, that totally freaked him out. Then he was like, no, no, no, I really like you! And then he was all, I've had meetings every night this week, I'm so busy, so, you know.

Now, it's just a lot of texting. No talk of meeting up, though.

—Melissa, 29, nonprofit fundraiser, New Orleans

MEET YOUR GUY WHO JUST BLEW YOU OFF

You've seen or read *He's Just Not That Into You*, and you know that this guy should not be in your gaggle. Whether he canceled your dinner plans, forgot to call you back, or never responded to the funny YouTube video that you sent him, the Guy Who Just Blew You Off is full of excuses and seems to have undergone a complete personality transformation while you were out of town for the weekend.

That being said, whether you actually miss having him in your life or just miss the excitement and anticipation of figuring out when you'll see him next, the Guy Who Just Blew You Off is still on your mind. You've watched guys pull the slow fade on your friends in the past. You are all too familiar with the increasingly common blowoff strategy of slowly returning fewer and fewer phone calls and texts and suddenly being busy to the point of extinction. But even so—he never officially declared that he lost interest in you. And, because you weren't technically dating, there was no breakup. You're sure that the evidence is there: he *was* into you!

You could be just one cute email away from clearing up whatever misunderstanding is plaguing your relationship; you're also one "Do I really want to be *that* girl?" email away from angrily demanding closure and an explanation of why his feelings have changed. Sometimes you partially blame yourself and can't help wondering if, in your initial excitement, you unwittingly forced him into the wrong gaggle role. Maybe he would be interested in playing a more casual role in your life? To be fair, it was *your* decision to invest in him as a Boyfriend Prospect, even though he claimed that he wasn't looking for a girlfriend and was seriously considering a cross-country career move. You find yourself weighing the pros and cons of sending him a late-night text message in an attempt to turn him into your Hot Sex Prospect, momentarily holding off because you're terrified of looking desperate.

In any case, you're on the verge of contacting the Guy Who Just Blew You Off at any moment. But rejection sucks. So you've promised yourself that you'll wait until at least Thursday to see if he reaches out to you first.

HOW TO HAVE A GUY WHO JUST BLEW YOU OFF (EVEN IF YOU DON'T WANT ONE!)

Sometimes in life, when something is painful and horrific and nonsensical and just plain wrong, the only sane option is to laugh about it.

Ladies, let the comedy show begin!

Please raise your hand if you've been the recipient of any of these real-life blowoffs (Yes, my hand will be going up! No one is immune to this.):

Via text:
- *srry i haven't been in touch. i thiiiiink i have a girlfriend now. but you're really fun and look great naked ;)*
- *so your cool and pretty but I dont think its worth it. thanks for coming out.*
- *Him: Hey—want to hang tomorrow?*
  You: Totally, where have you been!?
  Him: Oh sorry, didn't mean to text you

Via email:
- *I just can't do it. I can't hang again tonight. I am just too committed to my professional life and need some time to myself. I am absolutely shredded tonight and just don't feel like hanging out. I am sorry about the tone of the email, but I am just feeling terrible. I'm sorry. You don't deserve this. I suck.*
- *just got your message. night was a bit wild. yeah, we could meet up for some joe. i probably have to do some penance for the rest of the weekend because of my last night's debauchery, but i might have things finished by Sunday afternoon. unfortunately, i have to be a bit vague and cagey at the moment because i don't know if i'll be able to get any momentum to get my work done. hit me up at noon or so tomorrow and we may be able to set up something.*

Via Facebook:
- *+1 Add as friend. (After having been Facebook friends for six years—defriended! Ouch.)*

Face-to-face:
- *"I've been on a couple of dates with a guy in my gaggle, and he asked me to come to a party with him on New Year's. Then, as the clock struck twelve, I saw him making out with someone else."*

Still laughing? Ha? Ha, ha? Yeah, ugh. Me neither.

Getting blown off sucks. The drop in the pit of your stomach when your phone buzzes and it's not what you were hoping for. The dawning realization that, wow, he's never actually going to respond to that email. The panic that sets in when you admit that, yes, he *has* been acting weird and distant, even though he swears nothing is wrong. The overanalysis that comes with believing that your fate is about to live or die by the *exact wording* of your next text or the *exact outfit* that you choose to wear next time you see him. The last-minute scramble to figure out something, *anything*, that will put your connection back on track.

Whether you've been rejected by the love of your life or by some guy you met at a party ten minutes ago, getting blown off messes with your mind and screws with your confidence. It chips away at your sense of empowerment. One stupid text message or canceled non-date can take you from feeling on top of the world to feeling insecure, unattractive, and doomed to a life of feeding your dozen cats and watching all your friends find love while you sit alone and yell at the *American Idol* contestants on your TV screen.

I'm here to promise you something: it's not only you. Every woman knows what it feels like to be blown off. Every woman is facing potential heartbreak around every corner of her gaggle. And every woman has to figure out a way to pick herself back up after experiencing rejection.

I have met and interviewed gorgeous girls (models included). Confident girls. Successful girls. Girls who always seem to be in relationships. Girls who are currently *in* great relationships. And all—all, all, all—of us have been blown off. And when it happens, all of us feel really crappy about it.

What does it mean to get blown off? We now live in a post-dating world, where the romantic rules, signals, and expectations have changed. The traditional advice regarding guys who blow you off—*Stop thinking about him! Never talk to him again! Cut him off!*—is not necessarily the right answer anymore. Our love lives have become more complex, and so has the experience of rejection, and potential rejection, and the fear of rejection. But the good news is that, in this brave new world of—

Hold up! Wow, that was sneaky. Don't think I don't see you there, itching to text that Guy Who Just Blew You Off. I can tell you're just planning to "check in" and tell him about that funny article you read, the one that made you think of that conversation you had that one time. But *please*, hang on for a minute. Let me finish. Promise me that you will read this section before doing anything.

No, really. Put. The. Phone. Down. Get off his Facebook page! Stop hovering over his name on Gchat. Listen to what I have to say first.

INTRODUCING THE DO-OR-DIE FREAKOUT (AND HOW TO HANDLE IT)

Let's jump back in time to the moment just before a definitive blowoff occurs, when it feels like your actions might actually affect how the pendulum swings with this guy in your life.

Of course, you can't force someone to want to see or talk to you— at least not in a genuine, lasting, based-on-authentic-feelings way. But you just might be able to set the scene for an ailing connection to have a real shot at working, if not now, then somewhere down the line. Be it tomorrow or in a few weeks, months or years.

As soon as you feel like a guy might be blowing you off, I want you to do one thing. This might be in direct opposition to what your instincts are telling you to do. But if there's ever a time to override your instincts, this is it.

I want you to give him some space.

When you're giving a guy space, you are *not* inviting him to a movie. You're not even inviting him to a friend's party. You are not shooting him a breezy email, just to see what he's up to this weekend. You are not posting the link to a new restaurant on his Facebook wall with a note saying, "We should try this place out!" You are not BBMing him a random funny thought you just had. You are not contacting him in any way that requires a yes or no response. And you are not asking him for answers or explanations about why he hasn't texted you in three days.

I know you may be tempted to do one (or all—ack!) of the above, because (1) you're hoping that you're totally imagining this blowoff, and that his response ("Yes, I'd love to watch the game together! I'm so glad you asked!") will serve as proof that, ha, you were just being paranoid, he's *so* into you! or (2) you believe the prevailing wisdom that says he's either in love with you or he's just not that into you, and that there's no gray area, so you might as well figure out *right this very second* if he likes you and if you two have a future together.

Well, number one is probably not going to happen. When was the last time a guy said *exactly* what you wanted to hear? I rest my case. And number two is *way* too black-and-white in the context of this post-dating world.

Contrary to popular belief, men are not always 100 percent sure about what they want, every single second of the day. Especially given the complexity, mixed signals, and miscommunications of the post-dating world, the changing gender dynamics between men and women of our generation, the endless ways that someone can display that they *are* into you . . . I could go on. Suffice it to say that adopting the oversimplified "he loves me, he loves me not" mentality is dangerous. It can cause you to imperil a real connection before it has the time it needs to flourish.

Let me shed some light on the truth for you. Sometimes, guys go through a freakout as they're getting to know you (and simultaneously sorting through their own gaggle). We'll call it the do-or-die freakout, because guys tend to come out of the freakout either committed to further exploring a connection with you, or really, seriously not. And your reaction to their freakout can play into their decision.

The do-or-die freakout often happens right as everything seems to be going so well. You and this guy appear on the verge of embarking on a real, legitimate relationship, and you can sense that you're reaching the next stage of intimacy and involvement.

And then, at that moment, he pulls away. *So* frustrating!

Why does he freak out at this point? Because if there's any tiny piece of him that's not 100 percent sure, at that very moment, that he's ready and excited to move forward with something serious, then he will start feeling like things are moving too fast and he will need to do a gut check—whether he realizes that's what's happening or not.

"Am I really into this girl?" is one question that he'll be asking himself. The other questions, which might feel even more pressing, are: "Am I ready to be in a relationship? Is this what I want right now? Am I prepared to uproot my comfortably single life? How do I feel about potentially never getting the chance to hook up with that cute girl at work?"

This freakout is not necessarily justified. The fact that relationships can seem like a chore, or a commitment to a set of annoying obligations, is a big problem with the way that coupledom is understood and portrayed these days. Nonetheless, these are the (often subconscious) thoughts that are floating around in his head. And whether he can articulate what he is feeling or not, he definitely has the sense that the walls are closing in on him every time your name pops up in his inbox.

When that happens, his newfound claustrophobia kicks into high gear. He was already getting nervous, but now the lights begin to dim and the freezing cold water starts rushing in at his feet. The sound of the waves becomes deafening. And suddenly, a masked madman appears, holding a knife to his throat and threatening to end his young, un-fully-realized life. No! It's too soon for him to go!

And just as he's trying to calm himself down and plot his survival, someone (aka *you*, with your "casual" phone call just to see "how he's doing") starts asking him to measure the floors and count the walls and estimate how many liters of water are filling the room. You demand to know how he's *feeling*, and what his escape plan is. And at that moment, he only gets more panicked. He seeks an exit door more desperately. He freaks out even more.

Because, geez, he just needs time to *think*!

And then, he bails. Whether he breaks things off with you or just pulls the slow fade, he goes MIA from you and the budding relationship you guys had.

A moment for the good news. Millennial guys aren't out to hurt you—they simply hold just as high a standard for relationships as we do, and they don't like half-assing their commitments. We all embrace the same admirable romantic values and standards. This is why a guy is now less likely to end up in a relationship without thinking it through and being certain that it's the best course of action for all involved. He wants to be the best boyfriend, partner, and *man* possible, the one he's always imagined himself to be. And let's face it, you want to be with that guy, too.

So when possible, it's in your best interest to grin and bear this do-or-die freakout when it starts to occur. From a distance. Because you need to give him space, remember? Step back. Keep yourself busy with other stuff. Give him a beat (or ten) to collect his thoughts.

Will a guy ever blow you off and then come back around? Sure. It really does happen sometimes—more often than you might think. But only when you allow him to come back around on his own time and terms. He needs to believe that it is entirely his choice to be with you. He needs to come to the realization that he wants more—and not less—of you in his life.

For example . . .

FIRST COME BLOWOFFS, THEN COME TWELVE MARRIAGE PROPOSALS (WAIT, *WHAT?!*)

One of my favorite interview couples was Shawn and Elaina, a late-twenties husband-and-wife team in Minneapolis. When I say "team," I mean it. As soon as I sat down with them, I could tell that they were a strong, functional, supportive, we're-facing-the-world-together-and-having-fun-while-doing-it unit.

This made the whole story of how they got together even more shocking.

"Our freshman year of college, I was an asshole to her," Shawn admitted while Elaina nodded in total agreement. "Huge asshole. We'd known each other from high school and were friends, and we were randomly assigned to the same dorm and the same hallway. I joined a fraternity, and there was a certain lifestyle that goes with that. I wanted to party and have a good time, and I thought I was too cool. So even when Elaina was always there for me, I wasn't always there for her. She was my rock, and I abused that privilege."

"He called all the shots," Elaina explained. "If he wanted to go to dinner, I would drop everything to go to dinner. But if I wanted to go to dinner, he wouldn't pick up his phone. We were living in such close quarters that it was really difficult. I was so hurt. It was an ugly, vicious cycle."

Despite all his bad behavior, Elaina still felt an impossible-to-ignore connection to Shawn. So how did she handle it? She didn't disappear entirely on him—but she did give him space. She explored her major, made some good friends, and got very involved in her sorority. She didn't try to force a relationship or give him any ultimatums, but she also put the brakes on any romantic or sexual tension they had. She took a step back and allowed him the opportunity to grow up a little.

And grow up he did. As Shawn remembers, "It wasn't until the end of that year that I realized, wow, I'm not happy. The party life only takes you so far."

While working together the following summer, their relationship finally clicked. Shawn stopped being an asshole and realized what had been right in front of him. As he tells it:

"I mean, I grew up. Sometimes you need to have a rough patch to really realize what you have. Like, I got arrested that year, and the only number I could remember was hers. That was a realization, like, wow, I can't even remember my parents' number, but I can remember hers."

Once he realized, on his own time and terms, that he wanted a relationship, Shawn was committed to it. He ended up proposing to Elaina . . . twelve times! Elaina was completely committed to their relationship as well—but once it became solid, she found herself in no rush to tie the knot. At her insistence, they took their time heading to the altar. They focused on strengthening their bond and becoming an established couple in their friends' and families' eyes.

After requesting a raincheck twelve times, Elaina eventually got to the point where she felt that "given our life, and the other things that we were doing at the time, it just kind of fell into place for us to get married." After his twelfth unaccepted proposal, Shawn had told her to just let him know when she wanted the ring he'd bought—so when she came around, he was more than ready.

Now they're happily married and continually building their life together. It's a good thing that Elaina didn't react to the original blowoffs by demanding answers, giving ultimatums, and forcing a romantic commitment when Shawn was living out his freshman-year dreams. It's also a good thing that she spent all that time building up the rest of her life and her confidence, instead of sitting around and waiting for him. Over the course of several years of friendship, Shawn came to the conclusion that he wanted to be with Elaina without any pressure from her. And he's been invested in their relationship ever since.

IF THERE'S MORE GOOD THAN BAD, THEN DON'T CUT HIM OFF

You might have noticed another element of Shawn and Elaina's story: while she didn't push him into anything freshman year, she didn't cut him off entirely, either. When he finally got his head on straight, she was still a presence in his life.

Your friends are probably telling you to never, ever speak to that guy who blew you off again. You only have so much time and love and energy to give, and he's sucking all yours away by not giving you his heart and soul right this very moment. Get rid of him!

I don't believe that, and you don't have to either. If he has blown you off in no uncertain terms, but you still enjoy his company and you're not feeling manipulated or taken advantage of, then why not keep him in your gaggle and see where things go?

Since when is engaging with a guy, even on undefined terms, a bad thing? There's a lot to learn and enjoy from keeping a guy in your life, even if you don't end up marrying him—especially if you've already taken the pressure off and are just (genuinely) enjoying each other's company. Welcome to the gaggle mentality.

If you're still hanging out with your Guy Who Just Blew You Off and truly enjoying it, then ignore the peanut gallery of people telling you that you're destroying your love life. Hang out with him, on terms that feel comfortable to you. Don't make him a huge number one priority. But find a spot for him that is suitable, and then just treat him in the same confident and friendly way that you treat everyone else in your life. Your openness will allow your relationship to progress in an unknown but organic—and therefore healthier—direction.

You are a big girl, and you can you stay in touch with your Guy Who Just Blew You Off without resorting to immature game playing. Don't sit there strategizing how to win him over the whole time and trying to read his mind. Instead regard him as one member of your ever-changing gaggle. Just live your life, rein in the intensity, and let him possibly come to the realization that his life is more fun with you in it. Because, obviously, it probably is.

THAT SAID, DON'T CONVENIENTLY FORGET THAT HE BLEW YOU OFF

We've all had that friend who keeps going back to a jerk. Honestly, most of us have been that girl, at one time or another. It's a thin line between keeping a Guy Who Just Blew You Off in your life and becoming his weak, pathetic plaything.

You must *always* be aware that you are treading this line.

We're not done with Shawn and Elaina. Even as their storytelling progressed to happier times, I couldn't stop putting myself in Elaina's shoes. Shawn had been such a jerk to her during that first year of college. How could she have known that he wouldn't do it again? How could she have known that she wasn't getting played and that he wasn't just making blind promises to keep her on the hook?

The answer is that she *wasn't* sure. She never kidded herself. She never forgot that he'd behaved so badly at a certain point in their friendship. She looked out for herself. And Shawn realized all this as well and fought for their relationship accordingly.

"He had a lot to prove," Elaina remembered. "He really did, and I think he still does, to this day, carry guilt about that period."

"One hundred percent," agreed Shawn.

Yet to Shawn's credit, he handled that guilt, and his growing feelings for Elaina, by deciding, *on his own*, to put his best foot forward.

After a summer spent working side by side, fostering a sexual tension that their coworkers now say could've been cut with a knife, Shawn and Elaina couldn't deny their raw connection any longer. But he knew that he had wronged her in the past, and that she would be taking a big emotional risk by allowing their relationship to turn romantic. He knew that he was working from a deficit. And he cared about her enough to work hard for her, man up, and convince her to trust him and be with him in an official committed relationship.

A key moment in Shawn's fight to prove his devotion occurred once they both returned to college that fall.

"When we got back to college for our sophomore year, it was hard. My guy friends thought I was absolutely crazy for being in a relationship. One of my friends even gave me a ten-thousand-dollar check and asked me to break up with Elaina. He told me that if I ripped it up, then he would know that I was serious about it. And I kept it for maybe an hour—because it was ten thousand dollars!—but then I ripped it up. I never got shit for it again."

Like Elaina, you should be wary of any guy who has already blown you off. Do not throw him back into Boyfriend Prospect territory just because he forwarded you the invitation to a mutual friend's birthday party, and do not enter blindly into an "are we or aren't we?" hookup situation. If he wants to prove that he messed up, fine. Give him a chance to do so. But don't be that girl who likes a guy so much that she'll take whatever she can get.

The painful fact is, we live in a time when it is so easy to get in touch with someone. Guys have your phone number. They have your email address. They have your BBM pin. They see you on Gchat. They're friends with you on Facebook. They're aware of your Twitter feed. Most of the time, you're probably only a text away. So if a guy wants to reach you, and especially if he wants to *fight* for you, then he'll know where to find you.

And if he's not getting in touch? Well, these days, that can be as much of a blowoff as an explicit one. Remember that fact, and use it as motivation to move on even faster. If it makes you angry, that's okay. He should be held accountable for his (lack of) actions.

Overall, be realistic. Don't constantly punish a guy for his actions. That's tiresome and will be a negative energy drain for you. But don't have amnesia, either. If he wants you back post-blowoff, then he's going to need to work hard for it.

DON'T SEE REJECTION AS AN ALL-ENCOMPASSING REFERENDUM ON *YOU*

Let's say that when all is said and done, the Guy Who Just Blew You Off is *actually* blowing you off. He's rejecting you. Your connection and all the potential that came along with it is dead in the water.

How are you supposed to deal? Are you supposed to turn on your go-to Taylor Swift playlist and sob? Curl up in your Snuggie and watch *The Notebook* on repeat, convincing yourself that no one will ever love you the way Noah loved Allie? Binge on retail therapy and buy yourself ten great outfits you can't afford so that the next guy will be sure to love you?

Thankfully, those are not your only options. Instead, you can take a cue from modern men. Even though it can seem like they are always the ones rejecting girls, it turns out that men have all gotten rejected as well, and have become pretty good at moving on. At least, they're approximately 1 percent less likely to crumble into a pile of insecurities and doubts and emotional goo than we are.

A key lesson in how to take rejection came from Jason in Minneapolis, who you met earlier as Maria's go-to Accessory. Remember when I said that he seemed to be getting a lot of action, when not at the farmers market with Maria? More on that.

After hitting up the city's bar scene with him and his friends, I could tell that he had a pretty decent handle on the ladies. It was easy to spot the girls who were into him, and yes, there were several. But he was an incredibly social guy, and I had to imagine that, because he met so many girls, they couldn't all be into him. Right? I asked him.

"Sure, I get rejected. But I don't get offended if a girl's not into me, or if she thinks we should just be friends. All I think is, she clearly couldn't be right for me, because the girl who's right for me would realize that we'd do well together. It's not like I'm sitting here saying, I'm so awesome, they're stupid for not liking me. It's just that the right girl will like me."

Rejection from one person is not a universal statement about your appeal to the opposite sex. Rejection does not mean that you're unattractive or unlikable. It just means that you and that specific person are not going to fall madly in love. And as long as you're cultivating your gaggle, then that person shouldn't be the last one left in your world anyway.

Post-blowoff, shift your focus to the other guys in your gaggle. If necessary, make a concerted effort to meet new guys to add to the mix. If you're still feeing some residual hurt, then fake it till you make it and force yourself to go have fun with other guys, even if you think you'd rather sit on your couch and feel sorry for yourself. Put on some feel-good music beforehand and do everything humanly possible to get a smile on your face. Because other men deserve you at your best and most confident. They're in your gaggle because there's a spark there, and they're *not* blowing you off.

Just think—how much more fun would your love life be if you weren't terrified of being rejected all the time?

IN CLOSING: A WORD FROM YOUR
120-YEAR-OLD SELF

Despite knowing all this, even I still feel hurt when a relationship with a guy in my gaggle takes a wrong turn. I tell myself that it's so unfair, and that I'm a great girl, and that his inability to see that just doesn't make any sense. I'm fun, I'm easygoing, and after a few beers I can speak pretty decent French. Who doesn't want that?!

Apparently, some guys. Bummer.

But after the initial stab to the heart subsides, I take a deep breath and cling to an India.Arie lyric from her song "Ready for Love," which has stuck in my brain for years. A few friends and I used to put it on repeat during college, while longing for perfect boyfriends, convinced that India was speaking directly to us.

(I know how cool this makes me sound, so please—contain yourself.)

I am ready for love,
All of the joy and the pain

After hearing this song for the first time, I was struck by one thought: wait, love involves *pain?* WTF?! Why hasn't anyone made that clear to me before now? But what India was saying is a universal truth. Pain is an integral part of the process of finding true love. It is part of the experience of feeling something so powerful. Experiencing emotions, be they positive or negative, is always a *good* thing. It means that you are alive and open to the world. And the sooner you realize that, the sooner all the ups and downs of your love life will fall into a greater perspective.

Sure, it would be great if every guy in the history of the world fell quickly and deeply in love with you. But that's just not very realistic. Luckily, when you're 120 years old and looking back on your life, you're going to appreciate the richness of experience that came along with every high and every low. You're going to remember having euphoric moments, and you're going to remember having moments where you felt so low that you were convinced you would never, ever put your heart on the line again. And at 120 years old, none of those singular memories are going to feel *that* serious.

So why not start realizing now that your love life is going to hit some rough patches that will hurt but not destroy you? Why not accept that these experiences will ultimately provide color, perspective, and variety to your story?

Rejection, and Guys Who Just Blew You Off, are a part of life. Don't worry so much about them. More importantly, make sure that when you reach your 120th birthday, you can sit back and know that you truly lived. That you took chances, put your heart out there, overcame pain, never played it safe, and always gave your all. Especially when it came to love.

KEY TIPS

For Making the Best Out of a Guy Who Just Blew You Off

1. Give him space. Don't demand answers, explanations, or one-on-one time. There is no better way to get blown off than to put pressure on a guy who is unsure of how he feels about you. Take a step back, put down your phone, and get busy doing something, *anything*, that doesn't involve him.

2. If he isn't giving you what you want but is still bringing more good stuff than bad into your life, then keep him around and in your gaggle. Ignore all those friends who are yelling for you to cut him off completely, and continue to engage with him in a way that seems safe and comfortable for you. Keeping the door open a slight crack might just introduce you to positive scenarios that you hadn't imagined yet.

3. Don't be passive-aggressive. He can tell, and it makes you look desperate. This means no calling him "Stranger" or uttering "Long time no speak!" Rise above those impulses like the awesome (and sane) woman you are.

4. If you *do* decide to keep him in your gaggle, just be smart and realistic about it. Don't think of him as a Boyfriend Prospect. Don't expect him to fulfill all your emotional needs. And remember, if he wants to become a key player in your love life again, then he should have to fight for it.

5. Don't see rejection as a huge referendum on you. When you're the one doing the rejecting, you're not necessarily deeming some guy universally unlovable, are you? You're just acknowledging that he's not *the* guy for you. Realize that one guy's opinion about you has very little to do with how other men will feel. Trust that other guys will be right around the corner, and that the right one for you—whether you know him yet or not—will fight for you when it counts.

THE CAREER BOOSTER

> A professional contact who makes your work or school day a bit easier. He offers access to power, resources, inside information, and an expanded network—or just helps you fix the copy machine—in exchange for a little extra attention.

There's a lot of overlap between the professional circles that I run in, particularly in the political arena. As much as you would say, "I'm not going to date where I work," when I was working at the Capitol, it's just such a culture, and everybody's in it, and everybody's around each other all the time. So the folks you work with, they become your friends, and you go out with them.

I was recently seeing a man who, again, came from my work circles, and politics is all he wanted to talk about. We would end up just defaulting to that, and I would constantly be like, "I don't want to talk shop, I don't want to talk shop." I finally had to tell him, "Look, I eat, sleep, and breathe politics. I don't want to come home and fuck politics!"

—Alexandra, 34, recruiter, Austin

MEET YOUR CAREER BOOSTER

In a brave new world where women are dominating classrooms and boardrooms and finally (albeit slowly) filling the top ranks of Fortune 500 companies, a woman's professional network has never been more vital to her success. Enter the Career Booster.

This guy may work three cubicles down from you or in an office across the country, but regardless of the mileage, you know that stopping by his desk on Monday morning to chat about his weekend or emailing him with a quick congratulations on his team's latest success may lead to a tip on the company's exciting new project, a coveted spot as his plus-one to the latest buzz band's concert, or an invitation to grab drinks with him and his friend, a young Web designer with whom he thinks you'll really click. You may not be attracted to the Career Booster, or you may simply be resistant to engaging in a romantic entanglement so close to the office. But you figure that a little fun banter is harmless and all part of breaking into the boys' club that still dominates most industries.

The Career Booster can also be the guy at your office who acts as your fan and your friend, adding an extra bit of support and fun to your otherwise stressful day. You can always depend on him to let you cut the line at the photocopier, grab you a midafternoon coffee on his way back from lunch, or listen to you vent when your coworker tries to take credit for the presentation that you were up all night working on. In turn, you champion him in his quest to win the latest promotion and sympathetically offer to help when you notice him trying to train his new assistant to use the scanner. This mutually supportive dynamic (see the Work Wife in the guy's gaggle for more) allows you both to stay relatively sane and positive at the office, even as you encourage each other to excel and reach new heights of professional success.

Of course, this is not the 1980s and you are not living on the set of *Working Girl.* You are careful to make impressions with your charm and wit and never with your body or the promise of sex. But climbing the career ladder is a sometimes complex and frustrating journey, and having your own cheerleader definitely seems to make the process more enjoyable.

HOW TO HAVE A CAREER BOOSTER

You were probably raised to believe that you could grow up to become anything in the world that you wanted to be. An astronaut! A movie star! A criminal lawyer! A fashion designer! THE PRESIDENT OF THE UNITED STATES!

(For years, I apparently went around telling people that when I grew up, I wanted to be "a doctor and an elephant." I cannot recall one person telling me that this path was unlikely—just further proof that our generation was constantly taught to reach for the stars, at all costs. Even if that meant shifting species.)

What is the inevitable by-product of this unconditional support and ego stroking? Boundless ambition to accomplish whatever you, as a unique individual, put your mind to. This means that you want to achieve at your highest level and fulfill your own personal potential to the max. ASAP. You want to innovate, in your own particular way. You don't want to be a cog in a wheel; you want to reinvent the wheel!

You may not be willing to toil for years and years in one job or at one company, biding your time until someone up above feels like giving you a promotion. Yet you are willing to work your ass off for causes, companies, and goals that you believe in. Long hours, an extra graduate degree, off-the-clock brainstorming, on-the-side entrepreneurial ventures . . . you throw yourself into projects you care about. You do whatever it takes when it comes to your passions and aspirations.

That all sounds great, right? Except for the fact that a lot of your hard work and laserlike focus is required in your twenties and thirties, right around the time when you're *supposed* to be figuring out your love life.

Think about it. Look at your schedule. Where do you spend the majority of your time?

At work. And gosh, it would be a damn shame if your gaggle lay dormant during all those hours, wouldn't it?

Well, thank goodness we striving, ambitious women are such talented multitaskers. We've got our jobs, but we've also got our gaggles. And as it turns out, men go to work, too.

Career Boosters to the rescue.

THE CAREER BOOSTER IS BASICALLY INEVITABLE

The unique dynamics of the Career Booster relationship were best laid out for me by Vanessa, the Austin girl we met with the toxic Ex-Boyfriend Who's Still Around. Her tales of working on the campaign trail and at the Austin Capitol reminded me of my own time working in the music industry—and they'll probably remind you of your time in any job that you gave your all to.

"Working on a campaign or at the Capitol is really awesome, and really horrible," Vanessa explained. "It's like wearing beer goggles. You're stuck with the same people constantly, working ten, twelve, fifteen hours a day in a little office, and you don't have time to meet anyone outside of it. It's your entire life. That's why campaign hook-ups are kind of a given. But I also know people who are in long-term relationships or married to people who they met on campaigns now, too. It can work both ways!"

Vanessa's observations were reflected throughout my nationwide interviews with happy couples. Many of them met at work. And of course they did! That's where they were spending most of their time and exploring their passions.

Aside from these effects of timing and proximity, there is an interesting quirk involved in workplace dynamics that can also play into your connections. In your personal and social life, you get to choose who you spend time with. But at work, that decision is made for you. And this can bring unexpected guys into your gaggle.

End up on a project with a male colleague, and you're going to be in each other's faces for the duration of the task. Get assigned a cubicle next to the new guy, and you're going to find yourself turning to him for support during a crappy day (or curiously peeking over the divider when you hear him laughing over a funny YouTube video). Crash your computer, and you're going to become best friends with the IT guy.

You care about your job. He cares about his job. You're often sharing a space or a goal or a group of coworkers or a pain-in-the-ass boss. Your friends (and the other guys in your gaggle) might not want to talk about your company's new social media strategy or those ridiculous shorts that your intern insists on wearing to the office. But that guy at work gets it. What a relief!

Here's some advice: you should get to know your Career Boosters better. While some of them may not initially be your type, they absolutely belong in your gaggle. You shouldn't be surprised when they become a huge part of your day, and maybe even your out-of-work thoughts. Because when you share interests and passions and networks and knowledge with someone, the potential for true connection is ripe.

THE CAREER BOOSTER IS A HUGE PERK IN YOUR DAY-TO-DAY LIFE

There are many facets of your professional life that are worth exploring, and your Career Booster can play a variety of roles in your development. For those of us who aren't quite a CEO yet, this may involve him escorting you down the path from bright-eyed, bushy-tailed ingénue to savvy, knowledgeable force-to-be-reckoned-with in your industry. In other words, your Career Booster may help you learn how to do your job, or at least do it better.

Take Eliza, a practice manager for an independent financial advisor who works in the Atlanta area. Smart, ambitious, and competent, she had recently started a new job when I met her, for "a real ballbuster" of a boss in an industry about which she knew nothing. We've all been there, right? Everyone has had some job that makes you feel like a clueless, panic-stricken idiot. But were we all lucky enough to have a Career Booster like Eliza's?

Meet Vendor Boy.

"I just started a new job in October, and it has been hell," Eliza admitted to me during after-work Friday drinks. "Vendor Boy works for one of the insurance companies we do business with, and he is my go-to guy when I don't know what the fuck I am talking about. Which is frequent for someone like me, who majored in journalism and is now working in finance. I know this might come as a shock to you, but I do not fully understand anything I currently do."

Been. There. Done. That. Having relied on my own version of Vendor Boy at my first office job, I could relate. So how exactly did Vendor Boy help Eliza out?

"He lives halfway across the country, but basically, I would not have a job if it weren't for him. He has unending patience for my ridiculous questions, and his sense of humor helps me get through every crisis I seem to encounter. Every afternoon, while the boss is away, I call him with a new horror story about how I messed something up or how ridiculous the intern was. And my favorite part? The way he answers the phone when my number pops up. Like he is genuinely happy to hear from me. And he always does his best to cheer me up and tell me I am good at my job."

There is no doubt that Eliza will one day actually *be* good at her job. But during this steep learning curve, her Career Booster has been there to support her and convince her that all hope is not lost when she mistakenly puts an undesirable call through to her busy boss.

Like Eliza, we are all strong women. We don't need men in order to succeed at work. But despite our tenacity and pride, it's okay to embrace offers of help and support. There's nothing wrong with letting someone make us smile, even just for a moment, during a stressful day at work. And sometimes that someone just happens to be a guy who appreciates our talents and wants to see us succeed.

And so, the Career Booster is a major plus in your gaggle. But don't take advantage of him! This should be a mutually beneficial work relationship. He has your back; make sure that you have his, too.

THE CAREER BOOSTER TEACHES YOU ABOUT YOURSELF

Conventional wisdom has it that men are intimidated by your ambition, smarts, and success. The media claims that your odds of finding a guy diminish with each pay raise. And now that you're getting a little older, your mother suddenly seems a bit worried about that, too (yes, the same mom who once forced you to do your homework and encouraged you to reach for that stellar job . . . weird). You've maybe even contemplated pulling a Miranda (*Sex and the City* alert!) and downplaying your job in order not to risk scaring guys away. You keep hearing that your professional awesomeness makes men feel less awesome about their own accomplishments, and that causes them to be less attracted to you.

Laaaame . . . but, is it true? Your Career Booster would beg to differ.

Sometimes, you might need a wakeup call that our generation of men can handle your ambition and intelligence. Because many of them can. They may have moments of confusion or uncertainty about their own professional journeys, but don't we all? Their ups and downs don't have to make *your* successes a romantic deal breaker. Go ahead and tune out anyone who would argue otherwise.

Instead, tune in to the story of the most ambitious woman I met in all of the Midwest: Amy, a twenty-seven-year-old marketing manager at a major multinational corporation in Minneapolis. Still in a sleepy coma after having dragged myself out of bed for our pre-work breakfast meeting, I was shocked to find Amy mentally alert, dressed for success, and ready to take over the world. At 7:30 a.m. After a holiday weekend.

This girl meant business. And as it turns out, she meant it at work and in her personal life.

"I feel like, starting out as a young woman, there's a divide: you're either going to be married to your job or married to your life," Amy explained. "There are the types who will go and get married, which happens here in the Midwest when you've been dating someone for a while and are ready to settle down and be a mom, blah, blah, blah. Then there's the flip side, where girls want to prove that they're career-driven and have to act so dominant, and pretend, 'I don't need a relationship, I don't want to get married, and I would never admit to wanting those things because it would be embarrassing, like a weakness.' And you're supposed to choose one or the other."

What path has Amy chosen?

"I want to do both! I'm ambitious, and I can see that my job gives me a sense of self-esteem that I can't get from another human being. But I've finally gotten to the point where I can admit that I want a relationship, too. You see more and more women starting to do both, and wanting it both, and I feel like it's okay to want it all. Yes, I want kids. Yeah, I want a demanding job as well. And I want a *great* husband. I think that's asking for it all, and I don't really care!"

Sitting there talking to Amy, I was inspired. Not only was she excelling at the office, but she had also just become "exclusive" with a great new guy. She was heading down all the right paths. Interestingly, her Career Booster had been along for the ride this whole time.

As Amy told it, "I call one of my oldest guy friends my 'career builder.' He and I go to breakfast a lot, that's our favorite thing to do. I'll go to him with work issues and say, 'Tell me your thoughts on this!' Because I absolutely trust his opinions, and he makes me feel good in that way."

What makes Amy's Career Booster a member of her gaggle, and not solely a professional sounding board? The fact that he wouldn't be quite as helpful and supportive if she were a big, old dude. There's still the teeniest, tiniest spark between them. A slight hint of ambiguity— but healthy ambiguity.

"I've never even kissed him, but he's a great-looking guy. I would talk him up to any girl," swore Amy. "But as compatible as we are, I still know my boundaries. I think I'm smart enough to know which buttons I'm pushing. Like, I only text him on weekdays. Anything more isn't my place."

Despite their professional compatibility, Amy and her Career Booster probably won't end up together, especially now that she's committed to another guy. But her Career Booster's insights have been critical to her growth, and even critical in her decision to give her new guy a try.

"Right after I met the guy I'm dating now, I went to my Career Booster," Amy recalled. "And seeing him verified my thoughts on the new guy. Not that the new guy would replace him, but that he could do the work thing as well. And I have more of a sexual pull toward him. But professionally, he also finds it interesting that I'm so into my job. I was, like, okay. What my career builder has, this new guy's got it, too."

After years of relying on networking-non-dates with her Career Booster, Amy truly understood what it felt like to be professionally supported by a guy and realized that this support was a requirement of any guy who was seriously going to date her. Luckily, she's now found a guy who fulfills her professional needs *and* turns her on in other, less PowerPoint-oriented ways.

Sounds like a post-dating promotion to me.

THE CAREER BOOSTER IS (SOMETIMES) A PRECURSOR TO DRAMA

You're ambitious—and since your job takes up so much of your time and thoughts, it seems like nothing could be better than connecting with a guy who fits into your professional sphere. Just remember: when that relationship goes sour, nothing could be worse.

While connections with Career Boosters should be cultivated with enthusiasm, they should be consummated with caution. Breakups, hookups, and unrequited Facebook flirtations are awkward by nature. Have them take place at work, and you may find yourself hiding in the storage closet, crying in the bathroom, or hurling expletives at the company holiday party. Not good moves for your career or your sanity.

For those of us who are pursuing our professional dreams in a workplace setting right this very moment, I offer a reminder: don't enter into workplace romances lightly. Don't unnecessarily complicate your professional relationships, and don't risk alienating supporters and colleagues. If you are exploring an intense connection that feels worth the risk, then fine. If it's love, then great. But for anything less, keep that Career Booster in your gaggle and go find a fantastic Boyfriend Prospect (or Hot Sex Prospect) elsewhere.

KEY TIPS

For Cultivating a Career Booster

1. Expect the importance of your Career Boosters to be proportional to the importance of your professional aspirations. Having lots of ambition will probably cause you to interact with lots of Career Boosters. Be ready to embrace them!

2. Really get to know the guys at your job and in your field—even if they're not your type. Long hours and similar passions often lead to surprising but genuine connections.

3. Absorb all the advice, knowledge, and cheerleading you can get from Career Boosters who are willing to help you improve your skills and make you feel more confident about your capabilities. We all need a little help!

4. If your Career Booster plays a major role in your life, then make sure that your next relationship is with someone who also supports and challenges you professionally. This is a core value for you. Keep an eye out for it.

5. Think twice before transitioning a Career Booster into a Boyfriend Prospect (or Hot Sex Prospect). If there's a genuine, undeniable connection there, then give it a try. But if your interest is simply arising out of fun or boredom or curiosity, then look elsewhere in your gaggle. Don't unnecessarily risk the workplace gossip, alienation, and drama that can ensue.

THE BOYFRIEND PROSPECT

> A legitimate romantic prospect who treats you with respect and seems to have long-term relationship potential. The one to watch!

Oh my god, I'M SO CRAZY ABOUT HIM!
—Becky, 28, WTF?! cofounder, Brooklyn

MEET YOUR BOYFRIEND PROSPECT

This guy is legit. He's really making an effort to get to know you, and you've both been taking it (relatively) slow. If you were to introduce him to people as your boyfriend, you're pretty sure they would think, "Ah, yes, that's exactly the kind of guy that I expected her to end up with." You have a lot in common, and he seems to be lacking the blazing warning signs that accompany most of the guys you like. You're not exactly writing his name all over your notebooks or declaring relationship status on Facebook yet, but the Boyfriend Prospect is the one to watch.

You might feel some pressure surrounding the Boyfriend Prospect, as you recently let your excitement get the best of you and have mentioned him, albeit briefly and with a choreographed nonchalance, to your friends, your parents, and your waiter at the local sandwich shop. Of course, *you'll* be the most disappointed if he ends up flaking in some major way, after you've allowed yourself a few ten-second daydreams about joining his family for their next annual ski weekend or showing him off at your upcoming college reunion. But you also know that he will be the guy everyone asks you about until they hear that you officially are or are not dating. Here's hoping that he continues to be as great as he has seemed so far!

HOW TO HAVE A BOYFRIEND PROSPECT

Ah, the Boyfriend Prospect. That guy who gives you butterflies and fuels your daydreams. His very existence makes getting up in the morning just a touch more exciting, and don't forget that warm, fuzzy feeling every time his name pops up in your inbox. You don't want to jinx it, but you might just be falling in love soon . . . like, any day now . . .

Sigh. Wouldn't it be great if every guy in your gaggle was a Boyfriend Prospect?

Actually, it can be tempting to think that every cute guy you meet *is* a Boyfriend Prospect. This is what traditional dating lore would have you believe. But in fact, your gaggle—and your entire personal journey toward love—will be much more fulfilling if you are able to differentiate between true Boyfriend Prospects and guys who belong in the rest of your gaggle. If you can acknowledge that some guys are not your Boyfriend Prospect, then your connection with the guy who *is* will be that much more thrilling and likely to work out.

Of course, every guy in your gaggle is a Boyfriend Prospect for one millisecond or another. That's the entry point to your gaggle— when you meet a guy, the first question you'll end up asking yourself (even if only during the first three seconds) is, "Do I *really* like him? Could he become my boyfriend?" If the answer is yes, then he's your Boyfriend Prospect. And if it's no, then you'll mentally shift him to another spot in your gaggle where he belongs.

Out of all the guys with whom you have some connection, which one is your Boyfriend Prospect? And since finding love is the ultimate goal of having a gaggle, what choices can you make with a Boyfriend Prospect that will leave you with a great, committed guy at the end?

First things first: run through this checklist and make sure that the guy in question is, in fact, a proper Boyfriend Prospect. If he's missing any of these points, then you're dealing with another gaggle guy and you should shift your mind-set accordingly!

A guy is your Boyfriend Prospect if:

☑ You *Really* Like Him.

You're striving for the best of everything—and that includes romantic relationships. You're not desperate to call just any guy your boyfriend or to end up in any ol' relationship. You don't want to settle. You want to find deep, true, exciting, epic love.

Do a gut check and ask yourself: Am I at least on the road to having very strong feelings for this guy? Does my attraction to him feel different than what I feel for the rest of the guys in my gaggle? Is there a *chance* that real love could be on our horizon?

If he doesn't tap into your emotional side, then he shouldn't be your Boyfriend Prospect. Very few things in life are as exciting as having an honest-to-god crush. Don't settle for anything less with your Boyfriend Prospect.

☑ When You Look Ahead, All You See Is Possibility.

Sure, you might see logistical issues. Distance, maybe. Inconvenient timing. Religious differences. Perhaps you're living in *West Side Story*, and he's a Shark and you're a Jet.

But when it comes down to the very raw, core connection between the two of you, the potential should feel unending.

You should *not* already be fixating on traits of his that annoy you or on personality quirks that you believe are going to make you incompatible over the long term. If you're going to be looking into the future anyway (and let's be honest, so many of us do once we meet a great guy), then you should be able to see a future with your Boyfriend Prospect and feel excited by what you see. It should be pretty easy to envision what a relationship with this guy would be like, and what a kick-ass couple you would become.

☑ He's Treating You Like a Potential Girlfriend.

This guy's treatment of you is key to the Boyfriend Prospect dynamic—and it can be tough to admit when it is missing. But if you avoid being honest with yourself here, then you're likely to end up massively disappointed and maybe even broken-hearted. So ask yourself: Is he treating me like I would want a boyfriend to treat me?

Your Boyfriend Prospect should be acting like he really likes you. This is a guy who you're considering building a relationship with—so he should be behaving like someone who is ready and willing to be in a relationship. He should be showing you that if you did in fact end up together, he would treat you with respect, consideration, and a massive amount of excitement that you chose him to get dinner with, or to text before falling asleep at night.

This doesn't have to mean that he's professing his undying love or taking you on helicopter rides across rainbows (unless you are on *The Bachelor*, in which case, there should definitely be helicopter rides). There doesn't have to be a date involved. But he needs to be treating you well. Ideally, he should be actively trying to impress you by putting his best foot forward.

You might not want to hear this, but even if you *really* like a guy, you should not be thinking of him as your Boyfriend Prospect if he's telling you, or giving you signs, that he's not ready to consider being your boyfriend. Take what he's saying at face value. If he says that he's not looking for a relationship, then that's fine—keep him in your gaggle and see where it goes. But at that very moment, kick him out of the Boyfriend Prospect role. He may be a lot of things, but at the moment, he's not boyfriend material.

BE YOURSELF AND DON'T TRY TOO HARD TO IMPRESS HIM

You really like a guy, you recognize the limitless potential of your connection, and you feel like he's treating you well. Great! He's your Boyfriend Prospect.

What next?

If you're going to turn your mutual interest into the relationship of your dreams, it has to be based on a strong connection—and not on games or tricks or manipulative theories about how to get a man to propose to you. It has to be based on two people being themselves, letting their walls down and being drawn to each other at their realest, deepest core levels. Hint: non-dates are great for fostering and exploring this kind of connection!

Many of the happy couples I met went one step further and actually had crazy "I never thought I'd meet somebody like that!" stories. Maybe they met on a group-non-date at a holiday pub crawl, where they were wearing ridiculously unattractive costumes or, as one Chicago girl's story went, "a Santa hat and a Christmas sweater that was three sizes too big for me and had penguins ice skating across it." Or maybe they connected through networking-non-dates at work, where they were too busy and stressed to put on their "sexy" vibes. Maybe they had their first play-non-date after dominating the kickball field, where dirt and bruises and ponytails brought their guards down a notch.

In any case, in these tales, the walls are often lower than usual at the very beginning and the fronts aren't fully up in place. These couples started off a bit more exposed, casual, and truly themselves than they usually were—and their relationships were the better for it.

Regardless of how you meet your Boyfriend Prospect, you should try to conjure a genuine dynamic. When you like a guy, it can be easy to convince yourself that you need to be at your best around him, all the time. But actually, based on the many stories I've heard, sometimes it's when you're at your worst—or at least, your weirdest or silliest—that true connection is able to break through.

If you're worried about your undone hair or your stained T-shirt, compare yourself to Alexa, an Atlanta girl who was in a great relationship that all her friends couldn't stop raving to me about. She attributes her relationship to one crazy weekend with her now-boyfriend at a St. Patrick's Day festival that included forgetting her phone, losing her luggage, wearing one outfit for multiple days, getting her period in his friend's borrowed pajama bottoms, spending time in Walmart looking for tampons, and facing a tornado and subsequent power blackout.

Yep, Alexa's story wins. And did I mention that this all happened the second time she and this guy had hung out?

I'm not saying that you have to court utter disaster in order to connect with your Boyfriend Prospect. But just realize that if Alexa's catastrophic weekend can turn into a relationship, *anything* can. So don't stress too much about what to wear, what to say, and what you need to do to win his interest. Put on that ridiculous outfit for the theme party. Meet up with him for a drink even after a stressful day at work that's left you frazzled and spacey. Share your quirks with him, purposefully and passionately. The more real *you* are, the more real your connection will be.

PUT YOURSELF OUT THERE

Not only should you be sharing yourself with your Boyfriend Prospect, but you should be pushing yourself with him as well.

Having a gaggle can be a pretty convenient way to play it safe. You can rely on Ego Boosters for comfort and validation, seek easy thrills with Hot Sex Prospects, and have deep conversations with harmless Unavailable Guys. You can feel fairly fulfilled, without ever having to step outside of your comfort zone.

Your Boyfriend Prospect should be the one exception to this. He should sort of scare the crap out of you.

You say that you really like your Boyfriend Prospect, right? There's real potential there. So take some chances! Force yourself to be vulnerable with him. Stop obsessing over whether you should send him that text and *just do it already*.

If things are moving a little too slowly with your Boyfriend Prospect, or you're worried that you're headed in a nonromantic direction after all, take a deep breath and be the one to give it a go. Do you really want to live with the thought that you might have missed out on an amazing connection? You don't need to push the envelope and face rejection with every single member of your gaggle. But with your Boyfriend Prospect—do it. Tell him you like him. Pay for the plane ticket to go visit him. Ask him to meet you for dinner. Show him that you have feelings for him, and that, yes, you feel like there's something special there.

There's a good chance that he's thinking the same thing.

WHEN IN DOUBT, FOCUS ON HAVING FUN TOGETHER

Relationships are supposed to be fun! And that fun should be part of the journey from Boyfriend Prospect to boyfriend. With all the pressure and expectation wrapped up into the word "relationship" though, it can be easy to forget that.

In Portland, I met Eva, a twenty-one-year-old student who had gotten married just a few weeks earlier. She was physically glowing as she talked to me about her new husband and how happy they were together. So I was a little surprised to hear that, at first, a relationship hadn't really been on the table for them. They'd met at a party in Brooklyn and instantly clicked. But . . .

"I stayed over the first night we met, and it was really cute and awesome and beautiful and moving," she described. "But he immediately said to me, 'Listen, I don't commit to anything, and I don't have any intention of this lasting.' Of course, I was anxious about that. But then I thought to myself, 'Okay, this is going to be as long as it is going to be, and I'm just going to enjoy it until it ends.'

"So I just kept enjoying it. And after that, we hung out every day. It was *him* calling, saying, 'Can we see each other? Can we see each other?' And things just changed! He stopped being scared about factoring me into his plans, and we went on to be a couple without even saying anything about it. He'd never had a relationship like that. Now it's two and a half years, and I'm the happiest I've ever been in my life."

I'm not saying that you should invest all your time in a guy who isn't ready to commit. But when you really like a guy and things take a slight turn for the unclear, sometimes you should just chill out and enjoy whatever you have. Stop thinking and planning so much, and just keep him around in your gaggle and see what organically develops instead.

In the post-dating world, labels can often fall a step behind what is already happening between two people. How many couples do you know who were obviously a couple before they officially started calling each other boyfriend and girlfriend? Instead of worrying about titles, whenever you're feeling impatient about the pace of your relationship with your Boyfriend Prospect, take a step back and have some fun together. Focus more on the connection part than on the label part—and watch as your connection naturally gets stronger.

And, of course, continue investing in the rest of your gaggle while you do all this! Your gaggle will help give you the patience and perspective you'll need to feel confident in whatever is going on with your Boyfriend Prospect. And I hear that some of those guys can be pretty fun to hang out with, too.

KEY TIPS

For Cultivating a Boyfriend Prospect

1. When you first meet a guy, ask yourself, "Could he be my boyfriend?" If not, then decide where else he lands in your gaggle for now. The gaggle is evolving, and he could always end up back there at some later point!

2. Make sure that a guy is worthy of being your Boyfriend Prospect. This should mean that you have real feelings for him, that you are not already envisioning the end of your relationship, and that he's treating you with respect and clear interest. If not, I can't repeat this enough—find another spot in your gaggle for him.

3. Don't succumb to the worry that your Boyfriend Prospect will only like you if you're perfect. Lower your walls and show him all the normal, quirky, and humorous sides of yourself. Only then will you be able to build the true kind of connection upon which the best relationships are founded.

4. Put yourself out there, and take some risks with your Boyfriend Prospect! Be vulnerable. Risk rejection. Avoid regret. This guy, above all gaggle guys, is potentially worth it.

5. Focus on enjoying each other's company and developing your connection, instead of on figuring out how to make him your boyfriend. A relationship will evolve naturally, if you're genuinely having fun together and simply don't want that fun to end. These days, labels usually come second. Stop stressing about them!

THE PROSPECT YOU'RE NOT SURE IS A PROSPECT

A maybe prospect who consistently sends you mixed signals, sometimes showing romantic interest and other times treating you with platonic ambivalence. His unpredictable actions probably drive you a little crazy but keep you intrigued and guessing.

There's a guy I met through online dating. He and I had the same interests. We slept together the first night, which was probably a bad idea, but whatever.

But then . . . it was like these platonic lunches. We would just have lunch, have a good time. No kiss or anything. It was his idea and he would pay. But I'd already slept with him! So I was just confused.

Then he disappeared for a while. But soon he came back and was really flirty and making all these sexual innuendos. And I was like, fine, let's hang out. And he would be like, when's good for you? And I would tell him, and then he'd be like, well, I'm sorry, those aren't good for me.

—Shanna, 26, teacher, Austin

MEET YOUR PROSPECT YOU'RE NOT SURE IS A PROSPECT

Your male friends will tell you that this guy is definitely a prospect, because really, can guys and girls ever truly be platonic friends? But despite their reassurances, you're not yet convinced that the Prospect You're Not Sure Is a Prospect is interested in you in a romantic way. Sometimes he seems notably excited to hear from you, and then other times he treats you with the same polite interest and attention that he shows everyone else in the room. You can't help but be confused when he invites you out for a drink but then spends a sizable portion of the evening filling you in on his latest romantic escapades. And you still don't know what to make of the party where he never left your side but then went home without even saying good-bye. Is he interested and just a little flaky? Or does he simply value you as a platonic female friend?

The Prospect You're Not Sure Is a Prospect is full of mixed signals, and you're never quite sure what his intentions are. However, he is definitely in your scene and on your radar, and you proceed cautiously but with interest, not letting yourself read too much into his compliments, dinner invitations, and the fact that he told you about his latest break-up before sharing the news with anyone else. You think there might be something there—if only you could get a more consistent read on how he sees you.

HOW TO HAVE A PROSPECT YOU'RE NOT SURE IS A PROSPECT

God, grant me the serenity
To accept the things I cannot change,
Courage to change the things I can,
And wisdom to know the difference.

The Serenity Prayer is a timeless plea, not only for religious folk and alcoholics, but for girls with gaggles, too.

If you've had a Prospect You're Not Sure Is a Prospect, then you've probably prayed for *something*. For clarity, maybe. For a sign that this guy is, in fact, in your gaggle. For faith that your confusing on-and-off connection will actually go somewhere.

I can often tell when a woman and I are about to start discussing her Prospect You're Not Sure Is a Prospect. The stories about this gaggle guy always take a while to get through, because there is no clear beginning, middle, or end. They are always a mix of "So he said X . . . but then he did Y, and I was like . . . WTF?! And at that point,

I was totally over it—but then he invited me to Z, although then he didn't even show up. So I figured Q, but my friend says that he meant W, but I mean, what if he was thinking V? Ugh. I don't know!"

Unfortunately, trying to read a guy's mind and suss out the meanings behind his mixed signals tends to be a frustrating waste of time. The more you try, the more likely it is that you will experience a moment of exasperation that leads to desperation. In a fit of emotion, you might even send him a passive-aggressive text or unsubtly show up at the store where he works or, god forbid, drunk dial him at 2:00 a.m. (and don't tell me you've never been that girl—we *all* have).

Bad idea. You are above all that—and the truth is, you are not crazy. The bipolar connection between you and this guy just is. And there is always hope! Thus, I want to leave you with a new prayer.

From now on, I want you to ask for the serenity, the courage, and the wisdom to deal with the Prospect You're Not Sure Is a Prospect in your gaggle.

SEEK THE SERENITY TO CHILL OUT AND TRUST IN YOUR CONNECTION

When a guy is sending you mixed signals, it's all too easy to get caught up in the drama and confusion of the situation. But remember: you *always* have a choice to stay sane. One hundred percent of the time! Throughout every single interaction. You can freak out about the ambiguity and stress yourself out by performing the mental gymnastics of "Does he like me? Why can't I tell?" Or you can recognize the mixed signals and relax, shrug your shoulders, adopt a bemused smile, and think with a chuckle and a good-natured roll of your eyes, "Well, this should be interesting!"

No guy, no matter how confusing his actions may be, can drive you crazy if you're not willing to be driven crazy. And on the flip side, any guy can drive you crazy, maybe without even meaning to, if you're determined to find drama in every Facebook status update . . . or if you're set on convincing yourself that he's just not that into you.

Next time you're tempted to overanalyze your Prospect You're

Not Sure Is a Prospect, remember that choice—and choose serenity. Choose to relax, and then alleviate any unnecessary pressure that you may be tempted to put on the situation.

If your connection is real, then you should trust that it will manifest itself in an organic way at the right time. Don't get stuck on the details of how he should be acting or what he should have said, if he really liked you.

Real-life example: are you upset that he didn't text you *personally* to invite you to his birthday party, but just sent you the Facebook invitation like everyone else? Well, who cares! A guy's initial intentions matter much less than what actually happens in the moment. Just pick an outfit that makes you feel confident, show up to that birthday party, commit to being your best self, spend some time with him, and let your connection do its thing.

If your relationship takes a step forward that night, then no one will remember how the invitation scenario went. Allow your connection to flourish, and the mixed signals will be nothing but a humorous footnote in your epic love story—because it's your connection, raw and real, that's going to propel you to the next stage of that tale.

Is this sort of laid-back attitude easy to pull off? Of course not. But I would recommend adopting the perspective of Rachel, the Chicagoan who earlier taught us about the art of appreciating Super Horny Guys.

When I met her, Rachel and her Prospect You're Not Sure Is a Prospect had been dancing around a palpable flirtation for over a year. They Gchatted all the time—but never hung out one-on-one. He asked her for advice about other girls—but then claimed to never really like them. He had hooked up with some of their mutual friends—but had never made a move on her. He invited her to a wedding during a drunken friend-non-date—but then awkwardly backed out when she emailed him to follow up about it later.

Rachel's conclusion was simple: "I cannot figure him out at all!"

And of course she couldn't! Just hearing all their back-and-forth made my head spin. But unlike some of the other women who I'd come across (and been, in my weaker moments), Rachel was just so calm about it. Perplexed, yes. But stressed, no. Her relaxed hands rested around her coffee cup. Her forehead remained uncreased. Her phone remained in her purse. She was a picture of ease.

"Yeah, yeah, it's all very confusing," she confirmed. "He's definitely somebody who, you know, there could be something there. Something may happen. Maybe one day, something will click, and we'll both be on the same page. But I'm also not forcing anything. I'm a planner, but right now, my whole mantra in life is just to be there, and to not get caught up in always thinking so much about things. I want to be there, be happy, be in the moment, and see what happens. And that's exciting! It's so fun to think that way."

I felt like I was sitting with a Buddhist monk! Despite classifying herself as "extremely single" at the very beginning of our interview, she seemed exceptionally serene. Her casual outlook was inspiring.

Rachel wasn't overanalyzing, and she wasn't wasting precious time succumbing to the insecurities that might present themselves if she let herself obsess over her Prospect You're Not Sure Is a Prospect. She was using her time and energy to advance her career, play golf, celebrate her sister's graduation, hang out with her friends, and meet me for coffee. And of course, to enjoy her relationships with the other guys in her gaggle.

There's a lesson here: when facing a Prospect You're Not Sure Is a Prospect, adopt Rachel's attitude. Go Zen. Be calm. Recognize the confusion that he's throwing your way, and choose to *not* get flustered by it. Neutralize it. Refuse to add fuel to his fire. You can find much better uses for that energy and focus.

And most importantly, if you still feel that hint of connection with him—keep him around and in your gaggle. Don't check in on him every other day or try to become his best friend, but explore your connection when the opportunity arises. And while this is all happening, view the ambiguity as entertaining and intriguing, and not as a mind-fucking deal breaker. You may not be able to change his actions right now, but you can change how you react to them.

Which brings us to . . . finding the courage to change the things you can.

SUMMON THE COURAGE TO ALTER
YOUR RELATIONSHIP

Only you can be sure of that moment when your Prospect You're Not Sure Is a Prospect's indecision (or his unintentional cluelessness) becomes too much of a pain to handle. And, yes—any time a guy in your gaggle causes you more stress than fun, you should consider making a change.

But even when you've totally had it with this guy, you don't necessarily have to cut off all contact with him. Having a gaggle is supposed to make you feel empowered about the relationships in your life. Running away from every guy who doesn't immediately make his intentions clear does not equal empowerment. It just equals insecurity.

If you're dissatisfied with your Prospect You're Not Sure Is a Prospect, then take charge. Try to make your relationship more to your liking, and see how that goes.

First, decide who you'd like him to be in your gaggle. Have you been secretly harboring real, potentially long-term feelings for him? (Boyfriend Prospect.) When you're bored in your bikram yoga session, do you fantasize about ripping his shirt off? (Hot Sex Prospect.) Do you find yourself smiling like crazy when you catch him charming your friends during group outings? (Accessory.) Are you just dying to pick his brain about your latest work project? (Career Booster.)

You get the point! If you could make him any guy in your gaggle, who would you want him to be?

Now, try to make him that.

You certainly can't force a guy to inhabit a particular role in your gaggle. There are no tricks or magic sayings that will hypnotize him into wanting to be your Ego Booster. And you probably aren't feeling too eager to make some big first move, like asking him on a date or pushing him against a wall and kissing him, since the intense ambiguity in your dynamic can make rejection seem a bit too possible. But you *can* foster settings that might make him feel more, shall we say, inspired to act in certain ways. Pick the non-date scenario that sounds most enticing to you, and instigate it.

And who knows—he may have been wanting to push your connection in that direction the whole time! He may have been thinking that his signals were clear, or that you weren't into him, or that he was just going to avoid the possibility of outright rejection for one more day (and then another, and then another). In the post-dating world, there are endless opportunities for men and women to rely on vague interactions instead of obvious and open signals. Sometimes it just takes one person—you!—shaking up the dynamic to actually make things happen.

THE WISDOM TO KICK HIM OUT OF YOUR GAGGLE (IF NECESSARY)

If a guy's mixed signals and unclear intentions are really, truly driving you crazy and detracting from your day-to-day satisfaction, then guess what? You're allowed to cut him off and spend that energy on less perplexing guys instead. It's *your* gaggle and *your* call.

You're a busy woman. If you know what you want, and you know how you want a guy to treat you, and a particularly confusing connection isn't going anywhere, then be wise and let it go. Feel free to stand your ground. You have a right to be choosy about the guys who populate your gaggle.

Ultimately, just be realistic and smart about how much ambiguity you're willing to tolerate, and then pick and choose the guys who make it into your gaggle accordingly. Don't be afraid to say, "Sorry, dude—I *am* sure that you're not a prospect, and not actually in my gaggle." Trust me, it'll be his loss.

KEY TIPS

For Cultivating a Prospect You're Not Sure Is a Prospect

1. Don't blame yourself for letting your Prospect You're Not Sure Is a Prospect confuse you, but don't fall into the trap of obsessing over every interaction and trying to read his mind, either. You're human, but you're also not an overly analytical psycho. Maintain your rationality and sanity!

2. Stop comparing his actions to how he *should* be behaving or his words to what he *should* be saying. Try to take him at face value and trust that, as long as you both are exploring your connection by continuing to talk or hang out, your dynamic might blossom organically and at a speed that works for both of you.

3. Remember that he is just one guy in your gaggle, and use that perspective to embrace serenity and an amused openness toward his ambiguous efforts to connect with you. The clarity of his interest is not a life-or-death issue. Your romantic happiness does not entirely depend on him. So when in doubt, laugh at his antics, roll your eyes, and keep your love life moving.

4. If the mixed signals begin to truly frustrate you, then decide who else you'd like him to be in your gaggle and start shifting your dynamic accordingly. Feel empowered to make a change and create a different type of relationship with him—or at least summon the courage to test the waters and see if that's possible!

5. If you're totally fed up with his games and his indecision, and if it's primarily making you feel upset, then be wise and cut him out of your gaggle. There are other guys out there who will be clearer in their intentions and interest, and they deserve your attention and a spot instead.

WTF (*WHERE* THE F*CK)
IS MY GAGGLE?

"Is there any sort of 'singles' scene in Green Bay?"

"No! It's . . . ugh. Really, going out to the bars is, like, the only way."

"Well, do you have guys in your life who you're not dating? Maybe guys who are just friends?"

"No. Not unless they're gay! There's really not . . . My friends' husbands, I guess? I'm pretty much the only one of my friends who is single. I don't know anybody who is single. It's hard."

—Marissa, 28, nurse and mother of two, Green Bay

I often wince when women tell me, "I want a boyfriend!" or "I want to be in a relationship!" or "I want to get married!"

Why? Not because the attainment of these goals is undesirable (of course not—we all want to find incredible love). Nor do I think it's impossible. It's just that these goals are daunting. They are tough to pursue right this very moment. If you're sitting here today, unattached, then it can seem unlikely that tomorrow, you'll have that boyfriend or relationship or marriage squared away and ready to go. Just the scope here can be intimidating enough to make you feel overwhelmed and throw your hands up in hopeless exasperation, opting to spend the next few days ordering copious amounts of Chinese food and catching up on TMZ gossip instead of investing energy in your love life.

But if you tell me, "I want a gaggle"? Done! You can get started on that right now.

I have met women throughout my travels who, even after hearing about every single type of guy in the gaggle, don't think they have one. Not many women, to be honest. Usually, those who think they don't have a gaggle start realizing that they do know some of these guys, once we start going category by category. But there are some women who go through the list and still come up empty.

In some cases, there are extenuating circumstances: maybe they recently got out of a long-term relationship, or moved to a new city, or currently work at an all-encompassing, all-female job, or live in a small town where everyone else seems to be in serious relationships. In other cases, women have clung so tightly to the rules and expectations of traditional dating that they have cut off every man who doesn't meet their husband criteria. Or in some cases, they have found themselves confused about how to connect with guys who are not explicitly trying to date them.

Regardless of the circumstances, some women don't have a gaggle, but want one. Here's how to make it happen!

STEP ONE: CONDUCT A GAGGLE INVENTORY

Start off by making sure, one more time, that you don't already know at least one of the guys in the gaggle. I admit; to this day, I have downtrodden moments where I feel like I don't have a gaggle. But then I force myself to do a Gaggle Inventory. And every time, I realize that my gaggle actually does exist—and it just needs a little cultivating.

Doing a Gaggle Inventory is easy: just run through the ten categories and ask yourself if there's any guy in your life who is currently filling that role. Or maybe there's a guy who hasn't played a big part in your life lately, but who might be just one email or text away from getting back into the mix and potentially playing that role. You'll often be surprised by who pops up, when you force yourself to open your mind to the guys around you and also to think back a bit to the guys who might be just out of your immediate reach.

But let's assume that even after your Gaggle Inventory, you truly believe that you don't have any guys in your gaggle. Ever the proactive woman, you can start changing that ASAP.

STEP TWO: MEET GUYS

This is the one moment where my advice might seem to dovetail with more traditional dating theories.

Here's some tough-love advice: you can't beef up your gaggle and learn about yourself and fall in love and all that great stuff without, you know, actively living in the world. Maybe you work really hard at your job all day and then you like to go home and watch TV with your roommate. Me too! But if you're wondering why your love life is boring, well, that's not rocket science, is it? You need to meet people. People with Y chromosomes. Don't make me tell my bowling story again!

You don't have to meet new guys with an eye toward dating them. You're not dragging yourself to a Western-themed singles mixer hoping to spot the man of your dreams in the middle of a line dance, or joining a running club (even though you hate running) in order to snag an athletic husband, or creating profiles on OkCupid, eHarmony, *and* Match.com to ensure that you don't happen to pass by the one and only guy for you (but what if he's on Plenty Of Fish?!).

Remember your casual non-dating mind-set, and adopt the perspective that you will not deem your socializing efforts a failure if you don't end up with a date for Friday night. Keep in mind that in the post-dating world, you're just trying to meet guys who could eventually play some sort of role, big or small, in your gaggle. No big deal. No huge pressure.

But meet guys you must.

Follow the best piece of advice that we all hear about meeting guys: do stuff that you already like to do, but do it socially. Do you read political blogs? Volunteer on a local campaign. Is your diary overflowing? Join a writing group. Are you a diehard fan of your local football team? Put on your jersey and watch the game at a sports bar with friends instead of in your living room. Did you go to college? Hit up an alumni event. Think you're funny? Take some improv classes. And in the meantime, show up at as many of your friends' birthday parties, group dinners, haphazard drinks outings, and lazy days in the park as you can. Expand your circles through their friends as well.

Just make sure that you inherently enjoy the activities you choose so that your plans don't end up feeling like a huge disappointment and waste of time if a Boyfriend Prospect doesn't immediately show up.

And where does online dating fit in to all of this? Especially since it has become the go-to "solution" for how to spice up a supposedly nonexistent love life? Well, I hesitate to recommend online dating as a method of getting things going. Because let's be honest: the fun factor here is not exactly off the charts. I've done it, as have many of the women and men I interviewed and know. And while it absolutely works for a lot of people, you often have to sift through an intense process of intricately crafted opening messages and awkward formal dates to get to the fun stuff. The potential for disappointment if you *don't* meet someone you really like can also be disheartening.

But hey! If you're in a rut and are looking to add some new people to the mix, then do online dating, too. It can be a great reminder that there are, in fact, guys out there, and that you have not met all of the eligible ones yet. As long as you're not relying solely on online dating as a quick romantic fix, and as long as you're pursuing every other social option you can think of as well, then perusing some other possibilities online is certainly not going to hurt.

Okay, you're meeting some boys! Great. Now, what to do with them?

STEP THREE:
EXPLORE EACH GAGGLE POSSIBILITY

For a while, you should be thinking of *every* new guy you meet as a prospective gaggle member. That does *not* mean you should be putting pressure and expectations on your interactions with him. It just means that you should feel empowered to try and push your connection forward in a way that feels appropriate and interesting to you. And you shouldn't feel like you have to wait around for him to take the initiative and become a real part of your life.

Once the pressure of dating is off the table, and once you're not looking at every guy as is-he-or-isn't-he boyfriend material, it should feel much easier to establish more casual relationships that will allow you to enjoy yourself and test the waters a bit.

Nervous about having to take the initiative? Do it anyway! This is your love life. No one else is going to take responsibility for it. And besides, these moves that you'll be making can be pretty small. You're not jumping off a cliff. You're simply stepping over a pothole.

And remember to explore your connections with more than one guy at a time. If one dude doesn't seem to be responding to your mostly friendly overtures, then whatever. He was just some guy who was potentially going to end up in your gaggle. Or not. Who cares! Moving on.

So take matters into your own hands and do whatever you would do if you wanted to simply become friends with someone. Send him a Facebook friend request. Include him on a big group email about an upcoming outing. Offer to lend him a book that reminds you of your conversation. Stop by his desk on your walks to the office bathroom. Encourage your mutual friend to invite him on your next night out. Pick a non-date option that sounds feasible to you, and make it happen.

Once you start interacting with him on some sort of regular basis, you'll quickly see where he falls in your gaggle—if he ends up being gaggle-worthy.

STEP FOUR: REPEAT!

As soon as you've got two guys, you've got a gaggle. And the more you get accustomed to thinking in gaggle mode, the more you'll meet new guys and start doing all this naturally, and the more your gaggle will expand and multiply. Soon you'll also be moving in new circles, and meeting new guys in those contexts as well, and then suddenly one day you'll realize that you're living in a world of post-dating plenty. And that's a beautiful feeling.

Remember poor Marissa in Green Bay from the opening of this chapter? The nurse and mother who didn't think she had a gaggle? It turns out that I probably should have walked her through her Gaggle Inventory more thoroughly when we met—because she definitely had one!

Mere months after our interview, I heard that Marissa had gotten engaged (Wow!). I asked her: Did she and her fiancé meet at one of the local bars she'd been frequenting? Did they find each other on Match.com, which she had been using at the time? Neither guess was correct. Instead, Marissa and her fiancé had met three years earlier. They were neighbors who had been living two doors down from one another the whole time.

After spending a full year floating around each other's gaggles, they suddenly fell in love. As Marissa said in her update to me, "Sounds kind of crazy, considering I've been looking for the perfect guy ALL OVER the place, and here he is, right next door! He really is an amazing guy. My advice to other women dating in smaller areas would be to look for the boy next door!"

And the gaggle strikes again.

Of course, the funny thing is that even when you think that you don't have a gaggle, you're almost definitely playing a role in some guy's gaggle. Or many guys' gaggles! Because, oh yeah: you didn't think that only girls have gaggles, did you?

Ha! Men have been exploring their wants and needs (and finding love) via the gaggle for much longer than women have. The roles that women play may be entirely different (there's no Super Horny Girl in the guy's gaggle), but being aware of a typical guy's gaggle can help you to better understand your relationships with the men in your life.

So then, who are *you* in *his* gaggle?

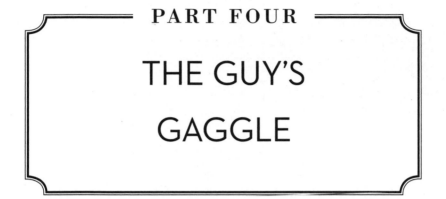

PART FOUR

THE GUY'S
GAGGLE

BRACE YOURSELF:
GUYS HAVE ONE, TOO

Talked to @jessmassa a few weeks ago about my nonexistent "Gaggle."
Turns out it's actually quite large. Fuck.
— @barringtongiles, 26, filmmaker, New York

A guy's gaggle? What must that involve, like, three categories? The girl he'd like to marry, the girl he'd like to fuck, and the girl he'd like to kill?

(Okay, "kill" sounds really extreme here. But we've all played that game while waiting on line at amusement parks, right? For the record, I'll go with marry Ryan Gosling, fuck Ryan Reynolds, and kill Ryan Seacrest. But that's just me.)

I questioned the extent of the guy's gaggle myself, when I first set out to discover the roles that girls might be playing in it. Women are complex; we all know that. But aren't we taught that men are simpletons? Aren't they brutes who just love to sit around and drink beer and talk football and sneak off to watch porn? And when it comes to women, don't men just meet them and instantly make the very basic decision: Do I want to hook up with her? Yes or no? 0 or 10? Hot or not?

Well, yes . . . and no. As I learned throughout my interviews, men often do think that their love lives—and their feelings about women—are simple. Many of them have also bought into this cultural stereotype that men exist in a world of black and white, while women drive ourselves crazy in our confusing world of gray (and sepia!! and mauve!! and teal!! . . . or is it aquamarine??).

As Peter, a thirty-two-year-old MBA student in Austin, told me:

"We believe ourselves to be simple beings, easy to figure out—and you guys, the females, are the ones who are difficult and have all the complex emotions. We believe ourselves to be nonemotional, one-track-minded, pretty straightforward to please sexually . . . simple."

But what else did Peter admit to me?

"I don't think that's actually true."

And here's where things get fun.

Most of the guys whom I interviewed initially assumed that their methods of categorizing women were basic. And sure, whenever they met a girl, the first thing they tended to do was register her level of attractiveness (see: Is she hot or not? Is she a 0 or a 10?). But what I found by listening more closely and connecting the larger dots was that, after this point, their interactions with women got more complicated.

Right from the start, I began discovering more categories in the guy's gaggle than even I had expected. And then a funny thing began to happen.

As I started to unearth the specific roles in the guy's gaggle, I would interview a guy, and he would tell me stories about the women in his life. I would suggest where they might fall, and we would discuss and debate.

And then, after the interview—sometimes hours, sometimes days later—that same guy would follow up with me. I would get an email or call or text or Gchat, telling me that he'd been thinking about it further and, in his opinion, I had possibly forgotten a category. Or two. Because you see, he was just talking to this girl, and he realized that they had *this* type of dynamic, and it was different than all those *other* types of dynamics, and here's how he felt about it . . .

These guys all thought that they were the only ones reaching back out to me. Just like so many of them told me, with a hint of shame and embarrassment (infused with a touch of pride), that they were the *only* guys who overanalyzed their love lives. Other men were actually simple, they assured me. According to each of these guys, he was the only exception.

But none of these guys were the exception. Introspection and overanalysis were the rule. And once I prompted them to start pondering the different roles that women were playing in their lives, it was like many of them couldn't stop. Because unlike us women, who regularly sit down together and psychoanalyze our love lives for sport, many of these guys just hadn't had anyone to talk to about all this. They had essentially shut those parts of their brains off, choosing instead to bond with their buddies over jobs and baseball and politics and movie quotes and whatever other surface-level subjects they felt comfortable shooting the shit about.

That said, while I was obviously thrilled by their enthusiasm and emotional outpourings, I still ended up having to turn down many of their suggestions—because really, the guy's gaggle couldn't have forty-seven categories, could it?

All this proved one thing to me: in this post-dating era of expanded networks, ambiguous interactions, and technological connectivity, guys' social and romantic circles have become just as complex as women's. So much so, that they now seem to be cultivating relationships with ten types of women as well.

And now here we are, ready to delve into the guy's gaggle. There are some strange waters ahead of us. Trust me, I was as shocked as you will be when I first saw the complexity, depth, and seeming contradictions within the male gaggle.

First of all, prepare yourself for the fact that the guy's gaggle is more inherently based on sex and sexual attraction than the girl's gaggle. Yes, there are more categories here than you probably expected, given the traditional belief that men are solely sex-and-offspring-driven creatures who either want to bang you, marry you, or blow you off. But that's still where their heads are at, most of the time. It just turns out that there are many different ways in which they want to bang you or marry you. Or hang out with you at work. Or use you as fodder to entertain their friends. Or treat you like a queen. Or slowly fade out of your life. Or put you on a pedestal to serve as a symbol of the great man they are trying to become . . .

As with the girl's gaggle, guys rarely have all ten types of girls at one time. The guy you're thinking of might have three Short-Term Investments, or two Girlfriend Prospects, a Last Resort and a Crazy Girl, or a whole cheerleading team of Friends He's Just Not That Into. Each guy's gaggle is its own unique entity.

BUT FIRST, A PUBLIC SERVICE
ANNOUNCEMENT

Before we reveal all, let's take a cold, hard look at how you should incorporate these ideas into your own love life. This is powerful information about guys, but we must use this power for good, and not for neuroses-fueled evil. We must *not* focus all our attention on figuring out how to become this or that girl in some guy's gaggle.

Most traditional dating books would be happy to provide you with their version of how to play the game and snag the man (remember, do X and Q to get *him* to do Y and S, but wait, stop, oh no, DON'T DO Z!).

That is not what this book is about. Leave all those well-worn tips about how to please a man at the door.

The most important thing for you to take away here is that *you* have a gaggle. This journey is meant for you to figure out who you are, what your needs and desires are, where your tendencies lie, and how you usually behave. And of course, where guys—and *the* guy you will ultimately end up with—can fit into all of that.

Yes, when you meet someone, it will be incredibly helpful to understand where you fit in his gaggle. But then the question will be, what do *you* want to do with that? How does that jibe with your own gaggle, and your own needs and desires, and your feelings for him within all that?

Cultivating your gaggle is a complex, somewhat circular process, and knowing more about each particular guy and where he stands is a big part of the enlightenment that the gaggle can provide. But at the end of the day, you shouldn't be obsessing over his gaggle and changing yourself to fit into it. He is in *your* gaggle. Being aware of your role in his gaggle can help you put all those pieces together and feel more empowered to make smart, informed decisions about your relationship. But the focus should always, always, always come back to you.

Okay! Glad we are all on the same page. And now, I present to you . . . the guy's gaggle.

THE GIRLFRIEND PROSPECT

A girl who he meets and immediately thinks, bam!—girlfriend material. While he probably isn't making the mental leap to marriage and kids yet, he knows that this girl deserves more than a drunken hookup, and he is courting her as such. Can he imagine spending lazy Sunday mornings with her and introducing her to his friends and family? Sure. Is he looking past the next few months? Whoa, now let's not get ahead of ourselves here.

My family's opinion is really important to me. So I know that I'm thinking of a girl as a potential girlfriend if I can already see myself introducing her to my parents and all of my brothers and sisters. I don't introduce them to a lot of girls.

Past that, I guess it's when I want to hang out with her on weekends. And it's always a good sign when I can imagine still finding her interesting for at least the next couple months. But past that, I mean, I don't think any further than that!

—Steve, 27, financial analyst, New York City

UNDERSTANDING THE GIRLFRIEND PROSPECT

Here's one way to explain it: a guy is thinking of you as a Girlfriend Prospect in *his* gaggle if he's acting like a Boyfriend Prospect (or Ego Booster, yikes!) in *your* gaggle.

When you are a guy's Girlfriend Prospect, you can often just tell. Not necessarily because he's asking you out on dates or declaring his love with roses and ponies, but because he's pursuing you in a relatively clear way. He's not making you work hard for his time and attention.

If a guy sees you as a Girlfriend Prospect, then does that automatically make him your Boyfriend Prospect? No! You get a say in this, too. The timing might be off on your end, or perhaps you're just not quite feeling it. Sometimes the nice guy really does finish last.

But not always. The nice guy can absolutely finish first as well. I heard many stories of guys making a strong positive impression on girls—girls who wouldn't have given them a second thought otherwise—*because* they were treating these girls like Girlfriend Prospects. Amidst the ambiguity and mixed signals of the post-dating world, the clear, flattering, mature attention of a guy who sees you as a Girlfriend Prospect can feel great.

HOW TO KNOW IF YOU'RE HIS GIRLFRIEND PROSPECT

He Is Asking You to Hang Out

If you are his Girlfriend Prospect, then he wants to explore your connection *now*. So he'll be trying to hang out with you *now*.

He might ask you out, like on a real date! But we are dealing with modern men here, so don't count on it. And anyway, who cares? The exact way in which he requests your time doesn't matter. It's the post-dating world: there are no straight-up rules here.

Case in point: I interviewed some guys who make special efforts to ask a girl to hang out in advance if she is a Girlfriend Prospect. But then I met other guys who told me they'd be more likely to hit up a Girlfriend Prospect at the last minute, to save their egos the potential blow of being outright, undeniably rejected by a girl they really liked ("She must have already had plans for tonight, and that's why she couldn't stop by the party I invited her to at 5:00 p.m.").

The point being, how he asks you to hang out is irrelevant and dependent on the guy. But if you're his Girlfriend Prospect, then he'll be asking. Even if you're also texting, emailing, and poking each other on Facebook, he's still going to invite you to join his soccer team, try to meet up at the concert you're both attending, or find an excuse to sit down for coffee. He likes you! He maybe-sorta wants to consider being your boyfriend, perhaps in the near future. So he'll want to start exploring that possibility now, in person. Romantic time's a wastin'.

He's Willing (and Maybe Even Excited) to Do "Boring" Stuff with You

Think about what it feels like to have a real crush. You want to do interesting, exciting things with that person, of course. But you also kind of want to do just about anything with them! You just want to be around them. Even the prospect of getting together to do the boring stuff in life can sound more tempting than catching a play or having a nice dinner with someone who you're not as into.

Not to mention that actual relationships are filled with boring, day-to-day stuff. And if you're seriously considering entering into one with someone, then it doesn't hurt to make sure that all that boring stuff will be more fun with them around.

If you're a guy's Girlfriend Prospect, then he won't only want to see you when you're looking your best and planning your most fascinating activities. He'll want to see you . . . whenever.

Take Peter, the Austin guy who admitted to me that men are not always as simple as they seem. A reformed player who had spent his twenties "chasing a high and looking for a thrill," Peter had recently decided that he wanted a girlfriend. And how did he envision that relationship?

"I'm looking for something very stable—you might almost call it boring," Peter declared. "Where we can go grocery shopping, or watch TV, or read—just joke around and be comfortable without having to make an event around it. Just sit in footies watching *Glee* and making fun of it. Fat, dumb, happy, and bored together."

Yep. Those are the kinds of things that boyfriends and girlfriends do together. So if your guy seems just as up for making a casserole as he is for an exciting night out on the town, then that might be a sign that he's imagining many more nights like that with you. As his girlfriend.

He's Trying to Show You What Kind of Boyfriend He Would Be

When I sat down with Jackie, an accomplished twenty-eight-year-old media executive who had been living it up in San Francisco for most of her twenties, she had just started getting to know a guy who clearly considered her a Girlfriend Prospect. How could she tell? Well, as she described it, he had immediately stood out in her gaggle for trying to prove that he could fill the role of every *other* guy in her gaggle.

"I feel like he's trying to show me all these different sides of himself," she explained. "When we talk, he points out everything we have in common. When I was going through a work crisis, he was emailing me suggestions and being supportive. When a group of us went out to dinner, he was being attentive and sharing his food and catching me a cab. And he touches me constantly. I feel like he's saying, 'Look at what a good boyfriend I could be!'"

If your guy is embarking on a full-court press to put on his best potential boyfriend show, then you're his Girlfriend Prospect. Especially if . . .

He Talks About the Future

And by future, I don't mean the real future. Not years, or even months, down the line. Don't be silly! I'm just talking about the typically male version of the future: you know . . . maybe a few weeks from now.

Most men are not known for making advance plans—at least not in their personal lives. So if he is mentioning events in the future (read: two whole weeks away) and hinting that you should be involved in them, then he's not planning on pulling the slow fade any time soon.

Jackie noticed that the new guy in her gaggle was doing this, too. "He's always bringing up these vague future plans!" she exclaimed. "Like, 'I might get tickets to this football game next month, but I don't know anyone who likes football.' Or 'I'm thinking of having a dinner party in a few weeks.' It's actually nice. It shows me that he's not just trying to hook up with me and then leave it at that."

Does he seem to want to hang out with you now—and in the future as well? This is good. This means that he's appreciating your personality and your company as much as he's appreciating the way you look in tight jeans, and wants more of all of the above.

KEY TIPS

For Increasing Your Chances of Becoming His Girlfriend Prospect

Demonstrate what an awesome, multi-faceted girlfriend you would be! Any girlfriend of his is going to be present in many areas of his life—so show him how much better all those areas would be with you around. A night out with his friends? More fun with you there cracking jokes. That work problem he's going through? Easier to handle with you as a sounding board. *Breaking Bad*? More tempting to order On Demand with you cuddled up next to him. Let him feel and experience how great it could be to spend more time with you, and see if he does the math.

For *Not* Becoming His Girlfriend Prospect

If a guy is showing you Girlfriend Prospect interest and you're not into it, then don't lead him on and don't take advantage of his attention. Respectfully turn down his invitations to hang out one-on-one, stop responding to every email, and nicely but firmly reject any generous favors that he may offer. As guys often told me, when they're interested in a girl, they'll look for an "in"—so don't give him one.

THE WORK WIFE

> A close colleague who is a fun and feminine presence at work. By day, he hangs by her desk, emails her to laugh about the latest officewide email, grabs her for afternoon coffee breaks, and Gchats her with updates on the sales report he just nailed. By night, he keeps his distance but never leaves his BlackBerry too far away. Who knows when he'll think of something work-related that only she'll understand.

I have a few Work Wives. I guess you could call me a work polygamist! But there is one special person I could not survive the hours of nine to five without. She's always up for happy hour or a midday Starbucks run, is willing to exchange no fewer than a hundred daily emails, and fully understands when I complain about my boss. We bond over work gossip, consult each other on office décor, and give performances at the annual Christmas party that are worthy of Dancing with the Stars.

I know that she dates other guys, which we talk about, but it doesn't bother me. Within the office walls, we're inseparable. Our colleagues tell us we should date all the time. The secretaries are convinced there's an impending engagement. But when work can be miserable enough as it is, why ruin a good thing?

—Jacob, 28, lawyer, New York City

UNDERSTANDING THE WORK WIFE

Married men often turn to their wives for day-to-day support. A guy needs advice; he asks his wife. He has a new idea; he tells his wife. He can't believe what that dumb neighbor said; he vents to his wife. He ate a good sandwich for lunch; for some reason, he thinks his wife would care to know that. And in return, hopefully, he provides the same support for her.

So it should come as no surprise that men often seek out a wife in the workplace, where many of them spend most of their time. We'll call her the Work Wife!

Having a Work Wife isn't about having a cute girl to flirt with during lunch (although there may be a little of that, too). It's about having a go-to, usually on the same professional level, for pretty much everything in the office. Cranky bosses, ridiculous emails, brainstorming sessions, gossip about the new assistant: a guy could turn to the dude in the next cubicle for that. *Or* he could rely on that female co-worker who not only gets it, but also laughs at his jokes and cheers on his successes and looks cute in a button-down. Right. Clearly the Work Wife is the more desirable option here.

Unlike a girl's relationship with her Career Booster, a guy's relationship with his Work Wife might be more immediate and office-based, and less connected to grander ideas of ambition and personal development and professional identity. Yes, your near-constant presence at work will inevitably affect the more complex aspects of his career path. You're not simply the Joan Holloway to his Roger Sterling, building him up all day so that he can take on the world. You've got way too much Peggy Olson in you for that. You're his professional and personal equal, and he knows that.

But when it comes down to it, his motivation to get close to you is probably not that deep. You just make his workday a whole lot better.

HOW TO KNOW IF YOU'RE HIS WORK WIFE

He Talks to You at Work a *Lot*

There are forty-plus hours in a workweek, and if you're a guy's Work Wife, then odds are that he's spending quite a few of those hours chatting with you.

Not every guy who buzzes your extension thinks of you as a Work Wife. If you're his Work Wife, then the communication should be regular and ongoing. He's not thinking twice about giving you the running commentary on the events of his workday, or changing his route to the meeting so that he stops by your desk. Checking in with you should feel like part of his routine, similar to grabbing his morning coffee or reviewing his assistant's to-do list.

If you're his Work Wife, then he sees you as a fixture in his day. Not only does he rely on you for regular support and validation, but his professional sanity partially depends on you.

When He's in the Office But Not at Your Desk, He's Keeping in E-Touch

A guy might not be lucky enough to sit right next to you all day, but why should that pause the conversation? Technology to the rescue! Even if his workspace is nearby, he'll probably still be hitting you up online. How else can you gossip about your coworkers in real time without them hearing you?

Gary, a twenty-seven-year-old software developer I met in Chicago, told me the story of how he relied on e-non-dates to bond with his Work Wife. When they first met, Gary had recently gotten out of an eight-year relationship. He was ready to meet some girls and start experimenting with life as a single man. Unfortunately, the art of approaching women felt "completely foreign" to him. After asking other guys for advice and finding most of it to be "asinine crap," he turned his efforts to one of the easiest social settings out there: the workplace.

Gary's story was a typical office story. He and "the girl in the green dress" both started in a new department at the same time. They bonded over her decision to order a Bass ale when some coworkers went out for happy hour. And then the conversations continued at the office.

"We crossed paths a lot," remembered Gary. "I always made a point to say something to her whenever I saw her, and kind of playfully make fun of her. And she gave it back to me.

"But the majority of our relationship was fostered through email.

We had this long email chain that lasted for a month and a half. I have it saved, just for sentimental reasons."

Email chains, BlackBerry Messenger conversations, IM sessions—they are all e-non-date tools for a guy to continue being in touch with his Work Wife while he's (cough cough) supposed to be doing work. So if your inbox is blowing up, then you'd better be ready to embrace those Work Wife duties.

You Are His Unofficial Plus-One to All After-Work Events

Is the work crew going out for drinks after a long day? You have to come! Has the company put together a softball league? Come *on*, it'll be so much fun. Is he dreading that birthday party for your strange coworker? He'll stop by your desk and you guys can grab a quick bite before heading over together.

Half the fun of socializing with coworkers is getting to laugh and gossip about it later. If you're his Work Wife, then he's going to push for you to be there, by his side, for all those work-related outings so that you can debrief afterward. The CMO's karaoke rendition of "My Heart Will Go On" *must* be reviewed and assessed, right? Cue the next-morning email chain.

But Your Connection Is Rarely Explored Outside of Work Settings

If you don't hear from him as often on nights, weekends, and sick days, that's okay. You're his Work Wife. He spends all day talking to you. So he's probably spending all night and weekend cultivating the rest of his gaggle.

Of course, guys often end up further exploring their connections with Work Wives outside of the office, for all the reasons that you, too, are drawn to your Career Booster. But if that starts happening on a regular basis, then you're no longer his Work Wife. Your relationship has evolved. And you're now playing another role in his gaggle.

KEY TIPS

For Increasing Your Chances of Becoming His Work Wife

Make yourself more of a presence in his workday and start giving him more opportunities to act as your Career Booster. Stop by his desk on a regular basis, forward him an office email with a funny thought, ask for his advice on an assignment, chat him up at happy hour, invite him to grab a midday coffee, or offer a friendly ear when he's struggling with a project. Aim to become one of his trusted people at the office and, if there's a connection there, he'll start consistently seeking you out as a balance to his stressful day.

For *Not* Becoming His Work Wife

If you want a guy to stop bugging you at work, gently blow off his overtures and tell him that you're busy, you know, doing work.

On the other hand, if the problem is that you're getting tired of your relationship's strict work-only boundaries, then reach out on off-hours and find things to talk about that don't revolve around the job. Shake up the norms of your dynamic by texting him on a Sunday, inviting him to a nonwork event, or introducing him to friends of yours who don't work with you. Make him a part of your nonwork life, and you may naturally become part of his, too.

THE SHORT-TERM INVESTMENT

One of the hottest girls on his radar—for now. He is very attracted to her on a physical level, but for whatever reason, he doesn't see her as girlfriend material, and is already pretty sure that true love just isn't in the cards this time around. However, that's not stopping him from putting in the work to keep her in his life (or, really, in his bed) for as long as the attraction lasts. It's not love, but it's certainly lust.

When I first moved to New Orleans, I was this guy with an Irish accent who just wanted to hook up with American girls. There was one girl that I was seeing. I met her during Mardi Gras, and she was a nice girl, but we didn't have much in common intellectually. But we hit it off physically.

She wanted a relationship, and I wasn't interested in a relationship. But I really wanted to keep sleeping with her, so I purposely avoided any relationship talk and just kept stringing her along.

I knew I was avoiding tough questions. I knew I was avoiding discomfort. I knew that if I was honest with her, that would probably be the end of it. But I was a bit selfish. I was getting something out of it, and I was happy.

—Charles, 28, entrepreneur, world traveler

UNDERSTANDING THE SHORT-TERM INVESTMENT

Ask any financial advisor, and she will tell you that your investment portfolio should be diverse. You should have long-term investments, which are typically the foundation of your plan. Those are the kinds of investments that take a long time to grow, but because their value is so high, they can yield a substantial payout down the line. And then you should also have short-term investments. These are the investments that might have lower yields and might not be part of your core plan years or even months down the line. But in the meantime, they make you some extra money and help you to deal with your pressing financial needs as they occur.

Another perk of short-term investments, from the investor's standpoint? They can be liquidated quickly. In other words, you can get out almost as quickly as you got in, with as little muss and fuss as possible.

Do you get where I am going with this? Substitute "guy's gaggle" for "investment portfolio," and you'll see the grander implications for your love life. Men are likely to invest in a diverse array of women, but it would be a mistake to assume that all of those investments are equal. And knowing which type of investment you are is important in understanding where you fit in a guy's romantic portfolio.

As I pieced together all the stories I had heard from men and women during my interviews, I had a realization. There was a role in the guy's gaggle that had the potential to be fun, empowering, and *hot* for the woman inhabiting it. The role didn't fit into an easy box; it almost never led to relationships, but it also wasn't founded upon quick-and-dirty booty calls or long, drawn-out "I bet they're going to fall in love at the end of this" friends-with-benefits scenarios. It wasn't true love, but it wasn't disrespectful no-strings-attached sex, either. It was something in the middle of all that.

This role—said by many men to be the most common in their gaggles—is the Short-Term Investment. It is based on a guy's temporary but very real physical attraction to a girl. It's kind of like the guy's version of the Hot Sex Prospect—except that often, a guy will put in more effort for his Short-Term Investment than a girl would for her Hot Sex Prospect.

And therein lies the conundrum of the Short-Term Investment. Because as soon as I figured out that it existed, I saw the ways in which men pursued (invested in!) these women. And I realized that women have been taught to misread these actions as signs of deeper, more long-lasting interest. We have been taught that these actions signify our status as long-term investments. And this fundamental misunderstanding constantly causes women serious confusion and heartbreak.

When you are a guy's Short-Term Investment, there are two trajectories that can take shape. On one trajectory, this guy is your Hot Sex Prospect. You both have a fantastic time getting it on during your play-non-dates. You appreciate each other in the realms of attraction, passion, and chemistry. Eventually this not-so-emotionally-deep connection is bound to fade, but without either of you taking too much notice. Not a bad deal, right?

But on the other trajectory, you misread this guy's signals from the start—in accordance with everything you've been taught to believe about how interested men act—and you assume that he is pursuing a full-blown relationship with you. You build up a host of expectations and assumptions. You swear that he is the Boyfriend Prospect in your gaggle. And then suddenly, seemingly out of nowhere, he begins slowly morphing into the Guy Who Just Blew You Off, and you find yourself exclaiming to your friends in a frustrated panic, "Everything seemed to be going so well, and he seemed so into me, and then all of a sudden he just disappeared and started getting flaky and now he won't answer my calls or texts. What could have happened? What did I do wrong?"

The answer is usually—nothing. You did nothing wrong! Except not realize from the beginning that you were his Short-Term Investment.

If only you had known the whole time, you could have read the situation accordingly and enjoyed it for what it was—or opted out, if you weren't feeling it. At least now, after absorbing some of the (brutally honest) intel that I got from my male interviewees, you'll know how to spot the signs that a guy sees you as a Short-Term Investment and not a Girlfriend Prospect.

Here's the number one thing you need to know: if you are a guy's Short-Term Investment, then he is going to pursue you in ways that have traditionally signaled that he really, truly *likes* you. You're going to be meeting him for drinks, texting with him consistently, and going out for pleasant brunches the morning after you hook up. And all this will happen regularly, and with respect. A booty call you are not! This boy is working for it.

This is why, if you don't know better, you'll begin thinking of him as your Boyfriend Prospect. You'll say to yourself, "This is fantastic! This guy is pursuing me, he's hanging out with me, and he's attracted to me. We must be one step away from falling in love!"

When, in fact, you are not. Because all this time, the guy is acting primarily out of a desire to explore a sexual dynamic with you, not a desire to be in a relationship with you.

Danger! What we've got here is a failure to communicate. Because as you will see, the distinctions between how a guy treats his Girlfriend Prospect and how he treats his Short-Term Investment are very subtle, but very telling.

HOW TO KNOW IF YOU'RE HIS SHORT-TERM INVESTMENT

He Is Trying to Hook Up with You

The very foundation of a guy's decision to see you as a Short-Term Investment is his physical attraction to you. He thinks you're hot. *Really* hot! He feels physical urges around you. He visualizes you naked. He wants to hook up with you. And he is going to invest however much he thinks he needs to, in order to make that happen.

If you are a guy's Short-Term Investment, then he will not hide his attraction to you for very long. He will not invite you on multiple networking-non-dates or spend months commenting on your Facebook statuses. He will go for it. He will try to hook up with you.

But what about everything I've said regarding modern men and their rampant insecurities and fear of making moves? That is irrelevant right now, because many guys told me that their insecurities tend to die down when dealing with a Short-Term Investment. A guy can feel relatively comfortable hitting on a Short-Term Investment in a clear and physical way. Actually, it turns out he's not that scared of getting rejected by her.

Because here's the catch: hot as she is, he doesn't really see himself falling in love with her. He doesn't feel about her the way that he would feel about a Girlfriend Prospect. He typically respects her and truly enjoys her company, but there's a lack of depth there—and thus, the entire experience sits lighter on his ego. This is why it's relatively easy for him to take a deep breath, suppress his nerves, and go balls-to-the-wall trying to make a little something happen.

He Is Asking You to Hang Out—But Not in Super-Meaningful Settings

Here is where we need to draw the major distinction between how a guy will treat his Girlfriend Prospect and how he will treat his Short-Term Investment. Because he is going to try and hang out with both girls—but the hangouts are going to look and feel very different.

When it comes to a Girlfriend Prospect, a guy is going to want to spend quality time (and remember, "boring" time!) with her, which will involve not only bodies and hormones but also brains and interests and conversations and emotions. Think concerts, book readings, BBQs at his house, sporting events, and cocktail parties. Friends will be met, coworkers will be introduced, and roommates will start bothering to remember her name.

On the other hand, if you're his Short-Term Investment, then you won't be getting too many invitations to these types of outings. Sure, you'll be making plans for nice dinners, or meeting up for drinks at a time that he has probably scheduled in advance. He's still trying to impress you. But he won't be trying to integrate you into the more significant—and social—parts of his life.

As one guy put it, "If I have a Girlfriend Prospect, I want to take her on double dates and integrate her into my friend base. I want to show her off, and I'm proud of not just her looks but her personality as well. But Short-Term Investments? They get the Wednesday night dinners, but they rarely get the 'Hey, come meet my friends tonight!' invitation."

Because—and this might be difficult for you to hear, depending on how you feel about this guy—if you are his Short-Term Investment, then he's not really *that* interested in getting to know you, or even having you get to know him. In the words of one man, "With this girl, you don't reveal much, unless it is helping your cause."

He wants you both to have a great time together, but he's not trying to establish a rich foundation of depth, connection, and *friendship* with you. He thinks you are attractive and cool, but . . . he just doesn't feel super emotionally invested in you.

It's important to remember here that not every single guy in the world needs to fall madly and deeply in love with you. That would actually be kind of annoying to deal with, right?!

But of course, a guy's lack of devotion can still be tough to face. You have so much intelligence, compassion, and wit to offer. The guy who sees you as his Short-Term Investment probably knows that, too, but he's mostly just focusing on what you look like in your underwear. When he thinks of you, his body reacts—but for whatever reason, his brain and his emotions just don't get all that riled up (see: how *you* feel about your Hot Sex Prospect).

Does this sexual compartmentalization make this guy an asshole? Sometimes, but not usually. Some of the nicest guys I interviewed had cultivated Short-Term Investments. Like Caleb, a twenty-nine-year-old Nashville musician.

Caleb's genuine, thoughtful, and overwhelmingly positive demeanor shone through everything he said during our talk, and he clearly held an exceptional level of respect for most of the women in his life. But even Caleb had pursued his fair share of Short-Term Investments—though he still felt kind of guilty about how some of those relationships had ended.

"It's so fucked up. I mean, this is where all the complexity happens, and where a lot of the hurt and drama comes into it," Caleb admitted. "Sometimes you meet someone really fun and beautiful and great. You might not feel that spark of 'Wow, this could be something really long-term or sustainable,' but you still want to spend time with her and, you know, satisfy those impulses."

For a self-aware guy like Caleb, this type of girl presents a conundrum. When he meets a girl who he is really attracted to, but for whom he doesn't have deep feelings, how is he supposed to proceed? As he described, "You're caught at this standstill, like, I like this person, she's beautiful, she's great, she's fun to hang out with, we're both sexually compatible and attracted to one another, so why not just live and have fun? I mean, are you supposed to cut off everything initially, just because this isn't The One?"

With that in mind, Caleb would invest in these girls in a casual but focused way. And for a while, it would seem like everyone was happy.

But alas, these girls would (understandably) have expectations of further commitment. The romantic norms had taught them that Caleb wanted to be their boyfriend. He had asked them out to dinner three whole nights in advance! But eventually, as happens with so many purely physical connections, Caleb would lose interest. He would decide to liquidate his investment. At which point . . .

He Starts Pulling the Slow Fade

You'll be as shocked—shocked!—as I was to hear Caleb confess to pulling the slow fade on multiple women in the past. He was a sensitive musician! We had just been discussing how important honest, genuine communication between the sexes was, and he had been schooling me on how the foundation of anything real was communication. But when I asked him if he had ever pulled the slow fade on a girl:

"Yes. Totally. Hey, I'm being honest!"

While the slow fade can be pulled on any girl in a guy's gaggle, Caleb shed some light on why this brutal nonbreakup tends to happen to Short-Term Investments the most. As he explained, "She doesn't owe anything to me, and I don't owe anything to her. We've hung out a few times, we've hooked up, it's been fun, I really like this person, I really respect her. But it's not something romantic, it's not a 'relationship,' there's no evolution, so . . ."

Faced with the prospect of actually saying all this to a (now former) Short-Term Investment, Caleb had often preferred to take the easy way out, even though he knew that this decision wasn't actually making things any easier on the girl. He admits:

"This is the contradiction: I appreciate communication, but at the same time, I can be really avoidant. I don't think it's that I'm trying to avoid drama, although that's a great thing. I just don't want to hurt her feelings. Even though the slow fade can actually be harder and more hurtful, because it drags out over a longer period of time, instead of cutting to the chase and being like, this just isn't going to work out . . .

"This leads into a lot of really bad, unhealthy situations where someone is hoping for something. I don't know what it's like from her angle, but maybe the girl is thinking, 'What did I do wrong? What's wrong with me?'"

Um, yes. Often, that's exactly what she's thinking.

Having a guy pull the slow fade on you is a painful experience, and one of the most common yet pernicious ones in modern-day romance (shout-out to the seven guys out there who don't do it! Keep on!). Because between the period when a guy really seems into you and the moment when you realize that he's just blown you off, there is a lot of time to question what the hell is going on. This confusion and disappointment can saddle you with baggage that can be difficult to not carry on to your future interactions with guys.

This guy was into you, until he suddenly wasn't. So who's to say that the next guy who shows interest isn't going to pull the slow fade, too? Maybe you should prepare yourself to be blown off? Maybe you should second-guess every guy's actions and motives from the start, to protect yourself? Doubt his nice words? Question his seemingly genuine intentions? Count down as you wait for the other shoe to drop?

And then you become a bitter, paranoid woman.

While these guys might not realize the extent of the damage they are doing to our generation of women, they are still self-aware. They know they are pulling a weak move. I witnessed their sheepish grins as they told me about doing it. But many of them confessed a terrible fear of awkward confrontation with their Short-Term Investment. They hated the idea of facing a tearful question from their erstwhile lover, such as, "What did I do wrong?" or, god forbid, "But I thought that night where we ate fancy lobster and then slept together *meant* something?" Many guys aren't sure what they would say to that. Whatever they're feeling is hard for them to articulate. So instead, they say nothing at all. This avoidance and fear of awkwardness is strong enough to keep great guys like Caleb from giving a girl even the most perfunctory (but at the end of the day, more respectful) of breakup explanations.

If you are a guy's Short-Term Investment, and that's what you want to be, then, great! You'll enjoy this light, fun, short-term dalliance. You'll be cultivating the rest of your gaggle and focusing on other (deeper, more meaningful) connections, and your relationship with this guy can run its course organically and not end with any hurtful implications for you.

What slow fade? You and that guy just haven't talked in a while. You've basically been too busy to notice. Oops!

But if you have confused your Short-Term Investment status for Girlfriend Prospect status, then you're really going to feel the slow nondeath of this nonrelationship. It's going to hurt. And you're going to have to face the truth: you were probably his Short-Term Investment all along.

Instead of wondering what you did wrong and how you must have messed up this amazing connection that was obviously destined for love, realize that you are blameless. The connection wasn't heading that way in the first place. Now go focus on the rest of your gaggle, keeping yourself open to a guy who sees the value of a longer-term payout with you.

KEY TIPS

For Increasing Your Chances
of Becoming His Short-Term Investment

There is much fun to be had in the short term with this guy if you're not interested in getting too serious with him. If you want to move in this direction, keep your communication on relatively superficial terms and turn down any offers to engage with him in more meaningful ways. If he invites you to his work party, say no but offer to meet him at a bar afterward. If he sends you an in-depth email, write back a perfunctory but still friendly and flirty response. And don't get upset if you notice him starting to lose interest after a while. You never wanted it to be that intense to begin with, remember?

For *Not* Becoming His Short-Term Investment

If you can tell that you're a guy's Short-Term Investment but you know that you have real feelings for him, then don't be willing to engage with him in a sexually casual way. Don't take "whatever you can get." Instead, set the standard that you need to be treated like a Girlfriend Prospect, and don't settle for anything less. Next time he wants to get a drink, turn down his offer and suggest a more personally significant outing instead. And if you set that tone and he doesn't seem to be following suit, then stay true to your feelings and drop him. If you keep him around under faux-casual pretenses, then you will have some unnecessary hurt coming your way.

THE LAST RESORT

This girl is a late-night booty call, to be hit up only when all other options fail. Whether scrolling through his phone or scanning the remnants of the night's party, he figures that he might as well hook up with her instead of going home alone. Luckily, he has a hunch that she'll be DTF.

Oh, ha ha! No, I don't have any girls like that in my life . . . but yeah, of course, all my buddies do.

—Pretty much every guy I interviewed

UNDERSTANDING THE LAST RESORT

Here's the good news: being a guy's Last Resort doesn't *have* to be a horrible thing. Maybe you're just looking for a fun, casual, non-committal hookup—and so is he. You want to get off. He wants to get off. Neither of you feel like working too hard for it. You're his Last Resort, and maybe he's your Super Horny Guy (turned temporary Hot Sex Prospect). This could be a one-night match made in heaven!

And now for the not-so-good news.

You deserve respect. Even if a guy is not in love with you, he should be able to see that you have great qualities and treat you accordingly. But that's not really how the Last Resort dynamic works. By definition, unfortunately, there's a subtle (or not-so-subtle) layer of disrespect involved in how a guy thinks of his Last Resort.

If you are a guy's Last Resort, then he is not seeing you as the cool girl that you are. He is not even seeing you as the cute girl that you are. Instead, he is simply seeing you as the willing girl during his time of need.

All too often, a guy is hitting up his Last Resort because he just needs to hit up someone. That's why, if any part of your ego—or god forbid, your emotions—are wrapped up in this guy, then you have to be realistic about what's really going on.

A guy's precise motivation to contact his Last Resort can be tough for us women to fully understand. In this day and age, men and women are obviously both capable of hooking up for the fun and sexy sake of hooking up. But a distinction that struck me during my interviews was that (generalization alert!) many men tend to be more willing to lower their personal standards in order to satisfy their sexual impulses. Yes, most women understand what it is to have a Hot Sex Prospect, but there is typically still a real attraction there. Men, on the other hand, can sometimes talk about sexual desire as if it exists in a vacuum, unconnected to any particular woman—just an itch that they are desperate for *anyone* to scratch.

As one of my male interviewees revealed, "I used to jerk off, and then fully in the midst of it, I would think of the ugliest girl in school. And then I'd think, 'Okay, would I fuck her? Like, at this point, would I fuck her at this point?' And I was never sure what the answer was. Sexual desire is a powerful thing, you know?"

You just don't hear that kind of thing from women very often. This is why we don't have the Last Resort in our gaggle.

If you realize that you're some guy's Last Resort and you're cool with it, then godspeed. But if you read this and alarm bells start going off in your brain, ditch this guy immediately and go hang out with a member of your gaggle who truly appreciates you instead.

HOW TO KNOW IF YOU'RE HIS LAST RESORT

He Woos You . . . A Little . . . At First

Many of the men I interviewed, possibly worried about making bad impressions, were reluctant to discuss their Last Resort experiences with me. Luckily, I have always had quite a few guy friends who never seemed to worry about that sort of thing ("Yo, Massa, did I ever tell you about that time I banged an ugly chick?"). So when I heard from female interviewees who had been treated as Last Resorts, I was usually able to pick out the dynamic immediately.

Case in point: Abby, a twenty-six-year-old teacher's assistant in Chicago. If there was one woman I met during my travels with whom I'd want to go out and party, it would be Abby. She was seriously fun, and had a huge, how-can-you-not-love-this-girl personality—which made it annoying to hear that some guy had tried to treat her as a Last Resort.

First, he had wooed her—because a guy has to somehow weasel his way into a girl's gaggle before he starts hitting her up for random hookups, right?

Abby had met Sly outside a bar. He chatted her up and immediately complimented her shoes (I guess some guys can still get away with a variation of "Nice shoes, wanna fuck?"). Overall, she found him to be "such a charmer. I was so smitten."

Sly proceeded to take Abby out on a few official dates. They listened to blues, danced to Frank Sinatra, talked about "everything," and hooked up. Abby was into him and began sleeping with him.

And then, once he had cemented a spot as the Boyfriend Prospect in Abby's gaggle, Sly started to change.

Once You're Interested, He Contacts You Only to Hook Up

Within a few weeks, Abby noticed that she was no longer being wooed. Instead, she was being booty-called.

"It very quickly turned from dating to an end-of-the-night thing,"

Abby recounted. "We weren't able to coordinate plans for a couple of weeks. I had a lot going on at the time, but when I tried to get him to commit to actual plans, he would call late and do the booty call at midnight. And I would be like, you have got to be fucking kidding me. Who do you think I am?"

Abby was pissed. She was no one's Last Resort! So why didn't she call it off?

We modern women all think that we can recognize a booty call from a mile away. We think we can tell when a guy is contacting us for sex without putting in the extra effort that he would for a Girlfriend Prospect or a Short-Term Investment. And if Abby had only heard from Sly when he was booty-calling her, then she would probably have cut off their rapport sooner.

But Abby's interactions with Sly tapped into a common misconception that many of us have about being the Last Resort. What you don't often hear is that even when a guy sees you as a Last Resort, he will probably have a trick up his sleeve that will confuse you just enough to keep you from kicking him out of your gaggle.

You Hear from Him Randomly and Intermittently Between Hookups

Even when Sly was booty-calling Abby on a regular basis, he was still in e-touch with her. He would text, and even call her every once in a while. Of course, making set plans with him had become impossible. But he was in contact just enough to keep her wondering about his intentions and open to receiving an invitation from him.

Most guys have evolved enough to realize that they can't booty-call women out of the blue. And technology has made it incredibly easy for a guy to take four seconds out of his day to check in with a "What's up? :)" text. So even if you're his Last Resort, then he will likely do what we're going to call "fertilizing," to keep you on the hook.

When I asked a male WTF?! guest blogger to clue our female readers into a "guy move" that he often sees women fall for, this is how he explained it:

"I apologize in advance to my entire gender, but here's a trick. It's known as 'fertilizing' or 'laying a foundation.'

"Unfortunately for us, having a gaggle of women who are *willing* to hook up with us can require some work. So we put in that work (to a point). Tuesdays and Wednesdays are great for a casual phone call, just to 'catch up' and see how someone is doing. But to be clear, this is all part of the 'fertilizing' process.

"Sometimes I hear platonic girlfriends complain, 'I don't get it! He called to talk, but he didn't really set a time to hang out.' Here's the truth: the guy has no intention of hanging out that day, but he knows that you can't just booty-call most women once every other week (unless she's fully on board with you being her Hot Sex Prospect). So we check in, in order to 'lay the foundation.'"

Yikes! If this guy is to be believed, then you should know that even when you are a guy's Last Resort, he will still put in a tiny bit of work to keep you around. But just because he contacts you from time to time, that does *not* mean that he is in love, or even in serious lust, with you.

Is he actually trying to hang out with you? If the answer to that question is "only when he's in the mood to hook up," then his e-communication doesn't matter. You're his Last Resort.

He Keeps Coming Back (and Playing the Same Game)

Desperate times call for desperate measures. So if you are a guy's Last Resort, then don't be surprised if he keeps treating you like his Hail Mary pass—no matter how many times you've laid down the law. From his perspective, what has he got to lose in trying one more time?

After one too many unwelcome booty calls, Abby cut Sly off. Lo and behold, three months later, he called her, told her how much he missed her, and invited her over to watch a football game. Of course, a few minutes into the game, "he started getting all handsy," prompting Abby to call him out.

"I was like, 'You've got to be kidding me! To reappear after three months and think that we can just . . . you know? Things are different, we're going to have to talk about this.' But he didn't actually think he did anything wrong!"

You would think that would be the end of that. But Sly gave it one more go. Abby explained:

"He contacted me almost a year later, on Facebook . . . and he essentially wrote, how have you been, I'm thinking of you, I really want to see you, I really miss you. It felt kind of validating, so we exchanged messages about possibly meeting up."

It ended in epic Last Resort fashion, of course.

Abby proposed a weeknight dinner. Sly pushed for a drunken weekend hangout instead and finally drunk-dialed her, trying to convince her to come over. When she responded with "Not a chance in hell," he offered to take her to brunch the next morning and dinner the following week if she would just come over now. She turned him down again but then followed up the next day to set up dinner for that week. His final answer? "A long-winded text explaining that he was going to be really busy for the next couple weeks. . . ."

If a guy reaches out to you weeks or months (or years!) after treating you like a Last Resort and waxes poetic about how much he misses you, maintain a healthy skepticism. Don't be surprised when he suggests that you catch up at 2:00 a.m. Realize that a booty call by any other name, after any amount of time, is still a booty call.

He Shuts Down After Hooking Up

Here's a cold, hard piece of reality: after a guy hooks up with his Last Resort, he wants to interact with her as little as possible. One of my male interviewees said, "Generally, I'm pretty disgusted with myself after sleeping with her, because now I'm thinking clearly. She's the girl you want *out* of your bed right after you wake up—or ideally, even before you're up."

If you're his Last Resort, there will be no post-hookup cuddling. No conversation. No move to the kitchen to get some food. The only thing there will be is sleep—if he even lets you stay that long.

KEY TIPS

For Increasing Your Chances of Becoming His Last Resort

Being a guy's Last Resort can be easy and fun if you're not looking for anything even remotely committed or serious with him. If this is the case, then respond to his booty calls when you're in the mood. Even feel free to hit *him* up for some last-minute play-non-date action. Stay realistic and emotionless, and get it on.

For *Not* Becoming His Last Resort

No responding to booty calls—ever. You will just reinforce his belief that maybe, if he propositions you nine times, he might catch you in a moment of weakness and get you to say yes the tenth time. Instead, treat yourself with dignity, show that you're not a doormat, and refuse to come through. Either he'll come to his senses and ask you to hang out in daylight or he won't—and then you'll have even more time to explore connections with the guys in your gaggle who actually appreciate you.

THE GIRL WHO IS OUT OF HIS LEAGUE

A girl who rests on the outskirts of his gaggle—but only because he is so afraid to talk to her. She is hotter, cooler, smarter, or more popular than he believes himself worthy of. His interactions with her generally take place in his far-off fantasies and solo pleasuring sessions, but this is probably best for all involved, seeing as the sweaty palms and racing heart that she induces in real life would probably scare her off anyway.

I got to class on the first day, and she walked in. I was like, man, she's fine! She's probably dating a basketball player or a football player or something. And I totally expected her to be kind of stuck-up, because she's so fine. I thought, she probably deals with dudes all the time. There ain't no way she'd be into me.

Then after the second day of class, she went my way, so I looked back. And she got in a Beamer, and I was like, dang, she's fine and she's rich! That's crazy, look at that!

Of course, later, I found out she got the car for less than a hundred bucks because her grandfather is a mechanic.

—Mike, 35, textbook salesman, Cincinnati,
speaking about his now-wife

UNDERSTANDING THE GIRL WHO IS OUT OF HIS LEAGUE

Is the Girl Who Is Out of His League even *in* a guy's gaggle? Despite the fact that he never plans on pursuing her? Yes! Any woman who can cause heart palpitations in a guy simply by standing in his general proximity deserves a spot in his gaggle.

Believe it or not, odds are that some guy out there—possibly even one who has never crossed your mind or entered your sphere for more than a brief second—considers you to be a Girl Who Is Out of His League. You are the blue tank-topped dream girl in his real-life version of *Can't Hardly Wait*. He could be your friend, your coworker, your mailman, your roommate's brother, or that guy who passes you on the street every day. Sorry if that creeps you out, but it's the price you pay for being an awesome woman who comes into contact with men on a regular basis.

Every girl plays roles in more guys' gaggles than she thinks. But how are you supposed to know if a guy has been secretly daydreaming about you? That is, if he's even allowed himself to daydream about you?

HOW TO KNOW IF YOU'RE THE GIRL WHO IS OUT OF HIS LEAGUE

He Doesn't Approach You (Even Though He's Aware of You)

If you haven't picked this up from the 873 times that I've said it so far, hear me now: men are not always the most confident creatures on the planet. Sometimes they are, but other times they are not. Men might typically be better than us at handling rejection, but that doesn't mean that most of them go out looking for it. So if a guy is convinced that you are out of his league, then he will avoid the inevitable (as he sees it) prospect of rejection and stay away from you.

The funny thing is, you're probably so far on the outskirts of his (realistic) radar that he barely realizes that he is choosing not to approach you. Just like the many men who told me that they always spot the 10 as soon as they step into a party but immediately go for the 7 or 8 instead, this guy has likely been conditioned to pursue women he thinks he might be able to get. Which apparently does not include you.

There is a theory in pop psychology that people generally end up in relationships with partners of the same level: 2s end up with 2s, 9s end up with 9s, and so forth. There is no scientific formula to determine people's levels (although facial symmetry helps), which might explain why Marilyn Manson and Salman Rushdie continue to pull hot women. But more often than not, people of a similar physical caliber supposedly flock together.

Needless to say, if a guy thinks that you are too far above his level, then he'll only barely register your presence. He might even convince himself that he's more into the girl who he thinks is a 7. But rest assured, he will still notice you. And if you're interested, therein lies your chance to push a possible connection.

When *You* Approach *Him,* He Is Clearly Excited and Eager to Talk

If a guy hasn't approached you and you want to gauge his interest, then approach him. If he's distracted or ambivalent, then forget about it. But if he seems really excited to talk, then he might just have thought you were out of his league.

When Carla, a twenty-five-year old publicist in Portland, Oregon, met Nathan in a small seminar during her junior year of college, she could tell that he had noticed her because she caught him looking at her in class a few times. But she also observed that, week after week of class, he did absolutely nothing about it.

"He would stare at me in class," Carla told me. "Our professor was a retired navy captain, and he used to stomp when he wanted to get our attention. So I would be looking at him, and Nathan would be looking at me, and the professor would stomp to get Nathan to look at him. And I was like, what's happening here?"

At the time, Carla was the president of her sorority and an exceptional student—"a force to be reckoned with," she called herself. Thus, when she caught Nathan checking her out, she guessed that he was intimidated by her . . . but still interested. Even though, by the end of the semester, his biggest move had been to compliment her final classroom project. Not exactly a bold declaration of romantic interest.

Luckily, Carla was confident enough to push him a little and read between the lines.

She got his number from a friend and texted him to see what he was up to over the weekend. Encouraged by his enthusiastic responses, she began inviting him on group-non-dates with her friends. He always replied promptly and came.

When Carla took the initiative, Nathan responded positively. Always. This is what *should* happen when you approach a guy who thinks you are out of his league. As a guy who works in publishing explained it to me, "If that girl opens the door of opportunity just a crack, most guys will kick it in. We already think you're incredible, so you don't have to do a lot of work here. Just pitch us an underhand lob, and we'll hit it out of the park."

And Then He Will Probably *Still* Do Nothing (Until You Make the First Move!)

The good thing about being out of some guy's league is that you get to call the shots. If you're not interested, then fine! He's not really going to be approaching you anyway. But if you are, then a strong nudge might be all it takes to make this Ego Booster more of a super-appreciative Boyfriend Prospect.

Back to Carla, who could sense from Nathan's responsiveness that he liked her. She could also infer from his inaction that he was still intimidated. "I recognized that I was the one holding all the cards," Carla recalled honestly.

Carla realized that nothing would happen if she left things up to Nathan, so she kept serving him beer one night until he finally got tipsy enough to admit that he had a crush on her. Four years later, Carla and Nathan are living together in Portland and completely in love. He'd gotten the girl he thought was out of his league—no thanks to him, of course. And Carla had recognized the signs that she was the Girl Who Is Out of His League and had decided to prove him wrong about that.

The lesson here? Keep an eye out for these signs in your life. Once you start looking at all the guys who *aren't* talking to you, you might realize that you've quietly caught a good one's eye. If so, follow Carla's lead.

KEY TIPS

For Increasing Your Chances of Becoming the Girl Who Is Out of His League

There's not a lot to gain from being some guy's unattainable girl, other than a quick ego boost. Boys who talk are more fun than boys who stare. But if you want him to be in awe of you, then put all the powers of your awesomeness on display. Embrace the exciting things happening in your life, flaunt the parts of yourself that make you proud, and show that while you're open to engaging with guys, your confidence and happiness aren't dependent on it. Trust me: he'll be intimidated.

For *Not* Becoming the Girl Who Is Out of His League

If you want him to take you off that pedestal because you're not interested in him, then it's easy: just don't give him any extra time or attention. That's pretty much what he's expecting anyway. But if you appreciate his high opinion of you and want to explore your connection, then take the initiative and show him that you might not be as far out of his league as he thinks. Give him special attention. Seek him out in a crowded room. Send him an unexpected email. Make the first move, and provide the confidence boost that he'll need to get more assertive with you.

THE FRIEND HE'S
JUST NOT THAT INTO

The guy's version of the Ego Booster. This girl is "just a friend" and claims to be happy with that, but she actually harbors a not-so-secret crush that tends to come out in her weaker moments. He may have previously hooked up with her in a moment of weakness/attraction/drunkenness, but he just isn't that into her and almost always treats her accordingly. He swears that he keeps her around because she's a good friend; however, he knows that it's only a matter of time until her romantic feelings ruin the whole friendship. Until then, he has to admit, it doesn't feel so bad having her around.

At some point, all my guy friends are like, "Why can't I meet someone like you?" And I'm like, hello. I'm *just like me. That's weird. Like, just date* me.

—Abby, 26, teacher's assistant, Chicago

UNDERSTANDING THE FRIEND HE'S JUST NOT THAT INTO

We all know what it feels like to have a crush on some guy that feels like it might be unrequited. But what happens when that guy is part of your social crew? When you see him around a lot, and maybe even find yourself on friend-non-dates together?

What happens is that his level of romantic interest can end up being tough to read. He might not be declaring his love for you (or even being particularly nice to you), but you're his pal: thus, he's usually not treating you like a jerk, and he's not completely ignoring you like a typical Guy Who Just Blew You Off, either. You actually get along pretty well! And so, you can easily convince yourself of all sorts of mutual feelings and scenarios that end with the two of you acting out your very own inevitable Ross-and-Rachel love story. When the truth is, you're the Friend He's Just Not That Into.

You probably keep hoping that he'll change his mind and start romantically pursuing you (I mean, look how much friendly *fun* you're having together!). You likely regale your poor roommates with stories about him, which are nearly constant because he's such a regular "friendly" presence in your life. And you definitely reminisce about that one time you both got drunk and kissed in a more than friendly way. Wonder how you can make that happen again?

For your sanity, you need to be able to recognize when a guy is treating you like the Friend He's Just Not That Into so that you can avoid the common mistake of considering him a Boyfriend Prospect in your gaggle and wasting months (or years!) pining away for someone who's never going to come around. Your general awesomeness as a friend is likely going to keep him from cutting you off in a clear way, and besides, there's that little ego boost that he gets from being around you. So you need to read between the lines, understand his subtler signals, and reconceptualize your relationship accordingly.

To be clear, you are only a guy's Friend He's Just Not That Into if he knows that you like him and he's trying to hold you at bay. There needs to exist a fundamental imbalance in your feelings for each other. If there's absolutely no attraction in either direction, then don't fret—you're just not in each other's gaggles! And if there's a slight, unrecognized, potentially mutual attraction, then you are a Possibility in his gaggle (more on that later).

But if there *is* a one-sided crush happening here, then that inequality needs to be understood and dealt with. No one's saying that you need to cut this guy off entirely. But you *do* need to be realistic about his feelings and your future together, so that you can free up that Boyfriend Prospect role for someone who deserves (and wants) it.

HOW TO KNOW IF YOU'RE THE FRIEND HE'S JUST NOT THAT INTO

You're Working Harder for It Than He Is

Here's the thing about crushing on a guy: if you get the distinct feeling that you are making more of an effort than he is, then that's probably true. And the longer that dynamic continues, the more painful the end will be for you.

He meets up with you to hang out—but is it always you extending the invitation? You chat over text—but do you usually text first, and is he the one who lets the conversation die out? Your heart leaps into your throat when you hear from him—but is that because it happens so rarely and unexpectedly?

There is a big difference between simply responding to someone's overtures and actually making the effort to get the ball rolling. If a guy knows that you are into him, and he still isn't taking the initiative very often, then truth be told, he might just not be that psyched to talk to you. He might enjoy your company when you're there but not be thinking much about you otherwise.

You might be the Friend He's Just Not That Into.

He Gets Uncomfortable When Other People Mistake You for a Couple

This Friend He's Just Not That Into dynamic doesn't only show up in casual friendships. It can also rear its ugly, confusing head amidst a much deeper bond—a bond that other people might deem worthy of a relationship (even if he doesn't!).

When I brought up the gaggle to Farrah, a thirty-year-old personal trainer in Denver, she first mentioned an old friend from back in her New York City days. In retrospect, she was aware of their particular dynamic right off the bat:

"I had a guy I thought I should marry, because he was like my best friend. He was the guy that I was in love with, that I spent years waiting on. I was always hanging on, waiting for him to like me."

When I met Farrah, she was over him—but I could still feel her pain. And one of the toughest parts of the situation for her had been that their mutual friends seemed to always be encouraging the connection that she already so strongly believed in.

"We had a marriage, in some ways," Farrah remembered. "And everyone around us was like, 'Why aren't you guys dating?' So that made it worse. Because it was like, well, why *wouldn't* you want to date me?"

Like Farrah, you might actually have a close relationship with this particular guy. Other people might see that connection and call it out, or even assume that you two *are* together. But how he reacts can be telling.

Does he put his arm around you and make a joke about being eighty-five years old together? Then you can at least rest assured that the idea of being paired with you doesn't scare the hell out of him. But if you are his Friend He's Just Not That Into, then he probably won't react so casually. Instead, he'll immediately clarify his unattached status or choke out a strangled laugh and excuse himself to the bathroom.

Why the bad reaction? If some part of him knows that he is stringing you along, even just a little, then these comments will hit too close to home and make him feel guilty or cornered. He might also worry that being publicly connected to you will mess up his chances with other women.

I know. Poor guy, right? Ugh.

He Talks—with Desire—About Other Girls to You

One of the reasons that a guy might be just not that into you is that he might be just that into another girl. Or a bunch of other girls. He'll want you to be aware of that, as a subtle sign that you shouldn't be expecting him to commit to you any time soon.

However, just mentioning other girls is not a guarantee that you're the Friend He's Just Not That Into. Every now and then, any guy could revert back to seventh grade and bring up other girls to get a sense of your reaction and interest. If you fill a desirable role in his gaggle, then he'll want you to know that *he's* desirable, too.

How can you tell the difference between a guy who is trying to make a positive point ("FYI, other girls think I'm hot, and therefore you should, too!") and a guy who is trying to make a negative point? ("FYI, I'm just not that into you and I like other girls more—see?") Especially when either move might be subconscious on his end?

Note whether he speaks about other girls with *desire* or not. Examples:

Positive:

> *"Yeah, she's into me but I'm not really feeling it."*

> *"I keep going out with these girls, but nothing clicks."*

> *"She's perfect—but it still feels like something is missing, you know?"*

Negative:

> *"It's going really well! I'm so into her. I could see myself falling for her."*

> *"I just noticed on Facebook that my ex got engaged—bummer :(Don't think I'll ever find another girl as amazing as her."*

> *"Sorry, I didn't hear what you said. Did you see that girl who just walked by us? Dayummmmn!"*

Basically, if he wants to leave the door open for something to happen between you two, then he'll let you know that the door is open and that no other girl is closing it right now. But if you're the Friend He's Just Not That Into, then he'll let you know that the door is being banged down by other girls and that he's psyched about it.

The subtlety of all these signals can depend on the guy you're dealing with and how introspective and honest he is with himself. But while most guys are fully aware that they are not romantically interested in you, a lot of the cues demonstrating that are being sent subconsciously.

When guys talked to me about girls who, from my female standpoint, were clearly into them, I often had to listen to them swear several times, "She's just a friend—it's not that complicated!" before they would finally admit that they knew this girl liked them and knew it was a problem. Therefore, I have gone on to assume that these guys just walk around most of the time, thinking to themselves, "She's just a friend—it's not that complicated!" in an effort to avoid the guilt and cognitive dissonance that comes from continuing to be friends with a girl they know wants more. Cue the confusing signals!

But there is one clear, unmistakable sign.

He's *Told* You That It's Not Going to Happen

Sometimes, when a guy is really trying to preserve the friendship, he'll do the unthinkable: he'll tell you that he's just not that into you. And ladies, if you hear this from a guy, *believe him!*

He is not going to feel differently tomorrow. His confusing actions don't overrule those words. He has made his decision. So take his word for it and move him to a lesser position in your gaggle.

"It's my own fault," Farrah insisted, when I asked how her nonrelationship with her guy friend had ended. "I'm not totally innocent, either. He said that he didn't want to date me, maybe two or three times, and I did the whole girl thing: 'He'll change his mind!' And then I finally just cut it out. I was like, I can't just be friends with you."

This is sadly what you might have to do if you're not capable of shifting this guy to a less fraught role in your gaggle. Ultimately, unrequited feelings are not empowering and they do not bring you all that much closer to finding love. And if he's looking you in the face and telling you that your feelings are unrequited, then they are. So cut your losses and open yourself up to the more fruitful and exciting possibilities around you.

KEY TIPS

For Increasing Your Chances of Becoming the Friend He's Just Not That Into

While you're probably not dying to fill this role in a guy's gaggle, it might be a good idea to find out if you're filling it anyway. If your friend is not romantically invested in you, then the more you push him, the more he will run away. So really go for it—admit your crush or moon over him even more than you already do—and if he balks and creates stricter boundaries for your relationship, then you know: you're the Friend He's Just Not That Into!

For *Not* Becoming the Friend He's Just Not That Into

You can't make a guy like you, especially if you're already friends; he has already seen all the wonderful sides of you, and for whatever reason, he's still not biting.

So if you've already pulled all the friend-non-date stops and nothing seems to be working, then stop being so available to him. Pull back and create distance. This may not make him fall in love with you, but it will eventually allow you to feel more in control of your friendship—and, hopefully, enable you to find a better spot for him in your gaggle.

THE CHALLENGE

A girl who's playing hard to get, inciting a guy's competitive instinct and making him want to win her over. She may not be the coolest or prettiest girl he knows, but her cat-and-mouse games and unwillingness to let down her walls keep him—and his ego—intrigued. She is a match to be won, and once he wins, he's usually over it. It's all worth it when he gets to walk away with a validated ego and a triumphant tale for his buddies.

So there's this psychological study of rats. If a rat pushes a button and gets a treat every single time, he will get the treat for a while and then lose interest and not push the button anymore. And if a rat pushes a button once and gets a treat, and then pushes it again and again and again and again and never gets another treat, he'll stop, too. But if he pushes it and gets a treat, and then pushes it three times and doesn't get a treat, and then pushes it one time and gets a treat, and then waits six times and gets another treat, he will continue pushing that button for such a long time.

—Maura, 23, media strategist, Salt Lake City

UNDERSTANDING THE CHALLENGE

There's a school of thought that says you can get a man by playing hard-to-get. You've heard all the rules, the tricks, and the do's and don'ts that comprise this not-so-complex theory of courtship. Yet, what the teachers of these lessons don't tell you (or maybe even realize) is that, most of the time, this advice will do nothing more than turn you into a guy's Challenge.

Being a guy's Challenge is, by many accounts, a pretty effective way to keep him on the hook for a while. You are treating him like that poor lab rat who has to push all those buttons, never sure if he's going to get the treat. As science has shown, this is certainly one way to keep a guy intrigued for longer than he might have been otherwise. But why?

As evolutionary lore has it, most guys have a competitive, ego-driven streak. They need to stake out their prey and go up against other hunters in order to feel that all-important rush of manliness. And when it comes to their pursuit of women, this caveman instinct can lead men to have a Challenge (or seventeen) in their gaggle.

The potential payoff for a guy here is huge: while his ego might take some small hits when his Challenge is making herself unavailable ("Why hasn't she responded to my text yet? Maybe she's with another guy?"), the ego boost that he's anticipating when he finally wins her over is substantial enough to keep him working at it.

As one male interviewee told me, "Sometimes, you have that girl you really want to get, or hook up with, just so that you can go back to your friends and high-five them and be like, yeah, I finally got that chick!" Some other guys seemed to care more about their innate confidence than their friends' opinions. But either way, the male ego takes priority in this dynamic.

Ladies, if you play your cards right—basically, if you play your cards like most dating experts tell you to, and aim to be strong, elusive, mysterious, busy, and guarded—then you'll offer just enough of a potential confidence boost to a guy to become his Challenge. Maybe you'll even inspire a few high-fives from his buddies. Quite the magnificent accomplishment, right?

But when you are the Challenge, what happens when you finally let a guy "get" you? Will his interest hold once the thrill of the chase is gone? Can your connection move on from all that game playing in a genuine way?

Usually not. If you present a guy with a game, then maybe he'll want to play. But once he wins, well, what is he supposed to do now? Go back to the beginning and play again? Hang out at the finish line for the rest of his life? Nah. More often, he'll take all that new pride and go find some other Challenge to take on.

Luckily, the gaggle can moderate this in some circumstances. The future of your connection with this guy partially depends on who he is in *your* gaggle (often a Prospect You're Not Sure Is a Prospect—hello, game playing!) and how *you* choose to further cultivate your connection. But a big part of exploring what other roles you might fulfill for each other depends on you realizing that, up until a certain point, you were his Challenge. At least in the beginning, your womanly wiles, mixed signals, and physical and emotional unavailability were the main draws.

In order for you two to evolve within each other's gaggles, you first need to know where you began.

HOW TO KNOW IF YOU'RE HIS CHALLENGE

He Is Trying to Impress You

Some guys are too insecure to even think of pursuing a girl who doesn't seem to be throwing herself at his feet. But for a guy who is more confident in his appeal, your unwillingness to fawn all over him can be intriguing. He knows that girls are into him. In fact, a significant chunk of his ego is probably dependent on this certainty! And if you don't seem sold on his cool factor yet, well, he's going to sell you on it. He can't stand to have some girl walking around the world not being into him. That could seriously mess up his whole self-image.

Also, for these typically confident guys, the game of trying to win someone over can be fun. It can bring a little excitement and curiosity to a guy's otherwise humdrum love life.

The existence of the Challenge was first unveiled to me by Asher, a twenty-seven-year-old marketing consultant in New York City who truly believed that no girl was out of his league. As off-putting as that sounds, he wasn't actually a cocky jerk. He wasn't picking up tons of women for sport and then dropping them carelessly when he got bored. He just had supreme confidence in his ability to win a girl over when he put his mind to it. Any girl, apparently.

Except maybe this one . . .

"I definitely think there's a type of woman that guys feel like they have to prove themselves to. I'm Gchatting with her right now," Asher explained to me over email. "Sort of an out-of-their-league type, but not because they're unobtainable based on looks or status. It's more that this girl just likes to make guys show that they're worthy before letting them see the real person she is."

And what would a confident guy like Asher do with a Challenge? He'd try to prove his worthiness.

"She's someone who really gets under your skin, but you can't help wanting her to like you," he admitted. "Not because you want to be with her, but because she helps you validate yourself."

Asher isn't the only guy with a Challenge in his gaggle: in fact, loads of the guys I interviewed had a girl in their lives who seemed somewhat guarded in an intriguing, compelling way. When guys described these girls to me, they would focus less on her particular attributes—pretty, funny, quirky, etc.—and more on the fact that she was just so, well, challenging.

Interacting with a Challenge put these guys into offense mode. When talking with her, out would come the stories about the money they made, or the academic accolades they'd earned, or the cool bands only they knew about. Whatever these particular guys were proud of, and whatever they thought would impress that particular girl, they'd share it.

So if a guy just happens to keep mentioning all the babies he saved in Kenya or all the miles he's been running in preparation for that triathlon, then you might be his Challenge.

Of course, no guy—especially no confident guy—wants to seem like he's trying too hard. Which is why, even while he's trying to impress you, you might get the feeling that . . .

He's Playing Games with You, Too

Just as we women are taught that we need to play hard to get, men are taught that nice guys finish last. And thus, it is all too easy for men and women to get caught up in games of, as one guy called it, "who can give less of a shit."

One moment, a guy might be trying to impress you, and the next moment, if you are his Challenge, he might be throwing the same faux-ambivalent game back at you. As Asher said, "It's sort of a cat-and-mouse game, but more of a breaking down of walls. You likely butt heads and have a mutual desire to have flirty banter until one of you concedes."

You didn't think you could just evoke the many complicated levels of a guy's ego and then have it be smooth, straightforward sailing, did you? If you are his Challenge, then expect him to make *you* work for it a little, too. Seeing you take one step closer just as he takes one step back is all part of the fun. And the little ego boosts that he gets when he wins one round are partially what keep him going in the chase.

Once He Thinks He Has Won You Over, His Interest Wanes

This is what all those other dating books don't tell you. Once you've played the game and snagged the guy, what happens next? Well, if your connection was based primarily on you being his Challenge, then once he's got you, he might not really want you anymore.

This doesn't have to be the case, of course. Throughout the process of trying to win you over, a guy can discover real, genuine things about you that attract him in more grounded ways, especially if you actually show him some of those things. But quite a few guys admitted to me that when their interest in a girl was totally dependent on the thrill of the chase, then after the chase was done, so was their interest. Because when a guy has been thinking of you in terms of "She actually showed up tonight—score! Pat myself on the back for game well played" instead of "Damn, that girl is so cool, I can't wait to see her again," then he will think of you less and less as he becomes more and more sure that you will actually show up.

To bring it back to science class, if the lab rat starts pushing the button and gets the treat nine times out of ten, then he'll only keep pushing if he's really excited about the treat itself. Keep this in mind as you consider transitioning from the Challenge to another spot in his gaggle.

KEY TIPS

For Increasing Your Chances of Becoming His Challenge

While I refuse to condone playing hard to get simply for the sake of getting some guy, a reasonable amount of keeping your cool and showing a guy that he needs to prove his worth can be a healthy way to explore your connection with a man who believes that women typically worship at his feet. Spend time cultivating connections with other guys in your gaggle, and you will naturally not be available to him 24/7. If you are living your fantastic life and spending time with other guys, then you'll become a Challenge (without having to obsess over dumb games and rules about how long you should wait to text him back).

For *Not* Becoming His Challenge

If you're tired of playing the slippery prey to his lumbering hunter, then start letting your guard down. Go ahead and show him more authentic sides of yourself. Don't immediately declare game over and offer yourself up: since you've been his Challenge all this time, he won't have progressed yet to seeing you in another way and will lose interest after his conquest is complete. But if you take a slow and steady approach to developing the more genuine sides of your connection and showing him that you are more than simply a prize to be won, then your relationship can evolve in any number of directions.

THE CRAZY GIRL

This girl is an irrational, unreasonable, insane (or so he says!) loose cannon. Often a former flame or erstwhile romantic prospect, she has since gone off the deep end and is making illogical demands, getting upset about unimportant things, and pursuing him in undesirable ways. To his friends, he wears her and her crazy antics as a manly badge of honor. But don't be mistaken: he's desperately trying to get rid of her! He just agreed to meet her for one more drink because...

I've decided that becoming a stalker is not going to help me. Calling every day, five times a day—like, you got my fucking message, right? You saw it. You said "ignore" . . . I just said to myself, "Look, I don't care what you feel right now, logic says that you're a fucking stalker if you keep calling, okay?"

But I definitely have insecure moments all the time. It's that moment where you're like, okay, I haven't heard from her in two days, I'll just send a "good morning" text. You don't get a response, and you're like, "Why didn't I get a response? Where the fuck is she? Hanging out with someone else? Maybe someone else is over there?" You just go nuts!

—Peter, 32, MBA student, Austin

UNDERSTANDING THE CRAZY GIRL

I know, I know. You were expecting a quote from a Crazy Girl! Not a Crazy Guy. But I wanted to make a point right up front. Because as we get ready to discuss the Crazy Girl, it deserves to be said that women *and* men can both be driven insane by this little thing called love. Women just tend to display their pending insanity a little more . . . openly. And maybe with more tears.

Yet, it's a fact: boys can be crazy, too. I heard stories from my female interviewees about men threatening to drive into walls after getting dumped, or drunkenly breaking into houses because they just needed to talk to some girl who had grown detached. My own mild-mannered father once crashed a party that my mother was attending after she briefly broke up with him, forcing her friends to form a protective shield around her as he crazily demanded another chance. No one is immune from irrational behavior when it comes to matters of the heart.

So then why does the Crazy Girl get such a bad rap? And why is she a notable member of the guy's gaggle when the Crazy Guy doesn't even get a mention in the girl's gaggle?

In the words of one very enlightened male interviewee, "I don't think girls are crazy. I think that's a cop-out. But it's like the easy explanation, where you don't have to question yourself and you don't have to question what *you* did. The answer is just, oh no, she's crazy. So I don't even have to think any more about it. It's not my problem. It's hers."

But cop-out or not, the concept of the Crazy Girl cannot be ignored. Everyone knows about her. She came up in almost every interview I conducted. And when in doubt, a woman's undesirable actions continue to typically be described by one phrase: whatever, girls are just crazy.

The ubiquity of the Crazy Girl has left most of us women terrified of becoming her. And can you blame us? The Crazy Girl, in as much as she actually exists, can be a dangerous creature.

When we slip into this role, we end up questioning our sanity and good judgment. And when guys find the Crazy Girl in their gaggles, they consider it evidence that, just as they had feared, women are inherently insecure and irrational. I interviewed one genuinely nice guy in Chicago who was so scarred by a Crazy Girl that he spent the following several years bouncing around between empty Short-Term Investment and Last Resort relationships, refusing to emotionally connect to anyone. Better to be guarded than to open yourself up to dealing with an unstable wreck, he'd decided at the time.

Like it or not, the concept of the Crazy Girl exists, and you'll want to realize when you are the Crazy Girl in some guy's gaggle—so that you can pull yourself together (or ditch the guy who is wrongfully writing off your reasonable, legitimate needs and desires as "crazy").

HOW TO KNOW IF YOU'RE HIS CRAZY GIRL

Your Relationship Is Volatile

If your dynamic with this guy is all smiles and laughter and nights spent gazing at the stars, then you're probably not his Crazy Girl. But if your dynamic with this guy was like that, then you probably wouldn't be reading this section so carefully, would you?

Do your interactions involve drama? Then he might think of you as a Crazy Girl. The major precursor to being a guy's Crazy Girl is that there exists some big issue on which you do not see eye-to-eye. All too often, that issue tends to revolve around the way he is treating you, and the way that you *want* him to treat you, and your chosen method of expressing that dissatisfaction. Disgruntled Short-Term Investments, Girlfriend Prospects, and Last Resorts: this might be the situation that you end up in—a situation colorfully described to me by Drake, a twenty-seven-year-old finance guy in New York City whose experience with a Crazy Girl was legendary among his friends.

When Drake and I met at a Starbucks, there was one thing he had to do before he could start telling me his story. He had to look around the rest of the Starbucks, with terror in his eyes, to make sure that his Crazy Girl wasn't there. And when I suggested that maybe she was hiding behind the coffee counter, he sneaked a glance back there too, nervously admitting, "That would not surprise me."

In his own words, this Crazy Girl was "not mentally stable. Very shaky, very insecure. Emotionally not all there. A control freak. She just has a crazy mentality."

Yikes! Even I started checking under the table, just to be safe.

Drake and his Crazy Girl had started off on the same page—a purely sexual page. Intensely physically attracted to one another, they slept together the first night they met and decided to keep things casual. He had just gotten out of a long-term relationship and so had she. So they agreed: they were never going to date. She was his Short-Term Investment. He was (supposedly) her Hot Sex Prospect. It should have been a hot, fun, temporary hookup situation.

And it was! Until he canceled plans to watch a movie at her place one night. Suddenly, the shit hit the fan.

"She freaked out," Drake recalled with a shudder. "One of the craziest freakouts you could imagine. She lost it. She started saying, 'How can you treat me like this? You treat me like the biggest whore ever!' So I went to meet her, just to calm her down. And then she said, 'Listen, I'm calm and I get it. But I'm still really attracted to you, so you should come back with me right now.' I was like, what the hell is wrong with you?"

Of course Drake hooked up with her that night, despite her crazy antics. Their sexual attraction, "a powerful and conflicting thing," knew no bounds! But thus began a toxic cycle. He would blow her off, she would freak out, he would calm her down, she would swear that she was suddenly satisfied with their casual dynamic, and then they'd hook up again.

This went on for almost a year and ended up being "one of the craziest experiences that I've ever had with anyone," said Drake.

Fights? Tears? Name calling? Freakouts? All volatile signs that, even if he's still hooking up with you, he's beginning to think that you're out of your mind.

He Avoids You More Than He Responds to You

Most of the time, a guy won't feel like dealing with his Crazy Girl. He'll consider her to be a lot of unnecessary drama for only a little bit of payoff (that payoff might depend on how equally crazy the sex is, and how much his friends seem to be getting a kick out of his "this chick is crazy!" stories). If a guy does not respond to the majority of your texts, calls, emails, and skywriting messages, then there's a good chance that he's sitting around thinking you're crazy. And the more you contact him, the crazier he will think you are.

Drake realized that he was partly to blame for his Crazy Girl's freakouts. At least, he realized that hooking up with her on a regular basis probably wasn't helping things. But from his perspective, he felt like he had been clear about his intentions from the start. And besides, she was hitting him up way more than he was her. She should have been getting the hint, right?

"She realized that we would only talk at nighttime, and most of the time she was calling me," Drake swore. "Then she started asking me to do things with her. Come over for dinner, watch a movie. And I kept saying, 'Listen, I am not ready to jump into a relationship. You know what to expect, if you want to continue this.' But I could see the switch flicking in her head, like, I'm saying one thing, but I'm going to do another, and then I'm going to do indirect things to show you what I want."

If a guy is avoiding most of your overtures to talk and hang out, and especially if he is telling you that he is going to continue avoiding them, then pay attention. If you contact a guy, then rest assured: he received your message. And if he didn't get back to you, that was a choice. The more this happens and the more you try again, the more desperate you seem and the more likely he's wondering why you're not getting the hint.

When You See His Friends, They Treat You Like a Potential Ax Murderer

The Crazy Girl tends to hold celebrity status amongst a guy's group of friends. He might not make the effort to introduce you, but rest assured, they know about you—because what guy doesn't love to tell his friends that some girl is bat-shit crazy obsessed with him? Of course, they usually think he should run away from you as fast as humanly possible.

"I lived with two of my best friends, and they knew very early on that she was insane," Drake remembered. "And they told me, 'She's fucking nuts! We know where this is going. Just don't let this get serious.'"

The point is that if you are a guy's Crazy Girl, then his friends have heard about you. He has regaled them with stories of your overly urgent voicemails and angry 4:00 a.m. emails. Therefore, when you see them, they are going to be slightly scared of you. They are going to keep their girlfriends and gaggle members away from you, lest the crazy is contagious. And they are going to generally avoid you, in an effort to avoid inciting a meltdown.

In their mind, if this were *Jurassic Park*, then you would be the T. Rex, ready to attack. And they would be all those kids who were instructed not to make any sudden movements and to avoid shining flashlights in your face.

That's the extent to which they'll fear you and your crazy ways.

You *Know* That You're Being Crazy

For me, the saddest part of hearing Drake's story was that, on the surface, his Crazy Girl didn't sound that different from me or my friends. In her defense, Drake described her as "really on point with stuff. Extremely intelligent. Really, really successful. Has it put together. Has friends. Goes out. Lives a normal life."

But her problem? "Emotionally, with guys, she's nuts." As she proved when she realized that he had detagged some Facebook photos of them from his birthday party and proceeded to have "the worst freakout times eight," thus effectively ending their disastrous on-and-off fling.

Drake's profile of his Crazy Girl as a mostly normal person reminded me that most modern women are not inherently, consistently crazy. Yet what my interviews confirmed is that many of us, at one point or another, can be driven a little crazy. Plenty of girls were able to pinpoint specific times when they had acted irrationally. And god knows I've had my Crazy Girl moments!

So maybe there need to be times when we use our smarts to own up to our own irrational Crazy Girl behaviors. Regardless of how certain men treat us, sometimes we might need to simply look squarely at ourselves and our actions and realize, without any external feedback, "Oh gosh. I'm being the Crazy Girl."

When in doubt, here are a few actions that women (bashfully) mentioned to me, when sharing their own Crazy Girl stories. No guy should have to tell you that these are signs you are acting a little crazy:

- ☐ You check out the Facebook page of every girl he's added as a friend—and let's not even get started on girls who post on his wall!
- ☐ You leave an article of clothing at his house to see if he mentions it without being prompted.
- ☐ You secretly check his phone or email to see who else he is talking to.
- ☐ You demand that he not hang out with his friends, family, or any girl who comes within a ten-foot radius of him.
- ☐ You fight with him in front of other people.
- ☐ You trick him into meeting up with you under false pretenses.
- ☐ You time how long he takes to text you back and have a set average in your head. More than two hours, and he must be with another girl!
- ☐ You count his condoms.
- ☐ You respond to an unanswered text by calling him. And then emailing him. And then showing up at his house.
- ☐ You cry. Often.

Ultimately, you know you are being a Crazy Girl when you are overanalyzing a guy's actions to death and desperately trying to read meanings that probably aren't there. So when you are obsessing over the potentially deeper meaning of some guy's retweet, remember this quote from Jason in Minneapolis and try to scale back the pernicious thoughts:

"Do I think girls are crazy? No, not on the whole. I just think that they approach things from a completely different angle, especially when it comes to all this stuff. Whereas I feel like I'm usually looking through a clear pane of glass, they're looking through a prism. They're like, 'But no, look! There's this and this and this!'"

When in doubt, close your eyes tightly and then open them again. Is that really a prism in front of you? Or can it be simplified to a pane of glass? Be honest and objective with yourself, and proceed accordingly.

KEY TIPS

For Increasing Your Chances of Becoming His Crazy Girl

You don't actually want to become some guy's Crazy Girl, do you? Well, if you're thinking of something that I'm not, then you know what to do. Scream, cry, worry, overanalyze, and text him until your fingers bleed. And do it all loudly. Yep. That should cover it.

For *Not* Becoming His Crazy Girl

At the sake of sounding like your parents' marriage therapist, it's all about communication! You should feel free to bring up tough issues with a guy, without worrying that you'll become his Crazy Girl. But there's a noncrazy way to do it.

Instead of being all drama, all the time, set aside a specific time to talk about whatever is bothering you. Give yourself this one opportunity to say whatever it is that you want to say, and say it calmly and rationally, as if this will be your last chance to get it off your chest. Then, whatever his response is, take it in stride. If he reacts defensively and calls you crazy, then drop him from your gaggle. If he seems to understand your point, then give him the benefit of the doubt and, moving forward, suppress any knee-jerk insecurities that might lead to craziness. And in the meantime, resume interacting with gaggle members who do not bring out your loopier sides to balance it all out.

THE (MAYBE) ONE

A girl he thinks is amazing, although he's not planning on actually exploring the potential of their connection until a later time. He says he will go after this awesome girl (who has all the qualities he supposedly wants in a lifelong partner) when he gets his life in order. Or when he's done playing the field. Or when he's more set in his career. Or when he's truly ready to settle down. You get the idea. He's not making a move on this girl yet, but he plans to do so someday in the future. This is why she is also often referred to as "the long-term plan."

Yes, I thought Elaina was cute when I first met her. And I knew that what I was feeling for her was different than what I had ever felt before. But I knew that if we started dating, it would be forever. And I wasn't ready to be forever. And if I had been, it probably wouldn't have lasted forever, at that point.
—Shawn, 27, psychologist, Minneapolis, now married to Elaina

UNDERSTANDING THE (MAYBE) ONE

The first time a guy told me about this girl, I assumed he was a strange exception to the male gender. When another guy brought her up, I thought, interesting story, I should remember to put this in my book. By the tenth time, I realized that something paradigm-shifting was going on.

As a woman, you probably act under the basic assumption that if a guy is romantically interested in you, then he will eventually hit on you in some explicit way. Because what men want, men go after, 110 percent, right? Isn't that what we learned from *The Rules* and *He's Just Not That Into You?*

Whoever presented these "givens" to us has obviously never spent time with Millennial men, because if my interviews made one thing clear to me, it was that these men think—a lot. About some seriously deep shit. Their dreams, their futures, their identity as M-E-N . . . and depending on how successful they're feeling on all these fronts, there's a good chance that they've got a (Maybe) One floating around in their gaggle. In fact, for these men-in-flux, their love lives seem to follow a simple calculus: the more highly they think of you, the less likely they'll be to start something romantic.

This equation can be confusing as hell for women. Having a guy treat you as a (Maybe) One can feel only teeny, tiny steps away from him being just not that into you. And we all know what *that* feels like (since we've been taught to default to that assumption whenever a guy has not delivered fifty-three dozen roses to our office on a Tuesday just to say hi).

There are differences, though, between a guy putting you on a pedestal and a guy being just not that into you. Read and learn.

HOW TO KNOW IF YOU'RE HIS (MAYBE) ONE

He *Hasn't* Made a Move on You (Yet) (or in a Really Long Time)

I spent a long time talking to Scott, a thirty-year-old who was in the process of embarking on a new career in Colorado, about his (Maybe) One. Over an hour into my interview with him, Scott just casually happened to mention, "I think I know who I'm going to marry." He'd apparently never said that to anyone before. (I was honored!) But . . .

Scott was single—"single as I've ever been." So wait, what? Who was this girl? And why wasn't he pursuing her?

"She's totally capable, self-sufficient. She has passion and love and sexuality in her, but she's not owned by that . . . and she's interested in me. She thinks I'm funny. She wants to hear what I have to say. She cares if I'm doing all right or not—but not where she's, like, dropping everything to bring me chicken soup. I just like hanging out with her, and she's one of the only people I know who I just respect through and through. I feel something is right. I feel at home. Coolest girl I know."

This girl—we'll call her Miranda—sounds awesome! Which is exactly why Scott wasn't pursuing anything with her yet. He "wasn't ready." Even though he'd already pictured her naked, of course.

"I'm honest with her, because we haven't had sex yet, so it's easy. We've never hooked up—always been friends. I'm not blinded by lust. Which is good, because I'm able to keep my head. But I think I know that when I ever do see her naked, it's going to look real nice."

I had to give Scott credit for not succumbing to his baser instincts and keeping his eyes on the more serious prize. He liked Miranda so much that he wasn't willing to cheapen their connection for a quick hookup. But if he wasn't making a move on her, then how was she supposed to know that he was into her?

He Hasn't Made a Move on Any of Your Friends, Either

Scott swore that Miranda must know that he had feelings for her. So what was his big signal that she was the girl he was considering marrying?

"I'm going after her, but it's a long-term game, and she's aware. Probably. Like, I'm deliberately not sleeping with her friends."

Interesting. Okay, so . . . anything else?

"One time her twenty-one-year-old cousin came to visit me, and she ran the most aggressive game I've ever been confronted with, like, demanding that I take her virginity. And I wanted to! But because of Miranda, I didn't."

And no man would turn down the opportunity to take a twenty-one-year-old's virginity, unless he was falling for her cousin, right?

Okay, fine. Scott's unwillingness to risk his (possible) future with Miranda by banging her cousin was a smart move. And while he and I ultimately disagreed on whether his chaste refusal was a strong enough signal to be sending Miranda, there is still a lesson here.

You shouldn't assume that every guy who has *not* tried to sleep with your friends or family is secretly in love with you. But, at least you know that if he has been making moves on them, then you are not his (Maybe) One.

He Is Regularly (But Not Constantly) in Touch—Always in a Respectful Way

When guys talked to me about their (Maybe) Ones, one word kept popping up: respect. And to show these girls respect, they had to actually be in their lives.

"I'm able to engineer the relationship that I want with her," Scott explained. "Of respect, of knowing each other. Like, we don't drink together. We have a book club together! We go out, and we have a good time. We can get together and talk."

To be clear, Scott has also had women in his life with whom he connects on more visceral levels. He had moved much faster (and even had intense relationships) with girls whom he calls, "shy, preppy, doe-eyed women who bring nothing to the table." But with Miranda, the connection was just different. There was respect there. And while their relationship might have been progressing slowly, it was still progressing. He wasn't disappearing from her life for huge chunks of time. He was around just enough to make sure that their connection never truly waned. And when he was around, he was engaging with her in a meaningful, respectful way.

When it comes to the guy who you're thinking of, ask yourself: Is he a fairly regular fixture in my life? Is his presence consistent, but not necessarily constant or rushed? Is he showing me that extra level of respect—even though maybe I've seen him be a jerk to other girls? If so, then you might be his (Maybe) One.

He Tells You That You're His (Maybe) One!

"I'm sorry, but you're just too good for me right now!"

If some guy you just met says this to you, *run.* He's blowing you off! But if it's said by a guy who has known you for a while, and if your connection is deep-rooted in real friendship, then he might just be speaking the truth.

One of my female interviewees in Cincinnati was shocked when a male friend told her that she had always been his "Bottom Bitch." I know, I was as horrified by this turn of phrase as you are. Didn't that have something to do with prostitutes? But it turns out that being a non-pimp guy's Bottom Bitch is a *good* thing.

As he defined it to her, "It's the girl who is like the baseline. You can go out and date other girls and have crushes on other girls and have other girlfriends, but if this girl was ever to say, 'I want to be with you,' you would drop everything to be with her. She's a girl you've been friends with, a girl you know to her core."

It turned out that my interviewee had been his Bottom Bitch for seven years. He'd been in love with her for ages! However, years before he declared this, she had made it known that she really liked him and wanted to be his girlfriend. His response back then? As she recalled, "No, you're too good for me right now—I'm not ready to settle down, I don't want to hurt you and I'm going to, if we get serious." Thinking it was bullshit, her response was "Fuck you." But actually, he meant it. Years later, he finally manned up and tried to make up for lost time by taking her to a Waffle House, where they slow-danced and he announced his feelings. Ah, romance.

If a guy tells you that he's "not ready" and then genuinely continues to pursue some sort of relationship with you, then you might be his (Maybe) One. So keep him in your gaggle, if you want to. But also give him the time and space that he needs. Who knows where your connection will end up? One day, you might even get to call yourself his Bottom Bitch.

Congrats?

He Is Clearly in a Transitional Phase of His Life

A guy might have a (Maybe) One if he feels unprepared to initiate the biggest, most important (potential) relationship of his life. So if you're wondering whether you fill this role in his gaggle, then observe the rest of his life and see if, in fact, there's a reason that he might not be ready for you.

Back to Scott! The question remained: why wasn't he pursuing his

(Maybe) One? What did it mean to be "not ready" for a relationship with Miranda? When he explained his struggle, I had to admit that he truly didn't sound ready:

"I think that timing, unromantic as it is, is almost everything. The ability of women to multitask is one of the things I respect most about them. It makes me feel like a fucking infant! Women are like, this is how I feel about you, and this is how I feel about my life, and I'm juggling that, and no, I'm not going to drop either of them.

"I just don't think men can multitask like that. I think we need a little more space and deliberation to plant our feet, at least in our heads. We don't have to have a career, but we have to be like, all right, this is where I'm at. I'm going to approach love now, and let it approach me, and not be blown off course. I need to be happy with myself, in order to give happiness to a relationship and let somebody love me.

"Men are insecure, and it makes it really hard for us to relax about achievement and who we are. There's always a struggle, as a man, to just reach some kind of pride, or sense of, okay, this is me, and this is enough."

Whew! Such is the mind of the modern man. We women might be able to figure all this identity stuff out while simultaneously exploring romantic connections—but apparently, that's a unique part of our charm. The same cannot be said for a lot of guys. In fact, the one thing they might be sure of is that they will mess it all up if they start something romantic with you, without feeling ready.

They might hook up—and even enter into relationships—with other girls. But for now, at least when it comes to a girl who they can really see a future with, they'd rather not risk it by starting something in the first place.

So where does your guy seem to stand, in his own life? Is he established, confident, and happy? Then he won't be topping off his gaggle with a (Maybe) One. But if he is in the midst of personal or professional transitions and treating you in all the ways that we've discussed, then he might be holding off on exploring your connection until he's gotten a little further along in his journey to manhood.

KEY TIPS

For Increasing Your Chances of Becoming His (Maybe) One

Keep it classy, friendly, and slow. No bang-'em-and-leave-'em play-non-dates. No pressure for your relationship to move faster. Instead, think long-term and gear your interactions toward settings and activities that encourage mental and emotional connection.

For *Not* Becoming His (Maybe) One

Tired of waiting around to see if this guy will ever get his shit together? If you're sick of being asked to sit on a shelf until the timing is more convenient for him, then push your connection now. Attempt to hang out more. Get increasingly flirty. At a certain point, give yourself an ultimatum: either he wants to be with you at this very moment, or he'll never get the chance.

THE POSSIBILITY

A girl who is on his radar and in his wider sphere, but not in an immediately present way. He finds her attractive, and she could eventually join the active ranks of his day-to-day gaggle. But for now, due to timing or distance or the fact that they just don't know each other very well, she is hanging out in the back of his brain. No need for her to feel discouraged, though, if she's a little into him. One significant moment or interaction could raise her profile and change everything.

Most of the girls I hook up with are mutual friends that I see enough. But I don't see them a lot. And you go out that one time, and it happens to be a good night. Maybe there's a mutual attraction, or they're attracted to me because they're drunk. Maybe I've been attracted to them, but I was never interested in pursuing anything at all.

Honestly, I don't know how it happens!

—Michael, 23, student, Baton Rouge

UNDERSTANDING THE POSSIBILITY

When you ask a girl how she and some guy got together, you usually get a long story. The tale typically gets unveiled along the lines of, "So he said this, and then I did that, because I was feeling this, and I could tell he was thinking that [and so on for five minutes] . . . and then we hooked up [and so on for ten minutes] . . . and then we became exclusive!"

That's not always what happens when you ask men.

Sometimes, when I ask a guy to tell me how a major event in his love life went down, I get a non-story—kind of like what I heard from this interviewee:

"I don't hook up with a lot of people, but when it does happen—I guess more than I would think—it's usually someone I've known for a long time, and it's just, like, wow, we hooked up. That's really crazy."

To summarize what he was trying to say: he usually had no idea why things happened with girls when they did. He just felt like the universe was making decisions for him, and he was along for the ride.

Sure, when I talk to guys about their gaggles, they tend to immediately mention girls who fall into certain categories—Girlfriend Prospect, Short-Term Investment, Work Wife, etc. These are the women who play an active role in their day-to-day gaggle. The guys are aware of their exact (for the moment) feelings about these girls and intend to interact with them accordingly.

But guys also have other women in their lives. These are girls who are not on their immediate radar but who, as I've seen in some of my follow-up interviews, often end up shifting into more prominent roles in the gaggle. Some of the guys think this happens because, oh, I don't know, they changed their contact lenses or something. Just all of a sudden, they really noticed her! All of a sudden, she seemed to be around more often. . . .

Here's the beauty of being a guy's Possibility: as a woman, you have a lot more say in those all-of-a-suddens than he may ever realize. When it comes to your dynamic with this guy, you have a wide-open playing field. He hasn't really decided how he feels about you yet. So once you figure out where he resides in your gaggle, there won't be much stopping you. You'll have the agency to make that particular relationship come to life.

This guy might not have fully recognized your potential yet—but he hasn't put you in a box, either. The possibilities (ahem) here are endless.

HOW TO KNOW IF YOU'RE HIS POSSIBILITY

You're His Friend

People love to debate the age-old question of whether men and women can be friends. The short answer is, of course they can! But it certainly makes it more likely that a guy will want to be friends if he thinks the girl is pretty.

There was a common sentiment regarding male-female friendships that I heard during my interviews with guys. These men swore that they were capable of having female friends whom they were not pursuing romantically or sexually. They had lots of women in their lives to whom they turned for great conversations, stellar advice, and common interests. But when push came to shove, they were willing to acknowledge that they found most of these women attractive.

That attraction would often exist in a vacuum. They were not pursuing these girls. But when asked, "That friend of yours—is she attractive?" the answer was almost always yes.

If you are friends with a guy, then odds are he finds you attractive. That base level of attraction makes you a Possibility in his gaggle.

He's In No Rush

A guy will have an end goal in mind for some of the girls in his gaggle. He'll want to date his Girlfriend Prospect, or hook up with his Short-Term Investment, or (maybe) marry his (Maybe) One. But when it comes to the Possibility, who knows! His brain hasn't gotten that far yet. He has no specific intentions in mind.

This lack of focus may leave your friendship feeling a bit casual. You get along, you enjoy hanging out, you check in with each other every once in a while . . . but there's not a sense of fast-moving momentum in your dynamic. Your relationship might not be progressing in leaps and bounds, and you might not be growing closer by the day.

But again, if you're looking to establish a heftier spot in his gaggle,

238 • JESSICA MASSA

this can be a good thing! You've got some open terrain here. You can go forth and gaggle.

He Seems to Have Many Women in His Life

You know how I've been telling you to explore any and all connections that you come across? Well, some guys out there have gotten that memo already. And the more women they know, the more Possibilities they seem to have. This abundance of options might partially account for why he seems to be taking his sweet time exploring your connection.

Take Walter, a twenty-six-year-old professional jack-of-all-trades in Atlanta. He told me that he interacted with new women constantly, and I was inclined to believe him, since we'd first met because he was my waiter the night before.

"I'd say that I always keep female friends around, and I meet women everywhere," Walter claimed. "I put that vibe out there every day. Like, in line at Whole Foods, I'll just connect so well with the lady checking me out. Or like yesterday, I was eating at this Mexican joint and I totally gave the waitress my phone number. Made her day, made mine. And it doesn't even matter!"

Walter wasn't a player, and he wasn't hooking up with most of these women. He was just getting to know them and filling his life with interesting people.

If you're friends with a guy like Walter—a guy who connects women easily and often—then you can probably just assume that you're a Possibility in his gaggle. Since he has only so much energy and focus to spread around, how could he put each and every girl he meets into a more specific gaggle category? He can't. So most women end up as a Possibility.

But make him a more prominent member of your gaggle, and see if that doesn't start to change. Because no matter how many women he knows, if he's not in a committed relationship, then he might still be out there searching for something. Walter told me that he didn't have enough romance in his life. Other men admitted that they were still seeking passion or intellectualism or someone who understood their weird music taste. If there's a void in your guy's life, then get to know him better, and you might just be the one to fill it.

KEY TIPS

For Increasing Your Chances of Becoming His Possibility

Becoming a guy's Possibility is easy: just get in his face! If he finds you the least bit attractive, and starts to consider you a friend, then you're in. Welcome to his gaggle. Now proceed as you see fit.

For *Not* Becoming His Possibility

If you're stuck in the Possibility role and want to explore your connection in a more immediate way, then turn back to your own gaggle. Who might this guy be to you? What role would he ideally play in your gaggle? Figure that out, and then start introducing elements of that dynamic into your interactions. Things might not go exactly as planned, but at least you'll be on the path to further defining your connection in a more enlightening way.

PART FIVE

LOVE IN THE TIME
OF TWITTER

IT'S NOT SEXTING . . .
IT'S TECHNO-ROMANCE!

One time, my sister and I were sitting in our kitchen and texting like mad to all these different men. And our mom was asking who we were texting and why.

And I said to her—"Do you think it's weird that we're in so much contact with so many people?" And she goes, "Yes, I do think it's weird."

But then she thought about it for a second and said, "But I think it's way better than when I was young, and I had to sit by the phone for two days to see if someone was going to call me."

—Maura, 23, media strategist, Salt Lake City

Now you've got your gaggle. And every guy in your gaggle has got his own gaggle. And you're all probably adding new prospects to your gaggles on a regular basis.

What a cluster(-non-)fuck!

How are you supposed to be cultivating all these connections while still, you know, finding time to get everything else in your life done?

By engaging in the great twenty-first-century romantic equalizer, of course!

TECHNO-ROMANCE (n.)

The rampant use of technologies to cultivate and explore romantic, sexual, and flirtatious interactions and even relationships.

In other words, yes, that text message counts. And so does that Gchat conversation. Don't be embarrassed by the butterflies that these technological communications can evoke.

You might have noticed by now that various forms of technology infuse almost every story in this book. In my interviews, I found that techno-romance played a prominent role in the love lives of everyone, everywhere, in every part of the country—from sexual progressives in Portland, Oregon, to the family-oriented young couples of Madison, Wisconsin, to the nervously unmarried Southern belles of Atlanta, Georgia, to the single parents of Louisville, Kentucky. A text here, a Facebook friend request there, an email here, a BBM flirtation there, an online dating profile here, a long-distance virtual book club there: whether we like it or not, technology has absolutely impacted all of our love lives. When it comes to romance and the gaggle, technology is omnipresent.

Now, is this a good thing or a bad thing?

People love to bitch about technology being the death of all things romantic and happy and holy. And of course, we've all had moments where we want to tear our hair out over some unanswered email or unclearly worded text message. So the jury still seems to be out on this point—but it shouldn't be! Because like all aspects of the post-dating world, techno-romance can work wonders for you, if you choose to embrace it.

Techno-romance is here to stay, and you should be psyched about that. You can own the role technology plays in your love life, instead of letting it make you feel like a slave to every beep and buzz of your phone. Used smartly and sanely, techno-romance is a fantastic tool that will make your love life significantly more vibrant and fulfilling.

I'll repeat: used smartly and sanely. Which, let's be honest, is not always the case.

TECHNO-ROMANCE:
USE IT FOR GOOD, NOT FOR EVIL!

I met her here in San Francisco, but she lived on the other side of the country—so we did a long-distance thing.

We texted all day. And you misinterpret a lot, right? So what we did was, we wrote down every text message that we sent to each other. And then we'd go back and say whether or not we'd correctly interpreted it at that moment.

And actually, we had this thing where I would send her a text message, knowing that she was asleep. And then she would send one to me, knowing that I would wake up to it. So we had this mutual thing where we would both wake up to each other's texts. Like, we'd be the beginning of that other person's day.

—Robert, 26, graduate student, Palo Alto

I get it: technology can wreak havoc on our love lives. It can cause us to miscommunicate, stalk, obsess, avoid difficult topics, and walk around with our eyes glued to our smartphones like our lives depend on that one email we're anxiously waiting for. And on the flip side, the ubiquity of technological communication can make the absence of it—otherwise known as silence—feel like the ultimate mind-fuck.

Technology drives us all nuts.

But technology can also present us with romantic opportunities that earlier generations could never have dreamed of. It can be used for good.

TECHNOLOGY CAN INTRODUCE YOU
TO NEW GAGGLE MEMBERS

One of the easiest ways to add some new flavor to your gaggle is to take your search online.

Online dating is, of course, the most obvious way to meet new romantic prospects. And as I mentioned before, as long as it's not the only way you're planning to expand your network, go for it! We all know friends, family members, and coworkers who have found love, or even just a little fun, via online dating.

But online dating isn't the only way to expand your gaggle technologically. Not only can you find potential group-non-date activities online—MeetUp.com groups, sporting leagues, activity-based gatherings in your city—but you can also use the social networking tools that you're already on to shake things up.

One woman I met in Chicago had met several of her boyfriends—and me—through Twitter, where she spent most of her online time and felt comfortable hitting up interesting strangers. Another woman in Chicago had performed an experiment where she changed her Facebook status from nothing to "Single" and found that even this slight shift had led to unexpected messages from men she hadn't heard from in years. And a girl I spoke with in Nashville was contacted by several guys from her past mere hours after breaking up with her boyfriend and changing her Facebook status from "In a relationship" to "Single."

If you are online in some capacity, then you are never without prospects. You just need to figure out the best way to reach and activate them.

YOU CAN USE TECHNOLOGY TO FACILITATE
E-NON-DATES

It's great to hang out with members of your gaggle in person. Necessary, really, when it comes down to it. But in between the time that you spend together, you can use technology to deepen your connection and strengthen your own unique dynamic with e-non-dates.

This can mean emailing each other interesting links or texting each other amusing thoughts—or for couples, interacting via BBM or IM throughout the day. For Robert, the neuroscience graduate student in Palo Alto, this meant coordinating a schedule of non-dates with his Short-Term Investment via an intricate and complex system of punctuation marks on the individual days of their shared Google calendar. In case you want to try this at home:

> *? = Do you want to hang out on this day?*
>
> *! = Yes, I do!*
>
> *?! = As much as I want to respect the fact that maybe you're busy, I really need to see you right now.*

Robert's story goes to show that if you want technology to fit your unique dynamic and sense of humor, it can even do that, too.

YOU CAN SIMULTANEOUSLY EXPLORE YOUR CONNECTIONS WITH MULTIPLE PEOPLE

From a gaggle perspective, technology is necessary for cultivating a group of romantic prospects in your life. How else would you find the time to simultaneously keep several guys in your sphere?

On any given day now, you can email with a Career Booster, text a Hot Sex Prospect, write on your Accessory's Facebook wall, and then maybe even go meet your Boyfriend Prospect for dinner. All while trying to ignore the fact that the Guy Who Just Blew You Off never responded to that direct message you sent him on Twitter.

Instead of spending several weeks talking on the phone and going out on dates with one guy, only to realize that he's not the right guy for you, you can romantically multitask.

YOU CAN BUILD STRONG LONG-DISTANCE RELATIONSHIPS

Not only does technology allow us to explore a greater number of connections than ever before, but once we do find someone who we care about, it allows us to invest in that relationship without having to account for geographic proximity right off the bat. You fell in love with someone who lives across the country? So be it! That's why God created Skype sex.

In this post-dating world, long-distance relationships have become a totally feasible romantic model. Even couples who live near each other often have to go through phases of long-distance love when someone gets temporarily relocated for a job, school, or family matter. Keeping up a connection across the country has never been easier.

In Nashville and San Francisco, I met women who used technology to maintain, and even strengthen, their relationships with boyfriends and husbands who were serving abroad in the military. I interviewed women in Green Bay and Denver who actually met their fiancés while they were living in different regions of the country and, thanks to technology, established long-distance relationships that grew so strong that they eventually moved to be closer together. Techno-romance has made the whole world our romantic oyster.

Tell yourself that technology is the end of romance, and you will create a self-fulfilling prophecy. But embrace technology, and you'll find that you have a whole new set of tools to create the kinds of connections that you want.

TO MOM AND DAD
(AND THE REST OF YOUR
GENERATION) WITH *SO MUCH* LOVE:
THANKS, BUT NO THANKS!

My parents work well together—but I don't want what they have.

They work as a team, and there's some love there—but they don't, like, go dancing like they used do. I've seen them dance once, and it was something I will never forget, because it was just so great to see them do their own thing. Basically, a family neighbor got married and they were invited to the wedding. And all of a sudden, I turn around and see my parents dancing, not really caring about whatever else. They just lost themselves. And that is a moment that is just, like—it was so good. So good.

But usually, they're too focused on their kids to, you know . . .

—Victor, 27, digital production artist, Seattle

Finding love—and knowing what to do with it once you've got it—are two very separate issues.

On that note, it is just a fact that the baby boomer divorce rate is a huge bummer. A bummer that left many of us growing up in broken homes. And it's hard to say whether married life is faring much better. Right now, if you turn on TBS, you'll probably catch a rerun of some half-hour sitcom that makes married life look awful.

When it came to long-term relationships, wherever I traveled, there was one topic that almost everyone could speak confidently on: their parents' relationships—and why they didn't want to re-create them. Disconcerting but true.

If you ask young people how their parents' relationships have affected their own romantic needs and wants, you'll get an earful.

For the record, most of my interviewees—and most of my friends, and myself!—truly adore our parents. We all appreciate the sacrifices and unconditional love that went into raising us to be the driven, well-rounded, mildly entitled grown-ups that we are. Almost everyone I spoke to thought that their parents had been pretty great parents.

They just didn't think that their parents had created inspiring romantic relationships.

Unsurprisingly, the children of divorced homes whom I met wanted to redefine the paradigm: their parents' marriage, at least by traditional standards, had failed. But unexpectedly, even those interviewees whose parents were still together seemed to feel notably uninspired.

The top concern that my interviewees articulated was that their parents were so focused on and committed to being fantastic moms and dads that they had often put their own romantic relationships second. Where was all the love? And the passion? And the fun? Were they hiding it in the downtime between running the kids to basketball practices and dance rehearsals and commuting home from work to throw together makeshift family dinners?

Parents aside, all of my interviewees had a different description of the love they wanted. We are all on our own journeys, and we have different understandings of what love means to us. We are figuring out who we are and what we want, in life and in love.

But then what happens when we find the person we want to build a life with? How can we ensure that this special love continues to get better and better with time? Do we even have enough of a template to work off of?

Luckily, our parents and their generation aren't our only role models these days. Some of our friends, family members, and peers are in amazing relationships. Many incredible and inspiring couples that I met on the road had plenty of advice about creating the relationship of the future—or more accurately, the relationship of *your* future.

Sounds like an Epcot ride, doesn't it? Even better.

Let's hear what they have to say.

THE RELATIONSHIP OF THE FUTURE

"Kevin and I started off as friends, which I think helped set the foundation for our relationship. Both of my parents have had three marriages. His divorced and refused to ever marry again. We knew that we didn't want to be like that, but we also knew that we needed to be open and not carry our parents' baggage."

"Sabine and I know it's not easy to grow together, and that we're two different people CHOOSING to go down the same path together."

"We're each other's best friends and biggest fans, and we support each other to grow as individuals so that we can then continue to grow together. But there's also more than that. There is no one in the universe that makes me feel like him. We wouldn't be together, if it weren't for the love—the love is the glue, and then it's the effort that makes us thrive."

—Sabine and Kevin, 27, teacher and audio engineer, Seattle, married

Sometimes, being in a relationship just doesn't seem that appealing. You have to "check in" with someone all the time. You have to give up other options. You have to take someone else's plans and preferences into consideration. And when you're constantly coordinating your life with someone else's, it's not as easy to escape the world and just curl up on your couch in sweats and no makeup and binge on *The Real Housewives of Whatever County*. Or to head out with your friends in a scandalously short skirt, dance all night, and make eyes at every cute guy you see.

It's likely that some of your friends are in uninspiring relationships, and as you watch them bicker, sulk, and bore themselves to tears, you may wonder: do I really want to be in a relationship? My life is pretty awesome as it is; do I really want to throw the hassle of another person's quirks and mood swings and annoyances into it?

And then you meet a couple like Mike and Sheria, and you think to yourself, "Oh, yes, I want what they have!"

Mike and Sheria—married with two children—are one of the most inspiring couples I have ever met. They've carved out a special little place in the world (in Cincinnati) for themselves and their family, and they emit a positive, welcoming energy that makes you not want to leave their presence. They're the kind of couple who remind you not to settle for anything less than, well, epic love.

Unlike many of the other optimistic, young-and-in-love couples that I met, Mike and Sheria were not new to the game. Their life together contained no hypotheticals, as they had already been dealing with the realities of marriage, kids, careers, and their own personal identities for the ten years they have been together. And yet, despite coming from broken homes, battling the insensitivities of their families and their city as a mixed-race couple, struggling at times to make financial ends meet, facing fertility issues, and all the while constantly encountering the belief of those around them that marriage is supposed to be boring (if not disastrous), their connection was as great as any I had seen.

Neither Mike nor Sheria had particularly good relationship role models. Mike's parents divorced when he was in seventh grade after his father cheated on his mother, and Sheria was raised by her grandparents after her mother had her as a teenager. To put it mildly, Mike and Sheria were starting from a blank slate.

"Before I met Mike, I was like, I am never getting married!" swore Sheria. "I'm never having kids, because my mom had so many kids, and I had helped raise my siblings. Instead, I'm going to be everybody's favorite aunt. I was like, no way. And besides, I thought, there was no way I could just hang out with one person, like, forever."

"I said I would never get married, too," agrees Matt. "Because everybody gets divorced."

Then Mike and Sheria met each other, and that all changed. But how to make that life-long relationship work? Whose advice to follow? In the absence of proven rules to abide by, they did what moderns couples have to do: they made up their own rules.

Like Mike and Sheria, when you embark on a relationship, you should join heads with your partner and, based on your own particular needs and desires, figure out some rules of your own. But if you're looking for a little guidance on how to get that started, dare I say that Mike and Sheria are on to something with many of the guidelines they have set for themselves! You might want to take notes. Because the standards they have set for their relationship revolve around themes and decisions that I heard throughout my talks with strong, happy couples.

Your ideal love shouldn't take "work," but it will take effort—along with thoughtfulness and a willingness to sit down, hash things out, and rewrite the rules to suit you and your partner. But it will all be worth it. These couples found authentic connection and happiness by ignoring the traditional expectations and creating their own norms and dynamics. Who's to say that you won't succeed in doing the same with your partner someday?

THE TEN COMMANDMENTS OF POST-DATING RELATIONSHIPS

I. Do. Not. Stop. Having. Fun. Together. Ever.

Fun shouldn't be the last thing you think of when it comes to your day-to-day relationship—it should be the first.

One trait I noticed with every happy couple I met was that they talked about their partners as if they were always a welcome presence, and not an obligation, in their lives. Whether they played a lot of Uno or traveled at every opportunity or swam together once a day, every couple figured out what was fun for them and made sure to do that as often as possible.

Every smart couple was aware that sometimes life is going to suck—or at least feel a bit boring, tedious, and complicated. There will always be errands and groceries, sickness and struggle. But young couples are making that whole experience of L.I.F.E. more fun for each other. One guy told me that he knew his girlfriend was "a keeper" when they went to do laundry and found that they could "roll with the punches, drink some wine, and make it fun." These couples who are able to find the fun in their time together will have a much better chance of withstanding all the ups and downs.

II. Remember That It's the Marriage, Not the Wedding, That Matters.

And actually, it's the relationship, not the marriage, that matters.

As I met couples, I noticed that the more they downplayed the importance of titles and labels and traditional guideposts, the less stressed they seemed to be. Have you ever seen someone trying to plan a big, fancy wedding? It's impossible to stay sane during all that!

For two married couples I met in Oregon, that meant basically eloping and then cuddling in bed afterward. For several Midwestern couples I met, that meant moderating the expectations, planning the best party they could, and simply enjoying all the love and celebration that their friends and family were sending their way. And for an unmarried mother in Wisconsin, that meant defying social pressures and dedicating herself to a committed, exclusive relationship with the father of her son for many years *without* tying the knot, as a promise to herself to keep up the effort and appreciation and passion that marriage supposedly kills.

Overall, every happy couple I met understood that the day after your wedding, there is a marriage to embrace. And really, that marriage is basically just a relationship that includes some extra health insurance. The piece of paper—and certainly the wedding—are always going to be less important than the connection and love that underlie them.

III. Shake Up the Traditional Gender Roles in Your Relationship—Or Don't—to Fit the Two of You.

In some relationships that I observed, the guys cooked while the girls watched football. And in others, the girls cooked while the guys mowed the lawn—and then they both played with their kids.

Sometimes the men were typically the more sensitive and emotional partners. And sometimes it was the women.

There is no algorithm for how modern gender roles should play out in relationships. But many new couples seem to be dividing tasks and activities based on their actual personal interests and abilities. One of you is probably pickier about the freshness of your fruits and vegetables, so maybe that person should do the grocery shopping. One of you cares more about the environment, so maybe that person should handle the recycling. One of you passes by the kids' school on your way to work, so maybe it's that person who should drive them.

By ignoring both traditional and postfeminist expectations about who should be doing what, we can all figure out for ourselves what works best for our domestic lives instead.

IV. Don't Be Afraid of Long-Distance.

In Houston, I met a young couple who were head over heels for each other. They couldn't stop touching each other and gazing into each other's eyes throughout our interview, and there was no limit to their mutual appreciation. He even went on (and on) about loving the way she smelled. But they were burdened by a huge worry: he was about to go to Hawaii to continue his professional kite-surfing career, and everyone was telling them that long-distance never works.

Well, I'm glad that I met them when I did! Because I had heard enough stories to realize that long-distance love can absolutely work these days—usually thanks to the ease and endless possibilities of techno-romance—and I told them so. In fact, the majority of couples I spoke with had experienced at least one long-distance phase through-out the course of their relationship. This might not always have been a blast for them, but instead of mourning the sure demise of their re-lationship, they often fired up that laptop, booked a few plane tickets, and thought of it as an opportunity to get to know some other sides of their partners a little bit better.

V. Learn How to Fight.

It's going to happen, so do it smartly.

Apart from never raising their voices, refusing to fight in front of friends, and being realistic about the fact that the same issues were going to repeat themselves, Mike and Sheria had one particular rule about fighting that I loved. As Mike explained:

"I like straight-up honesty, so I made a rule. I was, like, look, if you want to bring up something that's older than two weeks, then I'm not talking about it. So if you're mad at me, and if I say something fucked up, then you have to tell me right then. And there'll be times when [Sheria] breaks something out, and I'm like, we can't argue about this. How long ago was that? This one is dead in the water—you should have argued with me about this a month and a half ago."

While this rule took some getting used to for Sheria, she now finds that it causes her to face and air her gripes as they are happening, instead of holding on to annoyances and letting them fester into larger issues down the line. They both swear it works!

VI. Take Turns Supporting Each Other.

I know, I know, you can't have it all, at least not all at the same time. But not only is that true as an individual, it is often true as a couple. Especially when both partners have dreams and aspirations that would be more than enough for even just one person to pursue.

Gone are the days when men's ambitions took precedence over their wives' dreams, or even when both partners worked so hard to pursue their own goals that they eventually found themselves on separate tracks with a lost connection lying between them. Instead, couples are creating a back-and-forth. They are helping, instead of hindering, each other's passions—often one at a time. And in the process, they are forming relationships that are ultimately stronger than the sum of their parts.

She got into the business school of her dreams? Time for him to be the temporary breadwinner and support her studies. He took a job with the army that will move him around the country every few years? Well, how convenient that she became a nurse because now she can travel with him and establish her own career and identity as well.

The happy couples of our generation are figuring out how to have their cake and eat it too, feeling empowered to pursue their individual dreams but also demonstrating enough dedication to know when their partners' dreams must come first. They are discovering that having a partner who mutually supports their endeavors can lead them to become even more successful than they would have been alone, and vice versa.

And thus, the new era of power couples is coming into focus.

VII. Find Ways to Buffer Against Jealousy—By Keeping Your Gaggle Around.

Every couple, and every individual, has a different standard for how much outside-the-relationship fraternizing they can take. Jealousy can be a personal thing. But luckily, trust, openness, and communication seem to be taking on new meanings in modern relationships.

Some couples I met had established a basic rule: they allow themselves to talk and flirt and be friends with other people, and then they tell each other everything. I interviewed quite a few couples who even made a habit of admitting to each other when they found someone else attractive. Not so that they could do anything about it, but so that there weren't any secret longings or forbidden interactions swimming in the undercurrent of the relationship.

Was there an initial discomfort with this openness? Of course. But each and every one of them told me that, once they had gotten past the initial jealousy that came with hearing that their partners were attracted to someone else, they felt liberated. They realized that their partners' attraction to others did not signify a lesser attraction to them. They began trusting their partners completely, knowing that there were no secret flirtations going on. And they started to appreciate and share their own attractions to other people, without ever worrying about whether that would destroy their relationship.

One way to say it is that they maintained a gaggle—and were totally honest about it—even after solidifying their relationships. Maybe they stopped cultivating relationships with overly charged gaggle members, like Hot Sex Prospects and Short-Term Investments. But the ones who were there to simply help them enjoy and explore themselves? Why not keep 'em around!

This type of agreement was explained to me by Holly, a PhD student in Chicago who had always loved to flirt and party. She had felt stifled by the strict exclusivity of previous relationships, so when she fell madly in love with her current boyfriend of several years, she was determined to feel good about their relationship—without sacrificing major parts of her personality. And as it turns out, her boyfriend loved to flirt and party, too—so they figured out a way to stay monogamous without making it feel like a drag and getting resentful of each other. They could flirt with other people and party . . . together! And take some of the unrealistic pressures off their relationship in the meantime. As Holly explains:

"You can't expect everything out of the person that you're dating. And maybe that's a misstep that a lot of people make, is that they demand everything. But they can't even fulfill that criteria themselves!

"So I don't close doors off to things, even though I am in a committed relationship and I live with my boyfriend, and neither does he. And we flirt! Like literally, my boyfriend and I jokingly cock-block each other. We have our own relationships, but we can still all hang out, too. And then not everything is put on me, and I don't put everything on him."

It's inspiring to see that if we are willing to think outside the box when it comes to our needs and relationships, then we can find solutions that will make each person in a relationship feel comfortable and safe.

VIII. Prioritize Yourselves and Your Relationship over Your Kids on a Regular Basis.

This was the whole problem with our parents' relationships, right? That they were too obsessed with *us* to find time to continue their own personal and romantic growth?

Many modern couples are doing their best not to repeat that mistake. They're loving their kids as much as humanly possible, of course, but they're also dedicating themselves to, well, themselves. They're sneaking in time for dance classes, baseball games, and reading and making sure that they remain whole people outside of their relationships with their children.

You can call our generation self-centered, and maybe we are, but the couples I met were not doing this simply to keep themselves entertained. Many of them told me that they believed this was one of the best gifts they could give to their children: to grow up with sane, interesting, fully developed parents.

And another great gift for the kids? As a couple in Minnesota put it, "To see what a good relationship is." And one of the ways that they're going to see that is by having parents who are in one.

IX. Ask for Help When You Need It.

It seems like modern couples aren't afraid of a little guidance when they think they need it. From sitting down with their rabbis to going to marriage counseling, plenty of couples were willing to acknowledge that, at a time when they seem to be rewriting the rules for strong relationships (or in some cases, feeling like they have to invent them from scratch), some tips from the pros can help.

They often don't wait to reach a dangerous breaking point before seeking help, either. Their standards for their relationships are so high that they want to nip any potential issues in the bud immediately. Of course, that means you might end up like Mike and Sheria, with multiple marriage counselors confusedly asking you, "Wait, this is it? These are your problems? That's what you guys fight about??" and then prescribing, "Um, you're good."

X. Believe That You're the Best Couple in the Entire World.

Every great couple I met believed that they were the *one* couple who was "figuring it all out" and was destined to make it. Of course, logically speaking, they can't all be the best couple in the world, but that presumption keeps them excited and committed to each other against all odds and despite all trials. And if they truly believe it, and make each other incredibly happy as such, then doesn't that basically make it a reality?

IN CONCLUSION . . .

There's so much to be inspired by in this post-dating world. People are building incredible relationships all around you, and if they get to have that, well, then dammit, so do you! You deserve to find the love you want—whatever that love happens to look like—and enjoy the process while getting there.

Now, at long last, you have everything you need to find it in this complicated post-dating world.

Trust in this process and be patient. Because you are going to put this book down and venture out into the world, all full of excitement about your gaggle, anxious to explore your connections and eager to whip out that phone and send your Accessory a photo of that hilarious sign you just saw on the street. But soon enough, you'll be reminded that all those old expectations, pressures, and insecurities still exist. Your boss is still going to ask you who you're dating, Mom is still going to look at you blankly when you tell her about the guy from volleyball, and some lame dude is still going to blow you off.

But you know better than all that now! And since we can't necessarily rely on support from the old folks, let's support each other. As young women, let's validate each other's love lives and embrace the craziness together. The more we rally and get each other excited about exploring these new opportunities, the fewer worries and doubts will seep into our brains and cause us to question ourselves. Either we go all-in as a group, and a gender, and a generation, or we succumb to the outdated expectations still burdening us.

Embracing the post-dating world through your gaggle *will work*. There are countless couples who have found love this way. And there are many women who aren't there yet, but who are still having a fabulous, fulfilling time—and learning tons about themselves in the process.

It's time. Just take a deep breath and do it. Embark on this adventure right now! Go "like" that Prospect You're Not Sure Is a Prospect's Facebook status. Nice.

Throughout your journey, try your absolute best to enjoy it. You have the rest of your life to relax in a secure (but still loving and exciting) relationship. For now, soak up the thrill of being uncommitted and having a gaggle. And learn as much about yourself as you can. This knowledge will only help you to create and maintain the relationship of your dreams a little further down the line.

Ready?

Today is the first day of the rest of your love life. So make sure to—oh, wait, hold on one sec, is that your phone buzzing? Better go check that text.

ACKNOWLEDGMENTS

Thank you to Becky, for everything.

Thank you to my parents, Alice and Fred Massa, especially for letting me sleep in your basement while we started this crazy project and for telling every single person you meet on the street about WTF?!

Thank you also to my wonderful extended family for putting your faith in me. And special thanks to my uncle, Mike DeLuise, for lending his advocacy to this project and for being the one to realize that you can totally say "WTF" on television.

Thank you to my interviewees! I can't believe you told all this crazy stuff to a complete stranger—but I'm so honored that you did.

Thanks to everyone who made the interview tour possible. Whether you hooked me up with your friends, let me crash on your couch, revealed your romantic quandaries on camera, or came out for our parties and events, I am eternally grateful. Thank you to Maple Street Book Shop in New Orleans and Green Apple Books in San Francisco for hosting our very first blog readings. Thank you to Jeffrey Wiegand for seeing the business proposition in all our crazy love lives. And special thanks to Dr. Brian Fallon for your guidance in designing an interview process that yielded more mind-blowing results than I ever could have anticipated.

A million thanks to Jessica West, Loren Posen, and Alison Steedman for believing in this project and dedicating your time and brilliance to it.

Thank you to our agent, Alex Glass, for taking a chance on this book.

Thank you to our incredible publishing team—Amanda Ferber, Trish Todd, Tracey Guest, Richard Rhorer, Jonathan Karp, and everyone at Simon & Schuster. And huge thanks to Kerri Kolen for immediately understanding our vision for this book and knowing exactly how to get everyone else as excited about it as we were.

Thanks to our wonderful producers, Merideth Finn and Michele Weiss, as well as Toby Emmerich, Richard Brener, Andrea Johnston and the team at New Line Cinema. Thanks to Nicole Page at Reavis Parent Lehrer for your wise legal counsel. Thanks to Ana Maria Lopez, Gabe Brosbe, and Charles Brack at Federated Media for seizing the online potential of WTF?! Thanks to Dana Paul of Shazamm for guiding our initial leap into the blogosphere, and thanks to Joshua Cliff and his team at Atrion for understanding our growing Web vision.

Thank you to all my friends who have supported this journey since Day One. And thank you to my trusted inner circle of overanalytical men who spent endless hours dissecting the male brain with me for the purposes of this book.

Thanks to the many of you who contributed directly to this book and project. Suffice it to say, without you, there would be no gaggle: Jocelyn Topf Abrams, Kemi Adewumi, Jenna Ahrens, Lynne Antinarelli, Laura Arandes, Rebecca Aronauer, Sarah Ax, Doug Baldinger, Chris Barnes, Andrew Barry, Andrea Bartz, Julia Bartz, Wendy Batteau, Dan Beers, Yoni Berkman, Carla and Cilla Borras, Kole Bosworth, Chris Bradford, Ashley Bryan, Tom Chiodo, Demetrios Costoyiannis, Cassandra Cummings, Jocelyn Davies, Anthony DiFranco, Alison Diviney, Tara Dunderdale, Lex Edness, Brenna Ehrlich, Gerrald Ellis, Scott Faries, Bryan Farrington, Lief Fenno, Jessica Filante, Ellen Freedman, Rob Freedman, Andy Friedland, Michael Garber, Jordan and Denise Glickson, Allison Goldberg, Chris Goldberg, David Grizzle, Scott Hagerman, Dan Hammond, Emmy Suzuki Harris, Beau Hartshorne, Ilsa Hazlewood, Kevin Hickey, Monica Huerta, Jen Jamula, Sabrina Jeffries, Emily Johnson, Justin Kan, Todd Kane, Jon Keilson, Kara Kelly, Rael Kenny, Gary King, Estee Kostant, Lee Kramer, Stephanie and Kyle Kramer, Logan Lee Lamson, Phoebe LaPine, Alex Lee, MC Joyce Lee, Shawn Leventhal, Lisa Lewis, Joy Lin, Lauren Lindsay, Yijian Lu, Matt Mager, Kirkie Maswoswe, Lisa Morales, Adele McConnell, Michael McCutcheon, Chaandi McGruder, Chris Miritello, Turpana Molina, Katie Moore, Dave Neustadter, Jenifer Nields, Lily O'Brien, Jennifer Johnson Onyedum, Okwui Onyedum, Andrea Pappas, Johanna Paretzky, Matthew

Price, Vijay Ramachandran, Marcail Riggs, Jennifer Riordan, Sam Roberts, Marc Rodriguez, Jordan Rogoff, Mara Rosenbloom, Helena Rozier, Marcos Salazar, Kamala Salmon, Sam Schectman, Michael Seibel, Amanda Seidler, Eric Seymour, Susan Shapiro, Emmett Shear, Ezra Siller, Jessica Spencer, David Stanley, Elizabeth Stanley, Adam Stockton, Julianna Connolly Stockton, William Stump, April Timberlake, Amanda Tomasello, Jeff Tomczek, Caitlin Tremblay, Jake Tuck, Michael Vinson, Kyle Vogt, Adam Wager, Lucy Wagner, Andrew Walker, Spencer Walker, Jessica Wallin, Wendy Wecksell, Aaron Weiss, Anna Lo Westlin, Dan Wiegand, Daria Wiegand, Emma Undine Wiegand, Frank Wiegand, Kathryn Donovan Wiegand, Natalie Wiegand, Shellie Weisfield, Leanne Williams, Amy Wiegand Wynia, and Anne Zelek.

And finally, thank you to all the purveyors of traditional dating lore out there who succeeded in making me so fed up that I finally had to do something about it. I know we're all just trying, in our own ways, to make the world a happier, more love-filled place. So cheers to that.